New Roots in America's
Sacred Ground

New Roots in America's Sacred Ground

Religion, Race, and Ethnicity in Indian America

KHYATI Y. JOSHI

RUTGERS UNIVERSITY PRESS

NEW BRUNSWICK, NEW JERSEY, AND LONDON

LIBRARY OF CONGRESS CATALOGING-IN-PUBLICATION DATA

Joshi, Khyati Y., 1970–

New roots in America's sacred ground : religion, race,. and ethnicity in Indian America / Khyati Y. Joshi.

p. cm.

Includes bibliographical references (p.) and index.

ISBN-13: 978-0-8135-3800-6 (hardcover : alk. paper)

ISBN-13: 978-0-8135-3801-3 (pbk. : alk. paper)

1. East Indian Americans—Ethnic identity. 2. East Indian Americans—Religion. 3. East Indian Americans—Social conditions. 4. Religious minorities—United States—Social conditions. 5. Ethnicity—United States. 6. United States—Religion. 7. United States—Race relations. 8. United States—Ethnic relations. 9. Religion and sociology—United States. I. Title.

E184.E2J67   2006

305.891′4073—dc22   2005023065

A British Cataloging-in-Publication record for this book is available from the British Library.

Manufactured in the United States of America

For Mom and Dad

thank you for your
faith, love, and support

CONTENTS

Acknowledgments   ix

   Introduction   1
1 Religion in America   15
2 Ethnicity and Religion   34
3 Facets of Lived Religion   62
4 What Does Race Have to Do with Religion?   89
5 Religious Oppression   118
6 Case Studies   145
   Epilogue   194

Appendix   199
Notes   205
References   221
Index   235

ACKNOWLEDGMENTS

No person is an island, and a book is a product not only of the author but of the minds and spirits of those around her. Along the long path from first ideas to final galleys, I benefited from the support and input of many, many gifted people.

My thanks to Suvrat Bhargave, Jayenta Dey, Sudevi Ghosh, Shelley Gupta, Ketan Sanghvi, Linell Yugawa, and others, who assisted me in identifying research participants. Maurianne Adams, Warren Blumenfeld, John Dean, Joyce Flueckiger, Jane Naomi Iwamura, Uma Majumdar, Gina Martino, Pyong Gap Min, Steven Prothero, Sonia Sharma, Munjal Shroff, Paul Spickard, and Danielle Sigler all read drafts of the work in many different stages and offered valuable insights. David Blumenthal, Phyllis C. Brown, and Jimmy Harper have provided much encouragement along the way.

I am fortunate to be a part of two groups of people whose feedback and support have been invaluable. First, thank you to all my friends and colleagues in the Asian Pacific American and Religion Research Initiative (APARRI) for sharing the idea that it's not crazy to want to pursue research at the intersection of race, religion, and ethnicity. Thanks also to my friends and colleagues from the 2003–2005 cohort of the Young Scholars in Religion Program at the Center for Religion and American Culture at Indiana University-Purdue University Indianapolis (IUPUI). My fellow Young Scholars and our mentors offered me valuable feedback and a chance to learn about areas of religion and history with which I was not yet familiar.

Material and ideas from *New Roots* were presented before audiences at the Center for the Study of Ethnicity and Race at Columbia University, the American Academy of Religion, Yale University's Asian-American Cultural Center, APARRI/PANA conferences, and Association of Asian American Studies. The students, audience members, fellow panelists, and discussants at these events helped me develop my ideas and sharpen my analysis.

Particular intellectual nourishment on was provided by Jigna Desai and Judith Hudson. Both went above and beyond the call of duty, and everyone should be so lucky to have such dedicated friends.

Fairleigh Dickinson University has provided a wonderful environment for research and writing. My colleagues at the Peter Sammartino School of Education have been very supportive during my time there working on this book. Special thanks in particular to Dean John Snyder of University College for providing the release time that allowed me to complete the manuscript. Librarians are a researcher's best friend, and Kathy Stein Smith and Mary Anne Sena of the Weiner Library have gone beyond the call of duty to help make this book possible.

I thank my editors at Rutgers, Melanie Halkias and Kendra Boileau, their editorial assistant Alicia Nandkarni, and my copyeditor Margaret Case for their guidance, patience, and support on my first foray into book authorship.

More people than I could possibly name have provided well-placed words and kind gestures that smoothed the path, and my nerves, throughout the process. My own ethnoreligious community in Atlanta, Georgia—especially the Vijays and Mainthias—also provided a tremendous amount of moral support.

Thanks also to my family in India for their love and support—the Joshis, Bhatts, Pandyas, Desais, and Buchs in Ahmedabad and Bombay.

Mom, Dad and Dad, sister Hetal, and brother-in-law Fergus have helped in so many different ways. Their encouragement, even a simple "how's the book?" made it possible to labor through the long days and nights of drafting and editing. Most important, they kept my son Kedhar very happy and content during his first year of life while his mother was finishing this manuscript. Finally, of course, there's John—my husband, my sounding board, and my late-night editor—who held my life together and without whom I would not be whole.

New Roots in America's
Sacred Ground

Introduction

The post-1965 wave of immigration—the largest in U.S. history—has brought an infusion of color that is challenging traditional understandings of race and racism, the so-called straight line assimilation theory of ethnicity, and the normative place of Christian traditions in society and religious scholarship.[1] After nearly half a century during which immigration was available only to people from the predominantly Protestant regions of Europe, the Immigration and Nationality Act of 1965 opened the gates for a wave of immigrants from beyond the Judeo-Christian pale. Indian Americans were a major segment of the first wave. Alongside the growth in racial diversity that followed the 1965 Immigration Act has come a dramatic increase in America's religious diversity. The increasing presence of followers of non-Christian faiths such as Hinduism, Islam, and Sikhism has reverberated nationwide in urban, suburban, and rural America. The influx of new immigrants and "new" faiths requires us to reconceptualize the relationship among ethnicity, race, and religion and the impact of each on the individual. Moreover, every immigrant generation is followed by a second generation, born on these shores but raised in the ethnic home environment, in the dominant society of neighborhood and school, and in a space of their own in between. This book addresses second-generation religious experiences and identities not in a vacuum but rather in the specific and unique context of ethnicity and race in the United States.

America is changing how it categorizes people. Throughout history, those who were different—the "them" as distinct from "us" (the majority)—were made an "other" and had their differences racialized. The Irish and the Jews, to name two major constituents of the last great wave of immigration, were thought of as racially different, until this view was finally overwhelmed by the force of white skin and social mobility. Nearly half a century after the Civil Rights Act was passed, more than half a century after *Brown v. Board of*

Education, old-fashioned racism is finally beginning to become socially unacceptable. At the same time, the rise of religious fundamentalism and its intrusion into the public sphere has given lie to the old sociological assumption that the arc of history was bending rapidly toward secularism. And it is not just Christianity that is on the rise: Indian Americans and other religious-minority populations such as Arab Americans are choosing religion as their primary identifier in proportions heretofore unseen. Yet despite the decline of Jim Crow racism, America still needs its "others," and despite the flourishing of non-Christian religions, we prefer our differences to be visible. So we racialize religion, as we always have. Unlike the Irish and Jews of a century ago, however, Indian American Hindus, Muslims, and Sikhs will not melt into whiteness after a generation.

Into these swirling eddies of embrace and exclusion, privilege and disadvantage, were born the second-generation Indian Americans. Indian immigrants were one of the the largest Asian ethnic groups to enter the United States in the years following 1965 (Steinberg 1989; Takaki 1989). The United States' Indian-origin population quadrupled in the 1980s, doubled again in the 1990s, and now stands at over 1.9 million people, with an additional 200,000 reporting Indian American in combination with one or more other races.[2] Indian Americans now comprise the third largest Asian ethnic group in the United States, behind Chinese and Filipinos (United States Bureau of the Census 2001). Thirty-three percent of Indian Americans live in the Northeast, 26.2 percent in the South, 24 percent in the West and 17 percent in the Midwest.[3]

The second generation and their immigrant parents in the United States are a part of a larger emigration pattern in which natives of India have spread to all corners of the globe. As a nonwhite and disproportionately non-Christian population, Indian Americans are minorities with respect to both religion and race within the United States. As children of immigrants, the second generation is exposed to a range of experiences that includes aspects of Indian culture—the traditions, experiences, and thought patterns their parents bring with them to the United States—and aspects of American culture. The home environment is often heavily Indian, but may incorporate aspects of both cultures, while the environment beyond the front door is profoundly American. The child's ethnic identity is shaped by both and by the interaction between the two.

The lives and experiences of the post-1965 second generation raise interesting questions about identity. Their parents can claim they are Indians because they were born and raised in India, were active members of the Indian society for years or decades, have much of their memories and histories in that society, "think and act Indian," relate to the Indian culture more than to the American culture, and in many cases still hope to go back to that society someday. By contrast, second-generation Indian Americans can invoke few if any of these markers of Indianness. How then do second-generation Indian Americans construct their identity? Is one Indian by being born to parents who are? Is Indi-anness about their behavior and attitude, or is it about the passport they carry and the schools they attended? Is it familiarity with an Indian language or Indian culture, a love for *dal* or *dosa*? Do language skills, or the cognitive and emotive identification with Indian culture and society, determine whether these second-generation people regard themselves as Indian, Indian-American, or American? How do religion and race impact ethnic identity development of second-generation Indian Americans? To what degree do they exhibit knowledge of or derive their values from their home religion, and what does this mean to who they are?[4]

Second-generation Indian Americans are an ideal population through which to examine the myriad ways race and religion interact, intersect, and af-fect each other in the context of ethnic identity development. Indian Americans are both a racial minority and a religious minority in a society where Christian-ity and whiteness are normative. At the same time, for historical reasons dis-cussed at greater length in chapter 4, they are racially ambiguous—neither black nor white—and their ambiguity is magnified by the relative socioeconomic well-being of the population and by the effects of the racialization of religion. Second-generation Indian Americans are the first cohort to come of age on American shores of whom all these things can be said. Their experiences there-fore offer us a window on the changing nature and effects of race, religion, and ethnicity—and in particular on how religion interacts with race and affects ethnicity.

Seeking Answers

As an undergraduate at Emory University, I took a class on Hinduism from Pro-fessor John Fenton. It was my first class with Dr. Fenton, but not my first en-counter. I had met Dr. Fenton as a teenager growing up in Cobb County, Georgia, when he made repeated visits to conduct ethnographic fieldwork at the temple and community center my family had helped build in the 1970s and 1980s. These data were presented in his book *Transplanting Religious Traditions: Asian Indians in America*.

Dr. Fenton's book was one of many about Indian religions in America and led me to seminal works in several fields of study. I read about Indian immi-grants like my parents: their histories, the communities they built on these shores, and their efforts to transmit culture and religion to their children.[5] I read about Hinduism, Islam, and Sikhism in America: how they were being prac-ticed and reformulated in a nominally secular but deeply Christian country.[6] I explored the experiences of the second generations of other "unmeltable" (Suzuki 1979) American ethnic groups such as Latinos, Filipinos, and East Asian Americans.[7] The nascent but growing body of literature on second-generation

Indian Americans informed my thinking.[8] As a way of understanding the different factors affecting a person's life, literature on ethnic and racial identity development models help understand how ethnicity, race, and other social identities shape the lives of people in the United States.

Each of these fascinating subject areas informs my scholarship, including the book you hold in your hands. But each of them—even all of them combined—still left me dissatisfied and searching for complete answers. The scholarship on Indian immigrant communities all but ignores the experiences of the second generation. In fairness, scholars like Fenton examined these communities at a time when even the oldest members of the second generation were only in middle school or high school. Works on Indian American religions in America, even those that applied sociological rather than theological lenses, nevertheless ignored a crucial component of the equation: race, and the status of these religious minorities as simultaneously racial minorities on the American scene. The second-generation works provided helpful insights on issues such as parental immigration status, socioeconomic class, language, and race. Still, few of the studies examined religious experiences, and those that did focused on groups that are Christians; in a Christian-majority and Christian-normative country like the United States, these works are limited in their ability to illuminate the "double-minority" experiences of Indian Americans who are not Christians.[9] The immigrants of a century ago experienced religious oppression and even had their religious uniqueness treated as racial difference—but they were also, in the end, "meltable" ethnics who became white in short order.[10] Most of the ethnic and racial identity development models, although they have become important elements of my own analysis, do not speak to the issue of religion; they are therefore limited in their ability to provide a complete framework for exploring the Indian American experience. Also, too many of them remain mired in a black/white paradigm that is harmful to adequate consideration of contemporary racial populations.

Indian American populations are among the fastest-growing Asian American communities in the South and the Northeast. Second-generation Indian Americans in these locales—like my research participants—did not grow up with access to major ethnic enclaves like Edison, N.J.; Jackson Heights, Queens; or Devon Street, Chicago. Why is this relevant? Consider the remark of one New York-reared second-generation Indian American: "It is hard for me to socialize with other [Indian American] folks who are always starved for Indian food. They have to go to an Indian restaurant to experience Indian culture! New York City is so different that sometimes I feel I have grown up in a space between India and the United States" (Khandelwal 2002, 148). The New Yorker's perspectives and experiences are important, but her space and the space in which my research participants grew up were dramatically different. As a proud Southerner, I wanted to put Indian Americans from my part of the country on the Asian

American map, and to put them on the black/white racial map with which Southern race scholarship in particular remains preoccupied. The way to do this was to explore in depth the lived experiences of second-generation Indian Americans. I did so by conducting interviews with forty-one people in two major U.S. cities.[11]

Of these, twenty lived in or near Boston and twenty-one lived in the Atlanta metropolitan area at the time of the interviews—but nearly three-quarters of them had grown up in the South.[12] (Note that although subjects were interviewed in two cities, and the sociology of place can be relevant to the ethnic experience, this book does not set out to compare the experiences of Bostonians with those of Atlantans.) I interviewed twenty-three women and eighteen men. All but three research participants identified at the time of their interview with their home religion, the religious tradition in which they were raised. Of the three who did not, two came from Hindu families but now identify themselves as Atheists and one was an Isma'ili-raised man who had converted to Sunni Islam. The overall religious breakdown of the cohort, as they self-identified, was: twenty-eight Hindus, four Christians, three Sikhs, two Muslims, two Atheists, one Sikh/Hindu, and one Jain.[13] All but one of the research participants grew up with both parents married to each other and living together; many also reported that grandparents and other family members lived with them and their parents for extended periods. Most of them attended public school for the entirety of their K–12 (kindergarten through senior in high school) career. Of those who did not, all three Catholic research participants—Irfan, Shiren, and Binu—attended Catholic parochial school, and the remainder attended secular private schools. The vast majority described their schools as "mostly white" or "predominantly white" schools.[14] All forty-one research participants attended college, more than 70 percent of them in the South. In terms of marital status, four of the research participants were married at the time of their interviews.[15] None had children. Today, the research participants pursue a range of vocations: physicians and other health-care providers; attorneys; software and information technology professionals; bankers; a nonprofit executive; a graduate student; a homemaker; and a pilot. As to sexual orientation, one is openly gay; it would be conjecture, however, to assume that all the others are heterosexual.

Not only are all of the research participants in this study second-generation Indian Americans but specifically they are members of what I will call "Second Generation A," as distinguished from "Second Generation B" (see below). This particular segment of the Indian American second-generation population has a few defining characteristics. They came of age in the 1980s and early 1990s. Most succeeded academically, as a premium was placed on education in their households. Their educational attainment and academic achievement is also connected to the socioeconomic characteristics and educational backgrounds of their parents. It is important to note the United States did not get a cross-section of Indians, but rather a cross-section of professional Indians—in particular, an overwhelming number of immigrants with MD and PhD degrees (Chandrasekhar 1982; Takaki 1989).[16] The educational background of the immigrant generation, and their resulting relative privilege with respect to socioeconomic class, has affected the lives of their children. In this respect, the Indian immigrants who parented Second Generation A are part of the larger post-1965 Asian immigrant cohort that resulted in the development of the "model minority myth" among Asians.[17]

The distinction between Second Generations A and B is important as scholars build upon the present work and continue to consider the experiences of second-generation Indian Americans, and as practitioners set policies and combat presumptions about educational achievement. The distinction is pervasive and nuanced, but can be summarized in broad brush.

Second Generation A	*Second Generation B*
Born between 1965 and 1978	Born between 1979 and 1992
Earliest political awareness: 1970s' oil crunch, Iran hostage crisis, Ronald Reagan	Earliest political awareness: First Gulf War, Rodney King beating, Bill Clinton
Prayed and took part in ethnoreligious community (when available) in homes or rented halls—wherever their parents could gather	Pray and take part in ethnoreligious community (always available) at freestanding mandirs, masjids, and gurudwaras
Only Asian American kid in the classroom	One of three or four Indian Americans in the classroom
Classmates had never heard of India	Classmates wear bindis and henna tattoos
Watched Bollywood movies on poor-quality bootleg VHS tapes; hated them	Watch Bollywood movies on high-quality DVDs with English subtitles; love them
Watched NBC and MTV	Watch ZeeTV and TVAsia
Parents are professionals, often in medicine or the sciences	Parents operate or are employed by a small business
Got to college and built ethnic (sometimes pan-ethnic) student organizations	Got to college and joined ethnic student organizations; building sectarian religious student organizations

The relevance of the distinctions and characterizations will become clearer to the reader later in this text.

Terms and Usage

Many of the terms that are central to understanding this book are often misunderstood or misused. There are three reasons for this: First, different disciplines use the terms in different ways. Second, even within a single discipline there are often disagreements on how terms should be defined or used. Third, the popular understanding of a particular term may be different—sometimes entirely different—from the way scholars use the term; particularly in interview-based qualitative research, this can vex reader and researcher alike. In this text, I adopt a specific definition when possible and fashion my own when necessary to clearly transmit the data and analysis on second-generation Indian Americans.

Let us start with the term *second generation*, which in this text encompasses two groups sometimes identified separately by other scholars. The term generally refers both to individuals born in the United States to immigrant parents and those who arrived here by about age six (Portes and Rumbaut 1996; Zhou 1997). Some scholars separately designate a "1.5 generation" or "one-and-a-half generation" of children born abroad who arrived in the United States after age five but before age twelve. In the interest of brevity and simplicity, I refer to the entire cohort as "second generation." This approach also avoids some of the artificiality of the 1.5/2 divide. For example, there are research participants who were born in the United States but returned to India so frequently that they have developed strong transnational relationships with Indian family and family; technically classified as "second generation," such individuals' outlooks and experience might be more like those of a 1.5'er. Likewise, individuals may arrive after age six and travel back to India infrequently; they may experience language loss and may not form strong relationships with extended family in India, two experiences commonly associated with the second generation.

Generally speaking, I use the term *Indian American* to refer to my research participants and others like them: Americans whose lineage can be traced to residents of the territory now within the borders of the Republic of India. Occasionally, I use the term *South Asian American*, a term encompassing people with lineage traceable to the other nations of South Asia.[18] I do so only when either quoting and discussing a research participant who used the terms *South Asian* or *South Asian American*, or discussing a social phenomenon, such as the post-9/11 backlash, that clearly affects the entire South Asian American community. This approach is part of a concerted effort to avoid using overly broad terms where their use is not warranted and where they may obscure rather than illuminate the truth.

Next, *religion*. I use the term to refer to "an experience to which a sense of dependency on or a link with God/the divine and the transcendent is con-nected" (Tamminen 1994 34). Thomas Idinopulos reminds us that religion is neither "reducible to or equatable with a set of formal beliefs" nor comprehen-sible by reference only to questions of what the individual believes (or does not believe) or what rituals she performs (or does not perform); and "faith is not a matter of what is believed or thought about, but rather what is done or felt or imagined."[19] This book struggles to avoid the easy trap of the visible—doctrine, rituals, practice—at the expense of the more important invisible (see also Orsi 1985; Hall 1997).

The existing research on the immigrant generation examines the activities undertaken to transmit rituals and traditions to their children. But what does this transmission look like, what are its effects, and what else is going on in the religious lives of second-generation Indian Americans? The term *lived religion* al-lows for a much more flexible understanding of religion: that religion, usually thought of as a rigid and static ideology or rule system, is found in everyday be-haviors and practices.[20] Lived religion encompasses not only ritual practices but also principles and tenets internalized and applied in daily interactions and de-cisions. It is not about whether and how second-generation Indian Americans "go to religion," but about how religion springs forth in their lives—"goes to them," in effect—and is felt and acted upon where they are. The lived-religion approach of this text thus rests heavily on examinations of how religion shapes the way second-generation Indian Americans make meaning of their lives. Lived religion is the best lens for a study such as this one, which considers religion's role in ethnic identity development and therefore deals with subjective and personal experiences of individuals (Wendel 2003) and with the individual's re-lationship with religion as a dynamic process. With or without ritual practice, the meaning the research participants make out of being Hindu or Sikh or Mus-lim, and the processes, dialogues (internal and external), and experiences of being of their faith, and soon, shape their lives. For those who do engage in practice such as attendance at a house of worship, the examination is not only of how they worship but of how worship is situated in their lives and affects their identity. The focus of this book is on the different ways these second-generation Indian Americans incorporate religious belief and practice into their everyday lives.

Bring up the term *race* in a discussion, and the result is often sweaty palms and frazzled nerves. But as Omi and Winant (1994) note, there nothing inher-ently positive or negative about race. It is nothing more or less than a part of everyday life in our society. That said, discussing race requires us to understand some basic points: Race is not scientific. But it is a social factor of great impor-tance; even lacking inherent negative or positive weight, it is used to categorize people in our society.

Although race "evokes the language of phenotype" (Edles 2004), race is not a biological phenomenon. Although phenotype as such may be hereditary, the social and normative values that are attached to "race" in the popular mind have no basis in biology or any other science. Nevertheless, different races— such as Asians, blacks, whites—have come to be seen as human subspecies. This tenacious idea is the product of a school of thought now commonly known as "scientific racism." Western scientists and philosophers of the eighteenth and nineteenth centuries developed theories (1) that certain races were inherently inferior and superior to one another, and (2) that there was a biological basis for these differences. They took external differences such as skin color and hair type, rooted them in biology, and attempted to link them to internal differences like athletic and artistic ability, intelligence, and even judgment and morality. Linking race with inherent biological traits served a major social function at the time, by providing a more acceptable explanation for the differential treatment of nonwhites—in particular, showing the "need" to enslave blacks and explaining the "savagery" of Native Americans.[21]

Although race is not biological, neither is it an illusion—something that will disappear in a utopic future. Race is a social and historical construct whereby human populations are seen as separate and different by virtue of some notion of "stock" or a collective heredity of traits. Michael Omi and Howard Winant (1994, 55) describe a process they call *racial formation*, "the sociohistorical process by which racial categories are created, inhabited, transformed, and destroyed." Race, they write, "is an unstable complex of social meanings constantly being transformed by political struggle. . . . Race is a concept which signifies and symbolizes social conflicts and interests by referring to different types of human bodies." As Omi and Winant's definition points out, our racial terms and their meanings are not only created but also *re*-created; they change over time in response to social trends, group movement (including immigration), and legal rules and decisions (see Haney-Lopez 1996).

Race matters in this book not because of skin color but because of the values and assumptions that skin color has come to connote through the idea—the "social construct"—of race. Race matters not because it makes people different but because it makes people believe they are different. By doing so, it has shaped the United States since before its founding and has created the social, economic, and cultural topography on which all our lives play out in the present day. And it continues to be an element of modern society with a range of impacts in the daily lives of these research participants.

To explore religion, race, and their interplay in the lives of second-generation Indian Americans, we must shed the assumption that religion is a changeable characteristic. Tseming Yang argues, and I agree, that the view of race as immutable and religion as flexible hinders our analysis of both phenomena. Although research participants might intellectually realize that religion and religious affiliation can be chosen, religious beliefs—conveyed in childhood by people of authority and linked to the concept of an all-powerful divine—can feel much more like something that chose them (Yang 1997). Likewise, treating race as unchanging improperly adopts popular society's view of race as biological rather than social. (As the reader will see in chapter 4, the Indian American experience illustrates well the mercurial nature of race in America.)

Whereas race connotes phenotype, *ethnicity* is "a social category that primarily refers to and evokes the language of place, i.e. 'Where are you from?'" (Edles 2004). It refers to an individual's sense of peoplehood, whereby individuals who believe they are members of a given group base this belief primarily on similarities of national origin, religion, language, and other facets of sociocultural heritage. Ethnicity is actively created and recreated by individuals and groups on a foundation of belief in and connection to a shared history (Spickard and Burroughs 2000; Phinney 1990).

The importance of clearly defining race and ethnicity is illustrated by the fact that most of the research participants in this study demonstrated perceptions and understandings of the two as one and the same. Many used the terms interchangeably. Many consider ethnicity, like race, to be a biological rather than a social product. Ethnicity is often perceived to be fixed, inherited, or transmitted over generations; it is meaningful because it comes from a birth connection.[22] Rather than speaking of ethnicity—whereby one adopts a label ("Indian," "Indian American") seen as static—it therefore makes more sense to talk about *ethnic identity*. This approach recognizes that one's relationship with the ethnicity (or ethnic group) does not exist in a vacuum and is subject to change, definition, and contestation over the life span. The concept of identity can also help us understand the distinctions and commonalities that link the concepts of race and ethnicity.

Ethnic identity represents an awareness of self as existing within a specific group (and, by extension, as an outsider to other groups) defined by some set of factors—such as language, cuisine, geography, history, and social values—that are collectively identified with a particular culture. An individual's ethnic identity develops over the course of his or her life span in a process that is neither linear (implying a starting point and a destination) nor static (implying the existence, at some identifiable point, of a finished identity). It is shaped by the individual's own experiences; the awareness of oneself as the product of a particular people, place, and time; and awareness of how one is perceived by the outside world. It is affected by intersecting with other social identities such as gender and sexual orientation. How second-generation Indian Americans understand these experiences also itself affects ethnic identity development. Ethnic identity functions as a cognitive, information-processing framework within which a person perceives and defines objects, situations, events, herself or himself, and other people. One is never "done" developing one's ethnic identity, and the relative salience of these various factors can change over time on the basis of personal choices and environmental influences across the life span.

Research participants' ethnic identity is related closely to the ethnic subculture practiced in their parents' home and in their parents' home country; by contrast, their racial identity stems from the consciousness of their nonwhite status in a white-dominated and white-normative society. Racial identity is based on the sociopolitical model of oppression.[23] It "refers to a sense of group or collective identity based on one's perception that he or she shares a common heritage with a particular racial group" (Helms, 1994, 3). Racial identity seems most often, however, to be a frame in which individuals categorize others, often on the basis of skin color.

Culture consists of an ever-changing system of values, traditions, social and political relationships, and worldviews created and shared by a group of people bound together by a combination of factors that can include shared history, geographic location, language, social class, and/or religion, and how these are transformed by those who share them (Nieto 2003). To return to Edles's typology, " 'culture' evokes questions like, 'What do you know?' " (Edles 2004, 44). In everyday social situations, we use culture to express and give meaning to our identity, which in turn is used to construct affiliations with and boundaries between other individuals and groups. Throughout, I use the term culture to mean an "Indian culture": those ideas and traditions, imparted to the research participants by their parents and other Indian immigrants, which allowed the research participants to feel a connection to India.

The stories of these research participants' lives cannot be conveyed merely by offering a collection of facts about their religion, race, ethnicity, and culture. Rather, the stories must be told by an examination of how these factors intersect and influence each other and interact with the research participants' life experiences and surroundings—and, most important, by an examination of the outcomes that result from these interactions and intersections. To use a baking metaphor, this is not a book about eggs, flour, butter, and sugar. It is a book about cake—what goes into it, how it's made, and what it tastes like.

Overview of Chapters

Chapter 1 presents a brief historical overview to map Indian American religions' place in the context of present-day America and discusses the concept of lived religion and how second-generation Indian Americans negotiate religion in their lives. Chapter 2 introduces the phenomenon of ethnic identity development and discusses the relationship between religion and ethnicity. It then describes two major influences on ethnic identity development of the second-generation Indian American cohort: family and ethnoreligious community. Chapter 3 examines the major ways in which religion is lived by second-generation Indian

Americans, and considers what lived religion looks like across the life span. Chapter 4 poses and attempts to answer the question, "What does race have to do with religion?" It presents theories of race and the ways in which Indian Americans' status as people of color affects and interacts with religion and ethnic identity development, and how the racialization of religion affects the Indian American religious experience. It contextualizes that status against the historical backdrop of Indian American racial ambiguity and presents the range of experiences and viewpoints on race reported by the research participants. Chapter 5 describes the religious oppression of second-generation Indian Americans and how Christianity's normative power in the United States affects their ethnic identity development. In Chapter 6, the theories presented are brought to bear on the life stories of three second-generation Indian Americans. These case studies, and the questions following each, allow the reader to apply the lessons of the first five chapters in a concentrated fashion to an individual life. In the epilogue that follows, I speculate on the course of the second generation as it proceeds through adulthood, consider the ramifications of my findings for educators and policymakers, and describe future research opportunities.

The Case Study Approach

The purpose of the case studies in the final chapter of this book is to provide a sociocultural analysis of each person. Case studies are an effective method of viewing and understanding the social realities of people (see Redman 2003; Nieto 2003) and, by extension, of others like them. The individuals in the case studies are both typical and atypical of their ethnic, racial, and religious group. They may buttress, challenge, or even shatter commonly held stereotypes. The issues and perspectives that arise in the lives of these research participants are similar to those of many second-generation Indian Americans. Yet typicality is different from generalization; none of these individuals is a walking stereotype. Each of their experiences is singular and should be understood as such. For example, Salim's life does not reflect the experiences of all second-generation Indian American Muslim men who grew up in the South. But describing Salim's experiences and their sociocultural framework can help us understand other second-generation Indian American and Muslim men.

Each of the three cases studies provides the reader with a chronological story of the individual's life, presented as much as possible in his or her own words. This is followed by a discussion of the experiences so described, applying the analytical lenses used in chapters 1 through 5. In this respect, chapter 6 illuminates what precedes it and vice versa. If the first five chapters present a collection of snapshots, the final chapter presents three short films, applying the theories developed in the first five chapters intensely to the breadth of a single life. In so doing, I further illuminate the theories that in the earlier chapters are supported with the isolated experiences of multiple research participants. Without the theoretical foundation and detailed discussion that takes place in the first five chapters of the book, the case studies may be too idiosyncratic to describe a "second-generation Indian American experience." Without the case studies, the first five chapters could be overly static recitations of phenomena that are dynamic and internally contradictory in real life.

Across all of the first five chapters, the reader's goal should be to understand the ethnic identity development of the individual over a lifespan, and to understand specifically how the role of religion waxes and wanes in the context on the individual's ethnic and racial identity development. Case studies are meant to challenge you to ask questions rather than to make assumptions about religion, race, and ethnic identity. They ask you to engage with the deeper struggle to understand people on their own terms. Some of the experiences, feelings, and statements of the young people quoted in this book may surprise you or even shake your most deep-seated beliefs. So much the better. On the other hand, they may reflect some of your own experiences or your knowledge of second-generation Indian Americans. In either case, what these individuals say should be understood within the context of their own lives—illustrative of some common experiences yet unlike any other person's before or since.

Conclusion

Although the material presented in this book spotlights how religion affects and interacts with ethnic and racial identities, I do not intend to argue that religion was the most salient identity or even the most important factor in the ethnic identity development of all research participants. Nor am I interested in measuring the research participants' retention of Indian culture or to gauge the extent to which they have adopted or assimilated into American culture; there are no authenticity tests these research participants were trying to pass. I disagree with the essentialist position that identity is bipolar and that the research participants must gravitate toward either the pole of nativism or that of assimilation. Nor am I attempting to analyze or describe in any substantial sense the new subcultures developed by second-generation Indian Americans in response to Indian and American cultural inputs.

Rather, I mean to describe the flourishing in this generation of seeds transplanted from elsewhere (Fenton 1988). I am embarking on an examination of how religious roots transplanted from India are growing and nourishing the second generation. These Indian roots have been planted in American soil, soil tempered with unique cultural norms and saturated with ideations of God. The nutrients and pests of this American soil will bend the roots and shape the trees, creating shapes and forms unlike those found in India or in the Indian diasporas of the Caribbean or the United Kingdom. The second generation, their lives and their myriad faiths, are the trees of my forest. What will these Indian Americans' lives and beliefs look like as they reach skyward?

1

Religion in America

One of the first things we all learned in elementary school was that America is the land of freedom—specifically, that people in the United States are allowed to practice whatever religion they want, because our nation grew out of a quest for religious freedom. This is one of the most enduring and powerful misconceptions about religion in American history: that America was created so that all religions could practice freely. In fact, the Puritans fled England in search of a place where they could practice their own religion without fear or oppression. I suspect—and early religious leaders such as Roger Williams would probably agree—that the Puritans couldn't have cared less about Catholics, Lutherans, and Quakers, much less Hindus, Muslims, and Sikhs. Whatever the precise contours of the truth behind this American creation myth, one thing is clear: Every facet of American society is shaped, informed, defined, or given its vocabulary and structure by religion. Concepts of religiosity and religious freedom are among those considered our most foundational. Indeed, the First Amendment's clauses on the free exercise of religion and the separation of church and state are among those most strictly applied by the courts.

A Brief History of Religion in America

Throughout American history, the experiences of immigration have been shared by new Americans of all national and denominational backgrounds, from Italian Catholics to Russian Jews to Norwegian Lutherans (Gaustad and Schmidt 2002). Indeed, religiosity itself—in addition to its role in cultural maintenance and perpetuation—is central to the formation of an American identity. Although the colonial era is traditionally associated with a single immigrant faith, Puritanism, in truth even that period was more complex: Quakers, Anabaptists, and other sects followed the Puritans in their own search for refuge.

Each immigrant community brought with it the sociological bundle of ethnic and religious traditions specific to its place of origin. Religion shaped, transformed, unified and divided these and subsequent ethnoreligious communities arriving on American shores. Like earlier immigrants, the post-1965 Indian immigrants brought their religions with them and used those religions as their primary vehicle for the retention and transmission of ethnic culture to the second generation.[1] The primary distinctions between the pre- and post-1965 eras involve not the religiosity of the new immigrants but the breadth and quantity of regions, religions, and races represented in the newest immigrant waves.

The Indian American story is one of new roots in American soil, because the majority of Indian immigrants did not arrive until after the Immigration Reform Act of 1965 reopened a door slammed shut half a century earlier. The presence not merely of Indians but specifically of married couples was crucial, as the homes and families they established gave these individuals relatively more ties with the U.S. and relatively fewer incentives to return to India permanently. These families built ethnoreligious communities and sent their children into the American school system in substantial numbers. The majority within each Indian American religious group is currently an immigrant and second-generation cohort. However, the pre-1965 religious history of America belongs not only to Christians and Jews; adherents of each religion represented in this study were present on American shores two hundred or more years ago. Each religion—its theology, global history, and encounters with the American milieu—gives unique characteristics to the experiences of its adherents and their place in contemporary American society. Although Hinduism, Islam, and Sikhism have all been present throughout the history of the United States, the breadth of their impact on American society and culture has come about since 1965.

The signposts on the historical path for Indian Americans include four crucial pieces of federal legislation. Spurred the nativistic sentiment born of the "ethnic" immigration waves of the late nineteenth and early twentieth centuries and by particular anti-Asian biases, the Immigration Act of 1917, also known as the Barred Zone Act and the Immigration Act of 1924, also known as the National Origins Act, made immigration from Asia illegal. Just before the latter act was made law, Indian Americans were stripped of their U.S. citizenship by the Supreme Court in *United States v. Bhagat Singh Thind*. In 1946, the passage of the Luce-Cellar Act granted naturalization rights to Indians and also set an annual quota of one hundred immigrants to arrive from India in 1952, the McCarran Walter Act relaxed some of the immigration restrictions, particularly for students. The sea change came in 1965, when the Immigration Reform Act wholly reordered how the United States calculated national origin quotas and led to the wave of immigration that brought all these research participants' parents to the United States. It was 1965 that marked the true watershed in

Indian immigration because it was only after the Immigration Reform Act that substantial numbers of Indian immigrant families—as distinguished from the laborers who arrived in the 1880s or, later, individual students or professionals— were able to immigrate.

Indian Hindu immigrants, mostly single men, first arrived on these shores over two hundred years ago to pursue agrarian labor, mostly on the West coast. As non-whites, they were noncitizens and therefore not entitled to own land. America's earliest encounters with Hinduism came not from Indians but from transcendentalist writers such as Ralph Waldo Emerson and Henry David Thoreau. Both authors looked to the *Bhagavad Gita*, part of the Hindu epic *Mahabharata*, as a significant Asian source for philosophical guidance. In 1893, Swami Vivekananda lectured on Hindu ideals in a public forum at the World Parliament of Religions in Chicago. Vivekananda emphasized the Advaita Vedanta philosophy and later founded the Vedanta Society in New York (see Eck 2001). This group was the first Hindu organization primarily designed to attract American adherents; like the International Society for Krishna Consciousness (ISKCON, better known as the Hare Krishnas), it remains a Hindu organization that serves a predominantly non-Indian population of followers. The small Indian Hindu population in the United States became even smaller after the passing of the 1917 Barred Zone Act, and only began to grow after the 1946 Luce-Celler Act and the 1952 McCarran Walter Act.

There are some parallels between the early Sikh migration and the Hindu story. Some of the first Sikhs to immigrate arrived on the west coast over two hundred years ago. The earliest to arrive came from small landowning families in the Punjab region of present-day India and Pakistan; later waves were rural peasants, driven out of Punjab by land rights legislation that created unfavorable economic and social conditions. American law forbade them from bringing their spouses from Punjab and further provided that any woman marrying one of these immigrants would lose her U.S. citizenship. Many Sikh men married Mexican women; many of their children grew up as Catholics, although a small and active Sikh community descended from these immigrants remains in Yuba City, California, to this day (Leonard 1992). Sikh immigration came to a halt in 1917 with the Barred Zone Act and resumed only after 1952, when Sikh students were able to pursue graduate education in the United States. A factor that distinguishes Sikhs from Hindus is that the former are a minority group in India that has faced persecution; Sikhs have therefore emigrated in proportionally larger numbers for centuries. In 1984, the Indian military besieged and occupied the Golden Temple in Amritsar in response to domestic political unrest. The events of 1984 caused an increase in Sikh emigration from India, with many arriving in the United States directly or via Canada. Because of this history of persecution, Sikh immigrants have a very different relationship with India than do Hindus (see Mann 2000).

Indian Muslims followed similar patterns of immigration, both drawn by economic opportunity and driven by political persecution. Indian Muslims arrived to find preexisting Muslim communities in the United States, but these communities were composed of Arab or African American—not South Asian—Muslims. Islam had arrived on American shores with African slaves and nineteenth-century Arab immigrants. The first wave of Muslim immigration ended in 1924, when the Johnson-Reed Immigration Act allowed only a trickle of "Asians," as Arabs were designated, to enter the nation. In the twentieth century there was a substantial increase in Muslim migration to North America, and the Black Muslim movement, which was later named the Nation of Islam, was introduced. Indian Muslim immigrants have been part of the wider global influx of Muslims since 1965.

Some scholars argue that because each of these three religious groups had a presence here before 1965, immigrants did not arrive to a country without Hindus, Sikhs, and Muslims (see Eck 2001). And indeed, Hindu organizations, the Yuba City Sikh community, and non-Indian Muslim congregations did exist before the 1965 act. In a few cases—such as the Hindu community in Atlanta, some of whose members worshiped at the ISKCON temple until the Indian American Cultural Center was built in Smyrna in the 1970s—Indian immigrants took advantage of these preexisting structures. However, these structures were of limited importance to most in the post-1965 immigrant wave, either because they were geographically distant or because the religious experiences and social capital available from these institutions were unappealing or irrelevant to new arrivals. When an adequate population was achieved in a particular geographic area, ethnically homogeneous houses of worship—or, sometimes in the case of churches, separate ethnic services in the same facility—were created (Haddad 2000; Williams 1996).

By dint of numbers and diversity, these new faiths now permeate American society: across professions and trades in the workplace, in the K–12 and collegiate classroom, and increasingly (albeit haltingly) in the mainstream media. Indian American ethnoreligious communities have built houses of worship in cities, suburbs, and small towns from coast to coast. In the 1980s and 1990s, gurdwaras (Sikh temples) were built in Detroit, Birmingham, and Reno, Nevada. South Asian Muslim communities went on to establish mosques geared specifically to their own ethnoreligious needs and interests. (Although most U.S. mosques remain nominally multiethnic, 64 percent of mosques serve one dominant ethnic group, usually South Asian or African American.)[2] Often traditional buildings sprang up to replace or supplement earlier establishments that—because they used preexisting or rented facilities—did not bear an external resemblance to traditional structures. For example, a mandir (Hindu temple) was established as part of the Indian Cultural and Religious Center in a former church building outside Atlanta in 1986; it is a rectangular building made of corrugated steel. In 1993, the Hindu

Temple of Atlanta, built to have the architectural style of Venkateswara temple in southern India, opened its doors to the community. Both mandirs continue to operate today.

These communities arrived in the United States at a time when the world was shrinking, and cultural diversity was finding increased acceptance in American society. They were, therefore, able to break some barriers to economic and social success and, to a certain extent, influence the host community opinions regarding themselves and immigrants in general. They were able to insure good education for their children and also set up mechanisms for elementary religious education. Until recently, however, immigrant Hindu, Muslim, and Sikh communities and their religious structures and practice remained largely invisible to mainstream America. They are now becoming self-aware as groups with national reach and importance.

How many Hindus, Muslims, and Sikhs live in the United States today? It is virtually impossible to know with certainty. Whereas the decennial census affords us a clear look at the ethnic and racial makeup of the U.S. population, it fails on faith. The law expressly permits the Census Bureau to collect data on religious affiliation, but the Bureau declines to do so on the basis of a law that prohibits "mandatory" questions about religion.[3] Some nongovernmental research surveys collect data on religion, but usually do so on the basis of congregation. This is problematic because for followers of Hinduism and Sikhism, religious observance is not centered around the house of worship or the regularized congregational practice typical of the Abrahamic faiths. The surveys will therefore undercount by design, even if they effectively reach the growing number of "de facto congregations" (Warner 1993) now developing in Indian American Hindu and Sikh communities. The American Religious Identification Survey (ARIS) tried to overcome congregational bias by using a random-digit-dialed telephone survey, but its substantial undercount of Hindus (766,000), Muslims (1.1 million) and Sikhs (57,000) as compared to other estimates raises questions as to the degree of its success.

However, by relying upon several data sources, it is possible to estimate with some confidence an approximate population of each religion's American adherents.[4] Hindus constitute the largest religious group within Indian America; it is believed that there are between 1 million and 1.3 million Hindus in the United States. Of the 5.5 to 6 million Muslims in the United States, approximately 25 percent are South Asians; this population includes Pakistani and Bangladeshi Muslims. There are between 250,000 and 500,000 Sikhs. It is virtually impossible to estimate the number of Indian American Christians, because of the difficultly in isolating them from the much larger pools—American Christians, immigrant Christians—of which they are part. Although statistically small, each of these communities is growing as rapidly as the Indian American population as a whole.

As the roster of mandirs, masjids, and gurdwaras above indicates, these religions are part of life all over the United States and indeed are a main-street phenomenon and not just a "New York-and-California" phenomenon, affecting only the cosmopolitan coasts of America (Eck 1996). Indeed this small research participant cohort includes Hindus from Kansas, Texas, and Louisiana; Sikhs raised in Maryland and Florida; Christians from Tennessee and Georgia; and others. This range of experiences and discoveries produced the immigrant activities that shaped the research participants' young lives.

The "New" Religions as Lived Religions

In his seminal work *The Madonna of 115th Street*, Robert Orsi spends very little time discussing the scriptural foundations of Madonna reverence. Rather, he focuses on how participants' lives are oriented around that celebration, from the faithful who partake of the shrine to local businesses that depend upon the flow of pilgrims. He situates the faithful within both the community of believers and the wider geographic and social community of the area. A lived religion approach to the experiences of second-generation Indian Americans allows the researcher to take a qualitative look at religion's role in their lives—to ask not "How Sikh is he?" but rather "How is he Sikh?"[5] This may enable us to understand how religion can shape the identity even of those who consider themselves irreligious, how similar experiences can lead one individual to disenchantment and another to fascination with the home faith, and how encounters in the public space can illustrate the difficult fit between how Western culture understands religion and how some of these religions are practiced—and what all this means for a second generation caught in the middle.

The scholarship of lived religion arose only about a decade ago, as a critique of religious scholars' focus on doctrine and congregational practice at the expense of "a recognition of the laity as actors in their own right" (Hall 1997, viii). This distinction illustrates the Christian shackles in which much of religious scholarship continues to be bound. Although useful in research on Christians and Jews, the distinction between congregational and individual practice would be a false one with respect to some of the religions presented here. For example, attempts to seek out Hindus at their places of worship in order to compare their practice to that of Christians are ultimately flawed in that they ignore most of lived Hinduism, which is not congregational and mandir-centered but rather personal and home-centered (Mazumdar and Mazumdar 2003).[6]

The data thus far available on religion and second-generation Americans is similarly limiting. Both Ebaugh and Chafetz (2000) and their colleagues researched a number of immigrant ethnoreligious communities in Houston and accessed them primarily via the house of worship. This Western and congregationalist bias may itself explain why Ebaugh and Chafetz's report Indian American

Hindu youth are found to be "less participatory" than Hispanic Pentecostal youth. Even if Ebaugh and Chafetz and their colleagues were correct, and not improperly applying the concept of affiliation with a religions institution to measure participation, this tells us little about what religion looks like in the lives of youth.

When examining religion in the lives of the Indian Americans, it is imperative to consider the sociohistorical context that shapes their experiences and dialogues. Experiences with religion may vary across space (for example, South versus Northeast, urban versus suburban) and time (the 1970s versus the 1990s), and be affected by events of global and local importance. Global events such as the first Gulf War, national events and political disputes, and local upheaval over issues such as school integration and court-ordered bussing all brought to the research participants' attention to their status as racial and religious minorities. The individual experience of these research participants is also situated within, and affected by, their experiences with ethnoreligious community and transnational ties. Most fundamentally, we must recall that second-generation Indian Americans are living religion in a society where Christianity is omnipresent and hegemonic. These research participants were raised with steeples on the horizon or megachurches on the corner, with school holidays at Christmas and Easter while they had to miss a day for Eid or Diwali, and with an entire vocabulary and imagery of religion that was profoundly Western and Christian in nature. Awareness of the context is critical to understanding American Hinduism, American Sikhism, and American Islam as well as seeing how non-European Christians negotiate Christianity as ethnic and racial minorities.[7]

Religion has been characterized as a flavor of ethnicity that fades over time. The notion of "symbolic ethnicity" (Gans 1979) or "symbolic religiosity" (Gans 1994) is certainly a part of the experience for some Indian Americans. Maira (2002) calls religion an element of "ethnic nostalgia," something that helps the second generation think about the essence of Indianness but which, she implies, will fade over time. In reference to second-generation Indian American Hindus, Fenton (1992) identified approximately one-third of Indian American students who enrolled in his undergraduate course on Hinduism as "culturally Hindu." According to Fenton (1992, 263), being culturally Hindu "is equivalent to the customs of the ethnic group accompanied by broadly Hindu or Indian moral principles." He further states "Hindu rituals survive for them as a second-hand celebration of ethnic heritage and as festival (fun and games)." But my data reveal that there is substantially more than nostalgia going on as second-generation Indian American approach religion.

Negotiating Religion

As we consider the experiences of religious minorities in the United States—here, second-generation Indian Americans—we must observe the context as well as the content of their religious lives: What does being in the company of an ethnoreligious community mean to the "religious self" of the research participants? How do they interact with the dominant culture that surrounds them day-to-day? For example, how do Hindu or Muslim students' concerns about following their religion interact with their fears of being "weird" in their classmates' eyes? How does a person apply the religious rules described by his or her parents to the moral questions of life in the American milieu during college and adulthood? Raised in the echo chamber of American religious vocabulary—scripture, commandments, salvation—how does the individual come to understand the tenets of the home faith?

Second-generation Indian Americans encounter hundreds of questions like these in the course of simply becoming who they are. How do they negotiate religion? At one level, this is the story of the research participants' home/school conflict writ upon their religious lives. Ballard (1994) has suggested that South Asian youth in the West are "skilled cultural navigators," moving comfortably between the home culture and wider society, just as bilingual people switch easily between languages. This very charitable observation does not fit my research cohort. The forty-one research participants in this study reported a decidedly unsmooth process with many bumps and bruises along the way: social miscues, embarrassments, frustration, and guilt.

Virtually all the research participants grew up in predominantly white Christian communities with very few other Indian American—or even Asian American—young people in their schools. Hindu, Sikh, and Muslim research participants grew up in a society that presented them with a competing religious worldview.[8] For these research participants, a major element of their experience with religion involved feelings of difference arising from the obvious contrasts between their home religions and the Christian hegemony in the broader society.[9] These non-Christian research participants reported feeling different from the dominant society because of their and their parents' religious beliefs and practices. In childhood, these feelings focused on specific events. When asked about feeling different as a child, for example, Anila mentioned "not going to church was something. People talked about going to church and I did not go to church." In adolescence—including the high-school and college years—they were manifest in concentrated attention to theological questions and ideas.

Doubt, denial, and discovery are all elements of "negotiating religion," as is the backdrop of the research participants' cognitive development and their evolving relationship with religious ideas and opportunities.[10] During the K–12 life period, across religion affiliations, all the research participants felt that religion was something they had to do. Their participation was most frequently derivative from their parents'; whether they jumped at the opportunity to participate in the ethnoreligious community or felt "forced" or "dragged" to worship (both words used by several research participants), they were never-theless most likely to participate with the same frequency as their parents. Likewise, their parents were their primary source of informal religious teach-ing. By contrast, college is a time of freedom and a stage of life when Indian Americans, like most young people, are pushing the boundaries of childhood rules—and even of societal rules—as part of figuring out what they believe and who they are. Religious practice in this period is rare except when research par-ticipants visit home, but deep thinking about matters of faith and transcen-dence is common (Maira 2002; Pascarella and Terenzini 1991). In college many "fell away" from practice as such due to distance from home, but all found new ways to approach, experience, and interact with religion: through study, thought, travel, or the simple acts of negotiating a college student's daily life choices. They also found themselves (most for the first time) in a position to engage with their Indian culture—which, as they participated less in the organ-ized religious practice of their home religion, they could begin to define in terms separate from their religious community identity—as more important than religion during the college period. In adulthood, the relationship to reli-gion is characterized by a new-found focus on family and legacy, by a certain degree of nostalgia, and by the continuing presence or absence of other factors such as an ethnoreligious community. Religion for Indian Americans meta-morphosed from something they were forced to do either by parents or be-cause of the school they attended to having the choice to participate or not and do it on their terms.

There is more to negotiating religion than merely finding a balance be-tween social worlds or competing theologies. The negotiation of religion also in-volves the effects of each world upon the other: America's Protestant Christian culture and ethos affect how research participants approach and understand their home faiths, and experiences related to religion shape the research par-ticipants' views of American's Christian majority and the society in which it is situated. The popular catchphrases for the phenomenon—"straddling two worlds," "living in the hyphen," and the like—imply more balance and stasis than the data here reveal. The experience of navigating religion is dynamic, nonlinear, contradictory, and as likely to be characterized by lingering frustra-tions as by happy mediums.

Christianity 24/7

It sounds like a truism, of course, but it must be said plainly: For the research participants, home life was very different from school life. At home they found multiple manifestations of Indian culture; it infused everything, from language to food to the art on the walls. At school, their home religions (except that of Christians) were invisible: There were few if any other Indian Americans, India and Indian Americans were absent from most history courses, and the school year was organized around the Judeo-Christian calendar of holidays. Even the word *Indian* was commonly used and understood in the school setting to refer to Native Americans and not to Indian Americans. As a result, the Indian American child's two epicenters of socialization carry dramatically different meanings, offering different models of success and fulfillment and sometimes producing opposing ideas and beliefs.

Perhaps all this is inevitable in a world where parents are outnumbered—numerically and by hours of they day when their influence is felt—by contemporary American culture, by the more liberal social rules imposed by the parents of their children's non-Indian peers, and by the influences of white Protestant American culture that shape public school pedagogy and curricula. Inevitable or not, research participants experienced socialization at home that often validated parts of their ethnic identity, but ended up not feeling proud of that culture because of the messages they received at school. The meaning and impact of the difference varies across the research participants cohort; in general, it seems to depend at least in part upon how extreme the difference is between home and school. For example, Avinash didn't feel very different, in large part because he went to a diverse school in the Philadelphia area, where he was one of many Indian American young people. Others, like Monali in Kansas, dealt with more extreme contrasts between home and school and therefore were more reticent about "being Indian" anywhere outside the home. Many research participants recalled being teased, and this continues today.

Other scholars have amply described the bicultural conflicts that Indian immigrant and second-generation students faced, the feeling out of place both at home and at school.[11] This conflict between two worlds involves gender expectations, social pressures, conflicting cultural norms, and parents' coping with new experiences—which interact in dynamic, crosscutting and contradictory ways across the lifespan.[12] For many of these second-generation Indian Americans there is also a third space, a physical, emotional and social space within the context of the ethnoreligious community, where research participants encountered people who shared their challenges and frustrations. These research participants negotiated the home/school divide in part by retreating periodically to the company of friends who also felt out of place in the two worlds, who shared both the anguish of being different from school peers and common complaints about parents' actions and expectations.

The research participants' day-to-day encounters with Christianity during the K–12 period, even when not oppressive or hurtful per se, nevertheless made them aware of themselves as different and therefore affected the ongoing navigation of religious identity. Substantial exposure to Christianity was found across the cohort, but one research participant had a particularly intense set of experiences that brings this issue into stark focus. By attending a private Episcopalian school, Leela—a Hindu—was face-to-face with dominant Christianity on a daily basis, which led her to experience sensations of turmoil, self-doubt, and questioning her parents.

> Every night we'd have Communion and [my sister and I] took it. It's interesting. . . . We learned more about the Bible, and I read the Bible forwards and backwards, than the *Gita* or anything else. At points, when I was a little bit older, I was like, "Should I be taking this or not?" I would go home and I'd ask my parents and they'd say, "obviously we are Hindu and this is what we believe in, but you can think of it in your head as if you're doing this for your god, too." Some Jewish people would not take [Communion], but I just took it. When I'd pray to a god [during the school's Communion services], I usually just prayed to my god.

This story illustrates with particular vividness the sociocultural context in which the research participants were raised: Christianity, and not their home religion, was omnipresent.[13] Even more interesting is how Leela reacted when she began to understand intellectually the difference between Christianity and Hinduism and to question her parents about how to deal with that distinction: "Should I be taking [Communion] or not?" Her parents told her to think "as if you're doing this for your god"—that is, to think of the Communion bread and wine as *prasad*.[14] Leela found herself doubting her parents' advice when she saw her Jewish classmates declining Communion. If other non-Christians reject Communion, Leela thought, why are my parents telling me to take it? She could not answer this question because she, like most other research participants, had not received enough education to overcome an information gap regarding the home faith. While it's fair to argue that Leela's Jewish classmates probably declined Communion out of a vague understanding ("that's part of being Jewish") rather than a clear knowledge that the Bible prohibits Jews from consuming foods offered to another god, Leela nevertheless felt an information gap. Jewish kids were standing up for their identity by not taking Communion, so why, Leela wondered, was she not standing up for her identity, and why were her parents instructing her not to?

Likewise, Vishali's experiences as a second-grader in a Connecticut public school were early and stark reminder—from a teacher, no less—that religiously she did not belong. In Vishali's second grade classroom The Lord's Prayer was recited at the beginning of class. She and another Indian child, together with two Jewish children, "were put out in the hall and we were all alone. That should not have happened. There was no reason that we should have been sent out. I remember asking people, 'Why are we out here?' We were the smart ones and I thought we were here to learn and we should have been the ones in there." It would be fair to point out that a second-grader lacks the cognitive development to understand the existential meaning of God or of her public schoolteacher's exclusion of her for believing in different gods. It would also be fair to point out that teacher-led prayer in a public school classroom in the late 1980s was flagrantly unconstitutional, and giving students the choice to step out of the room did not remedy its unconstitutionality.[15] But this is not a story about theology or legal issues; it is about lived religion. Even if Vishali could not conceptualize God and religion as an adult could, and had only the child's understanding of God as a vague, distant and benevolent figure, she understood and remembered twenty years later this message: On the basis of a part of who she was, she was not welcome. Something was happening in her classroom, in her school, that did not involve her and that she had to exclude herself from in order to be true to herself. Although Vishali might not have understood the line between religion and culture in second grade, in hindsight she realizes the marginalization she faced was because of religion. Because of what religion now means to her—its evocation of transcendent reality, a supreme being, and other concepts of sacred significance—her second-grade experience exerts a continuing effect.

Experiences did not have to be so blatant as Leela's and Vishali's. Priti, another Hindu female, attended public school in Pennsylvania; she described feeling awkward during in-class religious celebrations because they marked her as different (albeit invisibly different) from her classmates: "In grade school on many occasions, when we would celebrate Christian holidays, I definitely remember feeling that I was not a part of that celebration. I mean every holiday— Easter, Thanksgiving, Christmas." Priti remarked that her public school's "curriculum at that point was very secular Christian."

Other research participants reported not only teacher-student interactions like these but also experiences on the playground and in the lunch room when there were not adults present. Brugesh talked at length about the way kids in school would "treat you because you are different religion, because you believe in different gods." Although "some of the kids wanted to learn," Brugesh said of most of his classmates: "Since it wasn't their religion or their background, they thought it was stupid." His classmates asked him why his god had an elephant's head (Ganesha), or why his goddess has eight arms; their intention was not to learn but to taunt and tease Brugesh for being different. Nikhil had a similar experience in his North Carolina public school. He was teased for not eating beef, and "whenever we talked about religion in our classes, someone would ask why we prayed to cows and [would criticize] the fact that we don't believe in Christ. That made me stand out." Religion-based teasing and ostracism reinforced research participants' existing insecurities about their identity and their place in the American scene. While hoping to "fit in" in the school social community, they faced classmates and sometimes teachers who make fun of an element of themselves that in another part of their life is the essence of what provides them comfort. For many of the research participants, such teasing reinforced their inclination to keep their "school" lives and "home" or "weekend" lives very separate, or to avoid those personal characteristics of a religious nature that would mark them as different, such as vegetarianism.

The Christian Norm and the Western Wish

The negotiation of religion for second-generation Hindus, Sikhs, and Muslims was also influenced by the theological and practical differences between their home faiths and the Christianity to which they were pervasively exposed. Being raised in the United States meant absorbing Western sentiments on what constitutes a religion and what the societal function of a religion is meant to be. The concept of religion as a rule-based phenomenon and of worship as a regularized congregational activity is Western and Biblical in origin. Christian tenets and the manners of practice and worship common to the Christian churches (such as the kneeling, hands-folded position in prayer, the legal and social recognition of Christmas as a national holiday) are normative in American society. For the research participants, therefore, their home religions were not only difficult to understand in the abstract but also visibly and strikingly inconsistent with the understanding of what religion says and looks like that the research participants absorbed as young Americans. Also, the research participants are American as well as Indian; an important difference between Indian immigrants, particularly Hindus and Sikhs and second-generation Indian Americans is that Indians from India "just believe" in their religions, while Indians raised in America seem to want to know *why* to believe it.

As a result, many Hindu research participants wished for what Anita called a "Ten Commandments of Hinduism." The research participants made sense of religion not only through the vocabulary of Christianity but also through its theological lens. Having learned their religions as a sometimes amorphous set of cultural phenomena and lifestyle guidelines—often divorced from their scriptural underpinnings and other senses of source—these research participants yearned for the types of hard information they saw in the overtly rule-based dialogue of contemporary American Christianity. When asked to explain how she understood "religion," for example, Anita said

> My definition of religion has become more of what would be almost along the lines of the Ten Commandments, or what's similar to them in a lot of the different religions. And I identify myself as being Hindu because that's what I know, that's what I grew up with. If I was going to pick a place to go to worship, it would be the temple [as opposed to a church or synagogue]. When I can, I observe holidays, just because, I mean, it, it's been a part of me. I'm just as religious, but less Hindu. For me now, it's more of a moral thing than it is the traditional thing.

Anita associates religion, but not Hinduism, with rules and the idea of following rules. Although it was expressed by research participants of various religious backgrounds, this concern about lacking rules and not having a clearly expressed set of guidelines to follow in life seemed particularly acute among the Hindu research participants. Here we see Anita continuing to identify with Hinduism because it is what she grew up with, but also expressing a yearning for a religion that fit into the concept of religion that she learned from American culture. The Hindu, Muslim, and Sikh research participants were, and are still, trying to understand and construct their religious identities in the context of a society that is not only dominated by Christianity but also renders Hinduism and Sikhism invisible and "terrorizes" the Islamic faith. (These phenomena are discussed in chapters 4 and 5.) Perhaps because of the presence of a dominant alternative theology—Christianity—or perhaps because of their academic exposure to Western rationalism, or perhaps simply for reasons of cognitive development and adolescent exploration, many research participants expressed a need to understand religious practices as a predicate to participating in them. Anita continued:

> My view of religion is very different than that [in which] my parents were raised. . . . I consider myself Hindu, but there are certain things I really have a problem with doing blindly. Like if there are certain traditions or way certain things are done, I'm always asking why. And if I can't get a reason of why things were done and it just doesn't make sense, I'm more likely to not do it versus if someone says, "Oh, this is why we do this." Okay, that makes sense, or it may not make sense in this day and age, but it made sense back then or probably when it started, so I can kind of go with it.

The "Sunday schools" of many research participants' childhoods, described at greater length below and in chapter 3, apparently did not rise to the occasion. Recently, in an apparent response to widespread feelings like these, Hindu groups have sprung up that mimic the programs of Christian youth groups. For example, *Bhagavad Gita* study groups—conspicuously similar to the ubiquitous Bible study group—have formed on some college campuses in recent years. Programs like these are developing as a response to the desire expressed by Anita and others, and offer a clue as to what American Hinduism may look like a generation hence.

For many research participants in this cohort, such wishes for a clearer view of the home religion sprouted into feelings of doubt about the home religion itself. It is not unusual during puberty and adolescence for an individual's approach to religion to shift from a rather unreserved acceptance (if not a particularly deep or nuanced understanding) of religious beliefs toward a more critical, even doubtful, attitude (Kooistra and Pargament 1999; Tamminen 1994).

Research studies on predominantly white Christian adolescents suggest an interplay between such religious doubting and the choices adolescents make to engage in, or disengage from, organized religion; they show that there is a decline in the frequency of attendance at religious services between eighth and twelfth grades (Regnerus, Smith, and Fritsch 2003). The inherent weakness of research that focuses on attendance of non-Judeo-Christians has already been discussed. Leaving this aside for a moment, let us consider the possible import of these data to second-generation Indian Americans. The drop in attendance might reflect growing autonomy as teens mature. Several of my research participants said they avoided attending ethnoreligious functions when they could as adolescents; those who continued attending during the high school years began to describe attendance as less a matter of parent-enforced obligation and more one of personal volition. Moreover, a study of adolescents in Iowa found that although frequency of religious service attendance—that is, Sunday morning church attendance—dipped during the high school years, levels of participation in other religious activities tended to rise over the same period (King, Elder, and Whitbeck 1997). This probably reflects the adolescent focus on religious gatherings as a social outlet; King et al. do not appear to have inquired how many of those young Christians who skipped church on Sundays attended church youth groups on Wednesday evenings. Likewise, Indian American "Sunday school" programs were attractive to the research participants primarily because of this social function.

Because of the contrast between what religion "should be" (the American Christian view) and what their religions looked like, and because of deficiencies in their own religious self-understanding, many Indian Americans reported that they began questioning the meaning of their home faiths late in high school and during the college years.[16] Anisa compared Hindus unfavorably with other Indian Americans with respect to religiosity, for example: "It means a lot to me, but some Indian girls couldn't give a shit. A lot of Indian guys are like, 'Whatever!' But my Christian Indian friends are very Christian, my Muslim Indian friends are very Muslim, and I look around and I wonder what is wrong with our Hindu friends."

Parents often could not provide an effective counterbalance in this negotiation. The research participants' parents had been raised in a Hindu milieu, but virtually none of them had actually studied their specific religion; they could not answer their children's questions in the way their children demanded. In this negotiation, participation was no substitute for knowledge. Thus, although he went to the mosque every Friday with his family, Salim—who identifies himself as an Isma'ili Muslim—felt he didn't know what it meant to be Isma'ili or Muslim. "I was learning about my own religion . . . through the media. You know, you just hear on TV. . . . I just knew that everything I heard about Muslim was bad." Anila too described her parents' laissez-faire approach to passing Hinduism down to the next generation: "Once or twice I went to church with my friends in second grade. In retrospect, it is very interesting that my parents just said, 'Yeah, just go.' My parents were never like, 'you are Hindu' and 'we are not Christian.' They never tried to teach us Hinduism." The insistence of the second generation that their home faith's practices be explained to them is a new and challenging demand on ethnoreligious communities whose immigrant members have never felt a similar need to intellectualize their understanding of religion.

Salim's and Anila's stories exhibit a very common disconnect between the immigrant and second generations. For the parental, immigrant generation, merely gathering with coreligionists and making efforts to transmit the rituals and heritage to their children is lived religion. For the research participants, who were raised in the American milieu, lived religion was incomplete without learning the whys and wherefores of their home religion. Raised in India, the parents want merely to continue being Indian. The research participants wanted to assert an Indian identity, and did not feel they could fully do so until they were prepared not only to act out rituals but to explain the rituals to themselves and others.

Negotiating Ethnoreligious Community as a Third Space

Religion functions as a way of relating the individual not only to God but also to those around him. As Hinduism and Sikhism are developing American iterations, religious gatherings are serving a function in providing the second generation with a community. For the second generation, ethnoreligious community and its formalized "Sunday school" programs—a term obviously adopted from the dominant Christian lexicon—have provided a third space, between the home and the dominant society. The community provides the space to express one's religious beliefs and, during research participants' K–12 years, functioned as a social safe haven and the first place second-generation Indian Americans could begin to develop a sense of their place within—and outside—the home and school worlds. In this space, those research participants who had access to such a community felt physically, socially, and emotionally protected relative to their experiences in the wider world. Throughout their K–12 years, the phenomenon of religious community as a place to come together and hang out with young people like themselves was for most even more important than the religious function per se. Anisa offered a typical description: "I went to Indian cultural school, which turned out to be my biggest outlet, because I finally had peers who were not my family friends, who I could get to know and talk to. I was so happy. I had something to go to every weekend. So they taught us a lot. It was predominantly north Indian, so some of the stuff I could not relate to. Given what I had, why not? I started going when I was fifteen. I have learned a great deal, so much that I still know today. It was very, very valuable."

Although research participants who took part in Sunday school uniformly reported looking forward to the weekly event, most kept it separate from their week-long school life. Nikhil carefully hid his weekend life from his schoolmates: "We'd go to the temple and I would never tell anybody that I went to the temple. If I had to wear like Indian clothes, I'd make sure none of my friends would see me. If my mom was ever wearing a sari while we were out at the mall, I would not hang out with her 'cause I was afraid that I would be seen by one of my friends or by a girl I was wanting to date."

Nikhil was not the only research participant who made the conscious decision to keep the Indian and American parts of their lives separate. With very few exceptions, the research participants reported that they tried to keep information about their home lives private from their friends at school because they were concerned with others' perceptions about their lives, and assumed the worst of those perceptions. To a certain extent, this was just another manifestation of the common childhood and adolescent inclination to keep home and school separate or to see parents as embarrassing household antiquities. But for most of these Indian American research participants, it also reflected a discomfort with the negative ways in which outsiders could see their home life—a discomfort which itself became part of their ethnic identity. Monali said she tried to avoid situations where her "Indianness [might] come out" at school. She also reported actively lying to her school friends about her weekend activities. She explained her deception by describing the contrast between her family and those of her friends: She noticed that on weekends her friends would be at home while their parents were out, and she was always out with her parents. Embarrassed by this difference, she would make up stories that she felt would make her weekends sound more like those of her school friends.

For some, like Aziz, the two-sided life was not a choice but a matter of circumstance: "On weekends, you have to go to religious education, you have to go hang out with this other community. And those kids don't go to school with me." For others, living a divided life meant going to school for studying, not socializing. The socializing occurred on weekends, when Sunday school provided their only meaningful social outlet. This partial social isolation also served their parents' goals: to create boundaries between their children and Americans' worst vices—sex, drugs, and rock-and-roll.

College meant new and different negotiations. Although still a Christian-dominated social context, college was the first time that many of the research participants interacted with large numbers of coreligionists and coethnics their own age and on their own terms. Collegiate Indian and South Asian student organizations and informal networks of coethnic roommates and friends came to function as the aforementioned third space while also providing the first time and space in which research participants could participate in fashioning a self- and group identity unmoored from parental designs. At the same time, research participants continued negotiating the balance and form of their religions identities in the presence of many of the same influences that they had encountered before: Christianity-based calendars and structures, Christianity's status as reference point for understanding religion, proselytization, and the like.

College as a life stage was also a time of religious reflection for the research participants' non-Indian peers. As a result, several research participants encountered a new factor in their negotiation: the positive attention and curiosity of outsiders. Smita, for example, had always kept her home and school lives strictly separated, and had never spoken to her white high school classmates about her culture or identity. In college, she observed an Indian American friend cooking Indian food for and describing Indian culture and traditions to her non-Indian roommates. Seeing her friend's experience showed her (as, perhaps, it showed her friend) that Americans who were not Indian could still be curious and enthusiastic about Indian culture:

> Before, everything I did with my Indian culture was always kept behind closed doors, and it was always with people of my same background. My American friends stayed away, and I never let them in, or never even asked them [to participate in any Indian event]. And for my friend to have done that—she had an American roommate, she was like, "this is Krishna," and just explaining to Evelyn, "this is what [ritual or prayer] I'm gonna do." Her parents lived an hour away, and they used to come every couple of weeks with food and we'd all just sit around and actually have Indian food with other, you know, non-Indians. That was a real shock for me.

This experience, of revealing her ethnic self and not being ridiculed or rejected for it, was surprising and encouraging to Smita. It opened a whole new set of thoughts in her negotiation, and ultimately made her less reticent about being "openly Indian" (my words) in the company of non-Indians. Nikhil reported a similar experience late in his high-school years:

> My friends start asking, about my beliefs and "why you believe it" and "why do you do things differently." I don't think I understood really until I started asking myself that. I started doing things because my parents said to do them, but I never really understood. The fact that my friends were asking these questions and I didn't know the answers, I think made me start recognizing that I needed to know more about my background and my culture. I think that was the thing that sort of, sort of pushed that forward. . . . I don't think my friends were trying to judge me, I think they

were just curious. And I think that stimulated curiosity in myself and I
recognized the fact that I didn't know as much as I should.

These interactions drove Nikhil to pursue academic study of religion in college.

The entire range of experiences discussed in this chapter have continued in
adulthood. As adults, the research participants find themselves negotiating
religion not only in the context of a sometimes hostile society but also in relation to the range of beliefs and observances of the other second-generation Indian Americans who could become their friends and spouses. The research
participants' current negotiations incorporate new factors—in particular, how
they want belief and religious identity to be part of their family life. Nikhil, for
example, is actively engaged in thinking about his religious identity and beliefs
and even engaging in religious practice—at home and at his local *mandir*—to a
surprising degree. This probably relates to the fact that he is about to become a
father, and is pondering whether and how he will be able to pass along Hinduism and his Indian American identity to his third-generation children.

For the adherents of these religions, at this historical moment, the processes and sensations of negotiating religion continues to define their life experiences and affect the development of their ethnic identities. The evolution of
each research participant's own beliefs, the effects of new developments in
their lives like Nikhil's impending fatherhood and others' search for a life part-
ner, and the impact of early twenty-first–century world events and social and
political movements are all crystals in the shifting kaleidoscope image within
which second-generation Indian Americans are negotiating religion.

2

Ethnicity and Religion

Scholarly work on the "identity question" for Indian Americans often springs from analysis of cultural, racial, and national-origin traits such as language, immigrant tradition, and assimilation. This theoretical approach, by itself, disserves second-generation Indian Americans. The importance of religion for Indian Americans must not be obscured because of scholarly discomfort with faith. Nor should religious beliefs or rituals be viewed as no more than ethnic traits. Religion divides most Indian Americans from virtually all non-Indians, including other racial and linguistic minorities.

What one discovers upon teasing apart the religious threads from the finely woven fabric of Indian American ethnic identity is this: Religion as a factor in ethnic identity development that touches research participants at profound levels, and in a variety of different ways, across the life span. Unlike other factors that affect ethnic identity development such as language, ethnoreligious community, or transnational experiences, religion—lived religion, in its practice, taught principles, and unspoken tenets—was powerfully present in the lives and identities of all research participants. This was true across life periods, genders, and religious affiliations, even (and sometimes especially) when research participants did not self-identify as religious.[1]

When I conducted interviews with these forty-one people, I got a snapshot in time. What they relayed to me were the things that had happened to them up to that point in relation to race, religion, and ethnicity. Understanding their identities is about looking back and looking forward. Their stories illustrated their identities at that moment while also offering clues about how those identities might continue to develop and change in the future. As Hall (1994, 394) tells us, "It is not something which already exists, transcending place, time, history and culture. Cultural identities come from somewhere, have histories. But, like everything which is historical, they undergo constant transformation. Far from being eternally fixed in some essentialized past, they are subject to the continuous 'play' of history, culture and power."

For second-generation Indian Americans, ethnic identity provides a sense of belonging and historical continuity; it encompasses and is informed by factors such as family, ethnoreligious community, language, dimensions of culture (such as food, clothing, and Bollywood films), experiences of racial discrimination, and transnationalism. Ethnicity's importance is that it connotes a set of experiences shared by others and thereby creates an emotional bond (with a community and with the past and future) and a sense of shared experience with coethnics. In everyday social arenas, culture gives meanings to identity, and an individual uses identity to construct affiliations with and boundaries among other individuals and groups. These affiliations and boundaries define (in part) who and what we are.[2]

The paradigmatic inquiry when discussing ethnic identity is "What are you?" In this respect, ethnic identity is also situational, and individuals will have a different ethnic self-conception depending upon the contrast with which they are faced.[3] Consider, for example, the different scenarios in which one might answer the question, "What are you?" with each of these labels: Asian, Indian, Bengali, or American.[4] Moreover, the same label can connote very different meanings across individuals. Ethnic labels chosen by individuals may at times be important and representative of the respondents' identity, but we must not focus on words at the expense of meaning. For example, over one-third of the research participants identified themselves as "Indian across" the lifespan.[5] This group included both males and females, and included Hindus, Sikhs, a Methodist, a Catholic, and an atheist. Several of the Hindu research participants cited their belief in and affinity for Hinduism as a major reason they were "Indian"; a Malayali Catholic respondent drew the same connection between Catholicism and her Indian identity. For Anisa, being Indian was a phenomenon based upon experience and sentiment; she reported feeling a connection to Indian culture because she attended cultural and religious school on the weekends "and would go to *pujas* with my cousins." By contrast, Mina identifies as Indian simply "because I was born to Indian parents"; Indianness for her connotes national origins and little more. Neha declined to describe herself as Indian in her interview, but acknowledged that she would often use that word to describe herself because "what they [people who ask 'what are you?' or 'where are you from?'] are really asking you is, 'What ethnicity are you?'" Moreover, most of these research participants were unreflective about their ethnic identity, defining it with a simple word or phrase—such as "Indian" or "Indian American"— not because this adequately described the full scope of their ethnic selves but because the term and the meanings they ascribed to it had been learned over years and decades of categorization by outsiders, acknowledgment (or nonacknowledgment) of their racial status, exposure to the expectations of the immigrant generation, and as a means to deal with their sensations of their own difference. When a term is defined so divergently, by reference to (or without reference to) so many various factors, its scholarly value approaches zero.

When we look beyond the label and hear the voices of the research participants, we can understand and describe the ethnic identity development process and the factors affecting it. Labels aside, most of the second-generation Indian American research participants, like many other second-generation Americans who are from ethnic and racial minorities, define their ethnicity by reference to traditional markers, such as religion, race, national origin, and language.[6]

Most research participants' ethnic awareness, their understanding of what it meant to be Indian, came from a small number of primary sources: family, their ethnoreligious communities, and transnational experiences of travel to India (including experiences with family there). A research participant's ethnic awareness could be further affected by any of a variety of factors: speaking their home language with relatives, eating Indian food at home, taking Indian dance classes and language classes, watching Indian cinema, reading books about India, wearing Indian clothing and jewelry, and attending ethnoreligious Sunday school classes.[7] Monali's eyes sparkled as she talked about Indian culture: "We had garbas, Diwali, temple, Holi. Any kind of function. People would get together consistently. What best *salwar kameez* can I wear. The *pyle* on my feet. The *bichiya* on my toes. When you are a kid, that is how you associate. Like my *choti* with the tassel on the end, I would wear that. Whose jewelry were you wearing. . . . Putting coconut oil on your skin and your hair. That is what I grew up with. Eating *dal* and rice every day. Every day." Not all research participants were so uniformly enthusiastic about Indian culture. For several, many dimensions of culture felt more like dimensions of differentness—palpable symbols not of their heritage but of the ways in which they were unlike their white, Christian peers who ate spaghetti, spoke English at home, and stayed out late on weekends. Either way, an ethnic awareness was gained.

Most research participants saw their ethnic identity as something inherited; they did not realize that their identities also developed in reference to their social experiences growing up in the United States. Ethnicity does not exist in a vacuum. The dominant culture and the subcultures one encounters shape both ethnicity itself and the meanings ascribed to ethnic identity. Just as ethnic identity may involve a sense of connectedness with one's national, cultural, linguistic, and religious origins, it may include the particular prejudices and cultural tensions that the individual experiences when coming in contact with the dominant white group.[8] These research participants' ethnic identities were affected by the experience of being categorized and marginalized due to their racial, religious, and immigration status; by parental and familial expectations; by interacting with peers and authority figures at school; and by bicultural conflict. A family's socioeconomic class could play a role. Where both parents of a research participant worked outside the home, the resulting time constraints affected the child's access to an ethnoreligious community. Geography—and the resulting ease or difficulty of accessing an ethnoreligious community—could also be a factor. Transnational experiences of travel to India also played a major role in developing the shape and scope of ethnic awareness.

Ethnic identity is not the sum of the experiences and influences described above, but rather the sum of their effects on the individual. The development of an individual's ethnic identity is a complex, continuous, and dynamic process affected by many phenomena. The identity of the individual changes in form and content across the lifespan, beginning with a young child's initial sense of self and awareness of others through and including older adults' summarization, integration, and evaluation of their life accomplishments (Erikson 1963). In between, second-generation Indian American adolescents may feel caught in a bicultural conflict, pitting their parents' ethnic values against those of the mainstream society, and young adults like those in this study may look to forge an identity that draws on concepts earlier rejected. Even at a single moment in time, no one identity (such as religion or gender) describes completely who a given research participant was or is.[9] At any given moment, elements of identity may be explored in depth or virtually ignored, committed to or rejected out of hand; most individuals even described feeling multiple or conflicting identities simultaneously. For some, there is continuity across the lifespan; for others, a factor that is salient at one point may be relatively insignificant at another.

For reasons obvious to anyone who has gone through it, adolescence, with all its physical changes and emotional turbulence, is recognized as a particularly important life stage for identity formation and individual development within a social context. Even during adolescence, however, an individual is not likely to explore all social identity domains at once; it is not unusual for an adolescent to be actively exploring one dimension while another remains unexamined.[10] The identity that becomes salient to the individual is often the one that is salient to the outside world. Because Indian Americans are a racial minority in the United States, and often members of a religious minority as well, they are more likely to be engaged in an exploration of their racial or religious identity than of another social identity (see Tatum 1997). Ethnicity and race exert significant influence on each other, so much so that the two terms are frequently conflated; more than one remarked, "My race is Indian." This response in itself reveals many things about how race is conceptualized; it shows us that race is understood by the research participants as a biological, or at least primordial, factor.

Racial identity in the United States does affect the ethnic identity development process (Adams 2001). Indeed, ethnicity and its components (such as religion) are frequently racialized; we cannot understand ethnic identity in the present without understanding the historical processes that racialize the factors affecting ethnic identity (Pierce 2000). Life experiences involving discrimination

often, but not always, exerted a particularly strong effect on the research participants' ethnic identities.[11] For other research participants, experiences of religious discrimination brought other social identities, such as religion, to the
fore. For still others, experiences of discrimination functioned at a more general
level—not generating attention to any particular facet of identity but reminding
the research participant of his differentness from others and therefore causing
attention to the "ethnic self" broadly conceived. Ironically, traditional ethnic
terminology—such as describing oneself as merely "Indian"—may both conceal
from an individual the role these contemporary factors play and protect him or
her from the most emotionally uncomfortable elements of cultural differentness from the American milieu. "Ethnic identities are not solely determined in
response to racial ideologies, but racism increases the need for a positive self-
defined identity in order to survive psychologically" (Tatum 1997, 165).

Intersecting Influences and the Passage of Time

During childhood and adolescence (which I will often refer to as the K–12 life
stage), many research participants experienced a heightened sense of marginalization, often having conflicting images of who they were and feeling a sense of
"not belonging" to either their "old" or "new" social worlds.[12] Others developed
what one might call a love/hate relationship with elements of their ethnicity.
Monali, who gushed earlier about ethnoreligious celebrations, also said that she
"hated Indian food as a child. Not that I didn't like it"—she loved the tastes, but
hated how it made her feel different. She also said she "felt very dirty compared
to white women" because of the color of her skin. Some responded by compart-
mentalizing their lives, participating in school activities and in a family or ethnoreligious community but keeping these two lives separate. Most felt their
home lives would be rejected by their non-Indian schoolmates. (Often, they
were right.) As a result, they experienced even greater alienation and isolation
at school. However, the reader should not assume that this separateness necessarily reflects shame about the home life. My research shows that most of the
second-generation Indian Americans who kept the two spheres of their lives
separate were happy when at home and looked forward to weekends when they
could socialize with their coethnic friends. This contrast of experiences itself
became part of the ethnic identity of many research participants.

Just as the ethnic identity development process is not linear, it also is not
constant. It proceeds in fits and starts, responding to critical incidents and other
encounters as well as to the arc of the individual's development as a social person.[13] Here, critical incidents can refer both to positive experiences with family,
coethnic peers, and the ethnoreligious community and to experiences of discrimination, exclusion, and marginalization. Critical incidents are characterized
both by their immediate emotional impact and the reflection and intellectual

changes they can engender and and thereby affect individuals' understanding of their ethnic self. But ethnic identity is not shaped only by identifiable and describable experiences; it is also shaped by those people with whom one has constant contact and by the unspoken norms and beliefs of parents and others in the ethnoreligious community. These rules and mores are themselves mechanisms of culture that help create an individual's sense of ethnic identity. Likewise, there is the American milieu, with its norms of Christianity and whiteness. Identity, and its emotional trappings like pride and shame, was shaped by constant subtle exposure to society's differentness and its stereotypes about their ethnicity and home religion.

For most research participants, the college years were characterized by ethnic discovery. With the exception of Parth, the oldest member of the cohort, the research participants found themselves in the company of more Indian Americans their own age than during the K–12 period. They experienced a separate, Indian American youth culture, engaging with ethnic elements on their own terms. No longer "forced" to participate in an ethnoreligious community, each could instead make the active choice whether or not to be part of the formal and informal networks of coethnics and coreligionists on their campus. Some leapt in with both feet. Vinay, a Sikh/Hindu male who grew up on the outskirts of Atlanta, said:

> I kind of had my own fraternity there, without even having to join one. This was something I realized early on my first quarter at Tech as a freshman. I'm sitting in the Student Center 'til two in the morning working on a lab and some guy who wasn't even Indian, he was probably Middle Eastern. He just kind of stopped and said, "Hey, what's your name." It was two in the morning and I couldn't figure out how to do this lab, and he stayed up with me for four more hours to finish this lab, and I had never met the guy before. And I'm sure if I had not been brown skinned, that he wouldn't have done that. And then I ran into him and he happened to have a lot of Indian friends, and, and I quickly realized that these people were there to help me no matter what, strictly because I was Indian. So being Indian meant I had a bunch of people there that would help me, if for no other reason, because I'm Indian. I had never had that before my freshman year in college. Wasn't long before I had all Indian friends that I spent most of my time with. . . . It's like you have your own co-ed fraternity, with a lot of people that just want to help you out and give you advice on what professors to take, and help you out with studying, and whatever you need.

Likewise, Binita said, "I hung out with [Indians] on a daily basis. . . . Whereas in high school, I didn't have that social life, [in college] I was meeting more Indian guys." Others were unimpressed by their new ethnic access. Neha avoided all associations with other Indian Americans, explaining that "there were all these Indian groups and there was a lot of peer pressure to go to the Indian American events. . . . I resisted that sort of grouping by skin color or by race." Between Vinay's total immersion and Neha's total rejection lay the balance of the research participant cohort. The largest group was those research participants, like Shabnam, who had a "rainbow of friends, some Indians . . . and some non-Indians." For those who chose to interact with other Indian Americans, ethnoreligious campus organizations and certain academic classes played a role in developing a positive ethnic identity, as described at greater length in the next section.

Transnational experiences of travel to India also played a major role in the development of ethnic awareness. In the K–12 life period, every research participant whose parents had arrived directly from India traveled to India. More than half went at least three times by the time they graduated from high school, and several went annually or biennially. These trips, whether loved or hated at the time, resulted in the development of familial relationships and exposure to other factors that shaped ethnic awareness.[14] They also created for the second generation a phenomenon Suarez-Orozco (1997) identified with respect to Latino immigrant children: a "dual frame of reference" through which immigrant children filter their experiences in the United States. The experience of transnationalism led the research participants to pursue academic and economic success as exemplars of their family or out of an appreciation for the opportunities they had as Americans. Monali, for example, said that "as an Indian woman, being an educated Indian woman, I felt like I had a responsibility towards the women in Indian who did not get the things that I got, like my cousins and even my aunts and my mother, for that matter."

Importantly, and contrary to the findings of Portes, Fernandez-Kelley, and Haller (2003), my data reveal that to a substantial degree the second generation is voluntarily maintaining substantial transnational ties. Half (nineteen of forty-one) of the research participants traveled to India at least once during college, and three-quarters have returned in adulthood. These second-generation Indian Americans cultivated relationships with family members, which resulted in even more return trips. In adulthood, trips to India function as a major avenue for cultural maintenance and rediscovery. Religion is a major reason for these transnational trends is a factor not considered by Portes and his colleague: religion drove many of these second-generation Indian Americans to engage in transnational travel because they saw India as the source and touchpoint for their home religion. (Most, but not all, of these research participants were Hindu.)

For research participants, late adolescence—a period that could span from late high school to early adulthood—was characterized by a time of self-reflection and attempts to locate a balance between an ethnic culture they understood as communitarian and what many saw as the preeminent U.S. cultural value: individualism. In college and beyond, a majority of the research participants began to "deprogram the self" (Thai 1999, 66). Growing up as children of immigrants, they had seen white, Christian, American ideals as appealing. Their own pathways into adulthood—with new ways of viewing family life, friendship, and intimate relationships—presented divergent feelings. With a small number of exceptions, the research participants are adopting an increasingly ethnic-oriented identity as they grow older.[15] For many, adulthood has been a period of active and intense ethnic recovery, which involved reassembling and reevaluating their own feelings about ethnicity, religion, and race and then seeking out opportunities to involve themselves with an ethnoreligious community. In contrast to the experience of the student organization—where ethnicity was "done" but the primary motivating factor was the social atmosphere—adult research participants are making and acting upon conscious decisions to maintain ethnic traditions and rituals. For second-generation Indian American adults, ethnic identity may involve a sense of connectedness with one's national, cultural, linguistic, and religious origins combined with a sense of despair at losing touch with those origins. Smita said:

> When I am sitting around the table with my family, I do understand Gujarati, but there are just times things will go way over my head. I have no choice but to sit there. . . . There's so many times that I desperately want to say something, but my *masi* [aunt] doesn't really speak English that well, and for me to try to say something would totally interrupt the flow of conversation. So, I just sit there and I feel so different, you know—just not fitting in with the group. They love me. I know that. They would do anything for me, as I would for them. But times where it's a family get-together and I can only follow the conversation, I feel uncomfortable and everyone's like, "Why don't you know Gujarati better?" Why didn't I realize that it would have been really important for me to learn this growing up, you know? Because now it's hard.

Also in adulthood, many research participants are reevaluating childhood experiences in light of adult understandings. Their greater ethnic awareness, combined in many cases with a racial consciousness brought on by life experiences, permits some for the first time to recognize racism and reinterpret childhood episodes in light of that understanding. In Espiritu's (2002) words, "experiences of racism are cumulative."[16] The same is true of experiences of religious discrimination. Nikhil, for example, described his white American classmates' ruthlessness when it came to teasing him for belonging to a non-Christian religion: "Kids teasing you [by saying,] 'you are reincarnated from a dog.'" As a child, that caused Nikhil to describe himself as "oriented toward being white" socially; he exhibited feelings of identification with the majority, religious doubt, and the like. Today as an adult, Nikhil is able to identify these experiences as ones of religious discrimination and reprocess his childhood thinking in light of new understandings.

Measures based on language retention or engagement with religious practice through attendance at a house of worship might show second-generation Indian Americans to be growing more distant from certain major ethnic markers. Their middle- to upper-middle-class background and levels of education allow them to socialize in mainstream white circles, and they generally converse among themselves in English rather than the home language. In fact, however, like the Asian American young professionals in Min and Kim's (1999) book, these second-generation Indian Americans exhibit a strong tendency—and an even stronger desire—to maintain ethnic identity. Many *do* speak their home language with parents and other extended family; most who do not, like Smita, wish they could. Most of them believe in and "live" their home religion. Those who were preparing to marry emphasized the importance of finding a coethnic, coreligionist spouse, while those who were married worried over how they would convey ethnic traditions and language to their third-generation children.

For this group, socioeconomics and technological development have made substantial transnational ties possible. Their parents' affluence (as well as their own, in adulthood) made it possible for ethnoreligious community centers and houses of worship to be built; many research participants' ethnic lives revolved around these centers in adolescence. Most research participants were children of well-to-do parents, who had the resources necessary to make the long and expensive trip to India. Those that could afford frequent trips reported particularly deep connections to ethnic culture, a result of their experiences in India, their connections with family there, and their relatively greater knowledge of the home language. This development was also a product of this modern world, where transoceanic flight, relatively inexpensive telephone and Internet connectivity, and other factors combine to make contact easier and more frequent than it was for immigrants a century ago.[17] Schools are also tending to appreciate and provide more services related to multicultural education and the needs of immigrant and second generation students—however haltingly—which has also had an influence. As compared to immigrants of the early twentieth century, contemporary immigrant families and their second-generation child no longer exhibit such a singular and powerful desire to shed the ethnic skin and blend into the melting pot.

As we close this discussion of ethnic identity development, it must be noted that whatever may be occurring in the lives of individual research participants, the larger sociocultural climate exerts a substantial effect on how ethnicity is formed, understood, and acted out. Sociocultural climate includes current events—such as court-ordered bussing to integrate public schools, the self-conscious public embrace of "diversity" of the 1970s and 1980s, and the first

Gulf War in 1990 and 1991—that impacted individual research participants' lives and affected how Indian Americans were viewed by and interacted with members of the wider society. It includes the relative invisibility of India and Indian Americans in mainstream culture at the time most of the research participants were coming of age. In the present day, it includes "Indo-chic." Elements of the research participants' ethnic niche, such as Bollywood films, are now becoming more appealing; DVD technology has made high-quality images and English subtitles available to a cohort that was accustomed to poor-quality bootleg VHS tapes with grainy images and tinny sound (see Desai 2004). Most research participants like Binita now in current times say they are proud to be Indian; this is both abetting their maintenance and rediscovery of the home culture and making them want to learn and participate even more: "Yeah, it probably started like when Madonna was using Indian tattoos, you know, henna. . . . I think now people are starting to recognize the influence of Indian culture. Clinton going to India, Silicon Valley Indian entrepreneurs—all of these things combined make me think, "You know, it's great to be Indian." We didn't have those role models. We did not have any role models that shared our culture. Now, I think, Indian kids have a lot of role models."

The almost inevitable outcome of the research participants' life experiences is a bicultural identity with affiliations with both the American mainstream and their ethnic community. Like so many other elements of identity where a duality is set forth, bicultural identity needs to be understood as a spectrum of outlook and experience. One may function in the mainstream culture but prefer to spend all of one's private time with coethnics and in ethnic institutions. Or, like Smita, one may feel "I carry a lot of the American ways, but . . . I am Indian too."

Ethnicity and Religion

Scholars have long recognized a substantial connection between religion and ethnic identity.[18] In this study, nearly all research participants, when asked about their connection to Indian culture or ethnicity, responded with an answer that referred to religion—practices, tenets, or mores associated with the respondent's home religion. They identified as Indian because they attended *pujas*, celebrated *Vaisakhi*, said the Lord's prayer in Malayalam. Indeed, a substantial proportion of research participants (particularly, but not exclusively, the Hindus) conflated their home religion with Indian culture. Across the research cohort, religion was understood to be a paramount marker of ethnic authenticity, and a concept so tied up with ethnicity and national origin as to be sometimes indistinguishable in the eye of the research participant. This idea is both cause and effect of their parents' use of religion as a vehicle for cultural maintenance. This too reflects the remarkably high salience of religion in relation to other factors such as language, transnational experiences, family, cuisine, and others affecting the ethnic identity of second-generation Indian Americans.[19]

For most second-generation Indian Americans, religion was a factor of paramount importance when it came to developing an ethnic identity. With a few exceptions, it is not their primary identity, but rather an "ancillary" identity (Williams 1988). Yet because of its association with the transcendent and holy, it carries a uniquely powerful cachet in the minds of most research participants. It is a foundational layer of their ethnic identity. The reader must keep in mind that the religion we're discussing here is lived religion—a rich area of inquiry because it is inherently subjective. An individual's sense of religion may either comport or contrast with the actual tenets and theology of the home faith.

Religion's importance is borne out by research on South Asians in Great Britain. This research revealed that for many young Hindus, Muslims, and Sikhs religion was the major facet through which they asserted their distinctiveness.[20] Its function as a marker of difference from the dominant milieu may be informed by experiences internal to the ethnoreligious community or by critical incidents involving religious encounters outside the community. But as easy as it is to say that religion affects ethnic identity, it is difficult to describe the exact nature of intersection between the two. For starters, the relationship between religion and ethnic identity varies dramatically over the lifespan. Moreover, to fully understand it and go beyond abstraction, we must consider the specific religion and specific ethnicity in question. Although common themes abound, and will be subject matter of much of this text, the experiences of second-generation Indian Americans are qualitatively different from one religious affiliation to the next, and thus religion's role in Indian American ethnic identity development varies by religious affiliation. The context and contours of the religion-ethnicity relationship depends on *which* religion and *which* ethnicity is being examined (Form 2000). The specific ethnicity and religion, in the context of the sociohistorical moment, form the backdrop for the ultimate question: What does the religion-ethnicity connection look like in the individual lives of second-generation Indian Americans?

For these second-generation Indian Americans, religion and ethnicity were linked like the strands of DNA's double helix. Dimensions of culture (such as vegetarianism or respect for elders) took on religious import, whereas manifestations of religion (such as holiday celebrations) provided the impetus and venue for engaging in Indian culture. For most, religion alone became a test of Indian authenticity. Religion's role in ethnic identity development went beyond its function as a vehicle and tool of cultural transmission. We diminish religion when we consider its functional role while ignoring the elemental power of individual faith. We diminish it again when we ignore or obscure the importance of religious identity for Indian Americans by viewing their religious beliefs as merely ethnic traits no more remarkable than cuisine. Religion was important to the research participants because they understood it (however imperfectly) as their connection to things transcendent and eternal. They observed the importance that religion had in the lives of their parents and grandparents, while also noting the cultural importance of religion in the American milieu. They internalized many of the parental values that had been characterized for them as religious (see also Peeradina 1996).

The United States offered each Indian American religious group a different set of circumstances upon arrival. Notwithstanding the small quota of Indians permitted to enter the United States between 1946 and 1965, the parents of these research participants all arrived to a land with few coethnics and became for the first time racial minorities.[21] The Hindu immigrants in the early years after 1965 found a country largely lacking houses of worship for, communities of, or familiarity with them and their coreligionists. They had come from a country where they were the majority, where they could be Hindu as effortlessly as an American can be Christian. From this milieu they arrived in a country where most people had never heard of Hinduism and those few who had heard of the religion understood it through one-dimensional lens of Swami Vivekananda, the Beatles, or the Hare Krishnas. On the rare occasion that Hindu immigrants found a temple nearby, it was likely to be a Hare Krishna temple. Lacking an Indian ethnic affiliation, these temples could serve immigrants' religious needs but did not function as ethnoreligious communities. Sikh immigrants also arrived in a country where they were both unheard-of and invisible; but unlike the Hindus, Sikhs were arriving not only *to* but also *from* a position of religious minority. Indian American Muslims also came from and to religious minority status, and they found themselves as an ethnic minority within the mosques and Muslim organizations they encountered, which were populated by Arab and African Americans. Until post-1965 Indian and Pakistani Americans built them, there were few if any Indian or South Asian masjids (Melendy 1977; Haddad 2000).

Unlike their coethnics, Indian Christians, both Catholics and Protestants, arrived in the United States to find religious institutions already in place—but, again, these were rarely ethnoreligious in character. Research participants Shiren and Irfan, both Catholic, were able to attend Catholic schools throughout their K–12 years, and white churches on the weekend. Even those who wanted to practice in ethnoreligious communities could sometimes do so through partnerships with preexisting churches; no building or other property costs were incurred as they were by Hindu, Sikh, and many Muslim observants. Still, their familiar religion was in an unfamiliar culture, with practical differences between their home faith and the Western Christian milieu. When resources and population permitted, some Indian Christian populations built their own facilities. Research participant Binu was part of a Malayali Catholic congregation with its own church building; in this respect, Binu's church community served all the cultural and religious maintenance functions that free-standing *mandirs* and *gurdwaras* did.

The myriad distinctions among Indian American religious groups affect the formation, geography, philosophy, and identity of the ethnoreligious communities that sprang up in the years since 1965 as well as the lives of the second generation. In particular, Hindu research participants have a different construction of Indianness from that of the Sikh, Muslim, and Christian research participants, and Christian research participants exhibit a qualitatively different set of experiences and responses in their relations with the dominant American culture. Ethnic history that ignores religion is surely flawed, but an ethnic history or analysis of Indian Americans that ignores the sociological place of the particular religion as within the Indian milieu *and* as within the American milieu is just as flawed.

With these caveats in mind, we can now pose the question: What does religion and its relationship with ethnicity look like in the lives of second-generation Indian Americans? Most of the scholarship to date has examined religion and ethnicity almost entirely in relationship to, and with typologies designed to consider, religious groups.[22] In part, this is due to a focus on the functional: the role of religion as a tool or forum for the performance, transmission, and maintenance of ethnicity.[23] Religious participation did indeed function to reinforce ethnic identity to varying degrees for most research participants across faiths, and had a highly significant role as a source of and support for emergent ethnic identity and group cohesion. But there is much more to the story: the way religion affects and is manifested in the day-to-day lives of these individual Indian Americans, whether experienced through membership or nonmembership in ethnoreligious communities. The focus on group functionality and congregational worship, although accurate and applicable as a lens through which to consider the role of ethnoreligious community in the lives of many research participants, leaves the examination of individual experience unfinished. Put simply, there's more to religion as a development factor in ethnic identity than group practice; there is the role that the individual's faith—belief in the tenets of and sensations of connectedness to the home religion—plays in ethnic identity.

To what sources can we look to find a theoretical foundation for this work? The large body of literature on religion and ethnicity in early-twentieth-century white immigrant groups such as Catholics and Jews (Herberg 1983) is of limited value in the study of post-1965 Hindu, Muslim, and Sikh populations for two key reasons.[24] First, the religious practices of the Protestant, Catholic, and Jewish immigrants were congregation-based. Hinduism and Sikhism remain likely to be practiced in private settings such as the home. This was doubly true two decades ago, when these research participants were children and few free-standing mandirs and gurdwaras were available. The same can be said of Islam, albeit perhaps to a lesser extent; the earliest immigrants, in particular, rarely had local coreligionists with whom to form a congregation. Even as Indian immigrant communities build temples, gurdwaras, and masjids, the nature of the tradition and the manner of practice still limit the applicability of earlier scholarship.[25] Second, the earlier Jewish and Catholic groups were "meltable" ethnics; Indian Americans, like many other the post-1965 immigrants, are people of color and therefore "unmeltable" (Suzuki 1979). This introduces a different and unique factor with respect to the post-1965 immigrants: the pervasiveness and irreducibility of race in America.

Despite its salience, and somewhat paradoxically at that, religion remains a component of the research participants' ethnic identity and not the other way around. Few—probably none—would say ethnicity is a component of their religions identity. Yet at the same time, religion is seen as the most authentic form and manifestation of ethnicity, and many would say it is the most important part of their ethnic identity.

Like so many, this rule is proved by its exceptions: four individuals who have an Indian ethnic identity but consider it entirely distinct and distinguishable from their religious identity. Among the Hindus in the study, Avya alone drew a clear distinction between her religion and her culture. This occurred because Avya had an extremely unusual religious upbringing: not in an ethnoreligious community, but in a multiethnic ashram community in upstate New York. The other three exceptions are individuals who in adulthood identify with a different religious belief system from that of their parents. Isma'ili-born Aziz converted to Sunni Islam in college in part because of the contempt he felt for the irreligion and materialism he observed in his childhood Isma'ili community. Aziz views religion as something distinct from and "one hundred times more important than" culture. For him, being a Muslim not only constituted his religious affiliation but also circumscribed his community as he understood it—a community both broader and narrower than his social sphere of coethnics. Finally, two atheists who were raised as Hindus demonstrate in their own way the intimate connection between religion and culture. Mina wants to be involved in Indian community activities but finds that they all revolve around Hindu holidays and worship; religion embodies her discomfort with her husband's pious family. Anand no longer identifies with Hinduism but feels that his culture is vicariously attacked whenever Hinduism, still the faith of those he loves, is attacked.

For some, religion is important because it is part of the package of Indianness of which parents and grandparents are exemplars; whether or not the research participant aspires to a parentlike connection to the home faith, the faith itself is seen as a marker of what is really Indian—in contrast to American culture, and to some degree in contrast to the personal culture of the research participant. For others, religion stands in equipoise to what they understand to be Indian culture. Shiren's experience is not atypical of this group; she understands that her coethnic peers see the distinction between Christianity and Indianness, embraces her home faith, and yet also self-identifies as Indian. Most Christian and Muslim research participants also had a more nuanced understanding of the relationship between their religion and their ethnicity, largely because they had encountered or were aware of a range of coreligionists who were not also coethnics. For some of the Christians, Muslims, and Sikhs, Indian culture and ethnic authenticity were seen as intimately tied to Hinduism, creating contrasts as well as mutual supports between the religious and ethnic elements of their identities.

Most Hindu research participants either conflated Indian culture and Hinduism, saw Hinduism as an inseparable component of Indian culture, or intellectually understood the distinctions but nevertheless considered Hinduism and Indian culture to be irreducibly related. For many there is an immutable connection between religion (or religiosity) and ethnicity. For example, Sweta said, "I want to know more about Hinduism because I feel that is the underlying fabric for a lot of my culture." Anya described Hinduism as "part of . . . a big package of being Indian." These research participants frequently responded to questions about culture with answers that evoked major Hindu holidays or teachings and responded to questions about religion by referring to India and Indians as if they constituted an undifferentiated group of Hindus. There are several reasons for this trend. The first of these was the inability of Hindu research participants in particular to see religious affiliation as a broader category than cultural heritage (and therefore separate from it); their experiences with their parents and other members of the ethnoreligious community involved the presentation of Hindu and Indian principles, characteristics, and history side by side and without a clear distinction being made between Hindu elements (Diwali, Bharatnatyam) and Indian elements (Republic Day). Second, religion extended beyond the singular situation and locale where it might be isolated: prayer in the house of worship. Instead, "everything" evoked a religious response: Sina talked about going to the temple for her birthday or when her parents bought a car. Smita said her parents performed a puja each time they moved into a new home and said she now does the same. Third, the border between Indian and not-Indian looked just like the border between Hindu and not-Hindu; both lay between life in the home and ethnoreligious community and life in the wider world.

The Christian, Sikh, and Muslim research participants also engaged in the conflation of Hinduism with Indian culture (but not with their own Indianness). Shiren, a Catholic, participated in Indian culture by learning Bharatnatayam dance, a Hindu devotional tradition. Irfan and Seema, also Christians, considered Indian culture to be synonymous with Hinduism. Both also chose the ethnic identifier "Indian" when asked. I asked Manish whether he wanted to learn more about Sikhism, his home religion. He replied, "Not really. I really want to learn more about Indian mythology." Here, Manish is not implying that Hinduism is more authentically Indian than Sikhism or than some other, nonreligious dimension of ethnicity. But he is failing to distinguish between "Indian" as a geographic, political, or ethnic designation and "Hindu," the religious designation that properly describes the mythology of which he spoke.

The tendency of research participants across religions to conflate Hinduism with Indian culture is explained by the unarguably hegemonic nature of Hinduism in Indian culture. India is Hindu just as the United States is Christian: legally secular but so imbued with religious structures and ideations that the connection between religion and culture is immediately apparent to a member of a minority religious group. This also may help explain the unlikelihood of Muslim and Christian research participants conflating—as opposed to merely describing a connection between—their religion and their culture. They know, from their parents' experience and often their own, that they are a religious minority in India.

The case of Diwali is a prime example of how this conflation operates in the second generation. Attending Diwali celebrations on campus was a collegiate cultural activity of choice for most of the research participants. Most described Diwali as a "festival of lights"; only a handful understood the festival to be a celebration of Lord Rama's victory over the demon Ravana and his return to Ayodhya to become king. Although some recalled Diwali pujas, religious services, as part of the holiday, all the research participants described Diwali as a celebratory season for their peers and families; as college students they celebrated Diwali with a cultural show (featuring, perhaps, traditional song and dance) whose primary function seems to be giving Indian American college students the chance to dress up in Indian clothes and socialize—that is, to perform ethnicity, not religion. Anya, a Hindu, took part in religious aspects of Diwali celebration in college, yet described it as nonreligious experience: "I did *aarti* [offering of a flame] at the Diwali show, but I did not think of it as I was participating in a religious event. I might do things that I don't think are religious, 'cause to me they didn't have much of an [religious] impact." Likewise, many research participants skipped the Diwali puja entirely in high school, spending that evening at the temple or at a private home socializing and attending the Diwali dinner that often followed the pujas. The cultural and social aspects—what Gans (1979) calls "symbolic ethnicity"—are what they remember from K–12 and therefore what they replicate in college. All three Catholics in the study also mentioned attending Diwali events while growing up and in college, and never made a distinction between religion and culture—that is, they never said "I went to a Hindu event." Thus Diwali has become a cultural landmark for young

Indian Americans, but has lost its religious import; it has gone from a Hindu religious holiday to a largely secular Indian American celebration.

Even those who understood intellectually the difference between Hinduism and Indian culture considered the two effectively interchangeable. Nikhil spoke for many research participants, particularly his fellow Hindus, when he remarked, "I still perceived Hinduism as more than just religion. . . . It's cultural, and I still feel that a majority of Hindu events, if you want to put it in that context, are more cultural, or as much cultural as religious." Therefore, Nikhil said, he goes to religious events in order to partake of Indian culture "more than for the religious aspects."

Those research participants who now identify as atheist face a conundrum: Mina said the "intrinsic" link between Hinduism and Indian culture was always a source of confusion for her. Since becoming an atheist in college, Mina is bothered by the tendency of her coethnics, including her husband and his family, to conflate Hinduism with Indian culture. Mina wishes to be culturally Indian without participating in Hindu rituals, yet every "cultural" event seems to be geared toward worship, the mandir, the taking of *prasad*, and so on. This conflation, and the unavailability of cultural events that are not linked to religious dates and traditions, vexes Mina. It should be noted that a comparison of Mina and Anand, the other self-identified atheist, shows the role of gender and marital status in compelling participation in ethnoreligious events. Anand is a single man. Mina, by contrast, is married and attending certain functions is often expected of her as part of her obligation to a family—her husband's—which is quite religious and actively participates in the ethnoreligious community. The fact that she is expected to attend ethnoreligious functions, where she feels uncomfortable, forments in Mina a sense of discomfort with ethnoreligious community as such and has also caused friction in her marriage.

Religion and Authenticity

Most research participants might accept the notion that they are in the process of constructing an identity that incorporates both Indian and American elements, creating a third space or hybrid identities, which are the product of religion, ethnicity, and the cultural inheritance of the immigrant generation, as well as the American sociocultural context and their own lenses of American and transnational experiences.[26] But hybridity is not what most of the research participants aspire to when it comes to religion. They are not interested in adapting to or developing an American Hinduism, American Islam, or American Sikhism. The home religion, as practiced by their parents, represents authenticity in a way that new traditions would not.

Regardless of whether religion is part of one's ethnic identity or is considered something separate from ethnicity, second-generation Indian Americans consider religion to be the most authentic form of ethnicity. *Authenticity* compares the individual or group to an idealized version of the "Indian." Because religion is seen as eternal and unchanging, it is particularly susceptible to being used as a reference point for authenticity. It is a primordial link to the history of the family and people with whom one wishes to identify. In the process of straddling two worlds and negotiating lives as racial and religious minorities, authenticity arises "from the angst we feel about the loss of self in the rapid currents of modernity that sweep us away" (see Rudrappa 2004, 134). For second-generation Indian Americans, the home religion—affiliation, knowledge, and parents' practice—is used as a measure of one's Indianness. This was the case for all research participants regardless of religious background. Even those Christians and Muslims who drew a distinction between their religion and Indian culture—which is shaped by (some might say dominated by) Hinduism— nevertheless experienced their home religion as a paramount vehicle for the expression, maintenance, and conveyance of culture.

The common impression held by most research participants is that religion is static—as unchanging as God. It is not. Religions are dynamic. Practices, tenets, and rituals change over time in dramatic and sudden and slow and subtle ways. Particularly in the context of immigration, evolution in religious tenets and practices may occur through loss of memory and through exposure to once-foreign cultures, languages, and traditions and the social and theological cross-pollination that can result. Moreover, religious practices in India will be changing at the same time; even if the research participants or their parents are performing their rituals just as they were performed in India when their parents left, practices have changed in India since that time. After traveling to India, Irfan, a male Catholic, came to realize this—not in the context of religion per se, but in the context of "morals" and societal rules:

> I think the culture that our parents preserved is a throwback [compared
> to] the way things really are now. My cousins in India, they're very liberal
> and forward in their thinking, they're very progressive. But from the way
> a lot of my friends were treated by their parents in terms of the strict,
> very, very, very traditional ultraconservative restrictions that were put
> on them . . . I think that the moral—maybe not the morals, but I think the
> restraints that were put on them are not, I won't say outdated, but I think
> our parents kind of brought over the 60s mentality and raised us in the
> 80s with those 60s mentalities.

Using India as the marker for religious authenticity implies that if one does not perform Hindu rituals "just like they do in India," one is therefore somehow less Hindu. Keeping in mind that it is impossible to maintain the religion in the United States just as it was in India, the real question is: Why is that so important? One reason could be that second-generation Indian Americans construct authentic identities, mostly based in religion, in order to combat feelings of "vacated or inauthentic identities in our contemporary world." (Cheng 2004, 171) Another reason could be because acceptance at the American multicultural table requires the defining of a "singular Indian culture" (Rudrappa 2004; Kurien 2004), and religion provides a more profound quality of anchor than other dimensions of culture. Americans understand nationhood by reference to monolithic groups with universally shared characteristics. The multiplicity of "Indian" identities is too much for the American multicultural mind to handle. By reference to previous well-defined immigrant groups, such as Irish Catholics and Russian Jews, religion seems a necessary element of the Indian American image.

Ethnoreligious Community

For most research participants, family also functioned as the gateway to an ethnoreligious community. The primary function of these informal social networks and official organizations was to transmit culture and religion to the second generation. They were also designed to provide a cultural and religious safe space for peer interaction that guarded against the evils outside of that space, defined by reference to what immigrant parents perceived to be corrupting aspects of American culture: crime, violence, drug use, divorce, and sexual promiscuity (Fenton 1988; Bacon 1996). These communities provide a social, physical, and psychological space where research participants developed relationships with coethnics and coreligionists of their own and their parents' generation. Community events, including shared dinners and holiday celebrations involving multigenerational participants, exposed research participants to ethnic activities and mores and caused most to develop a sense of attachment to Indian culture. They also reinforced the idea of such ethnic manifestations as positive and worthy (or at least shared) things.

With relatives a long distance away but other coethnics and coreligionists nearby, these communities also functioned as extended families. The resulting networks served (and serve) as social capital, offering a focal point for ethnic gatherings, celebrations, and the re-creation of ethnic language and customs. Many of these ethnoreligious communities began as pan-Indian organizations, which were created without regard to region, caste, and language.[27] Ultimately, as the Indian American population increased and more subpopulations achieved the critical mass that enabled them to create and support their own cultural and religious institutions, the popularity of pan-Indian organizations has been eclipsed by those serving regional or sectarian interests.

Religion and culture coexist and interpenetrate in these ethnic organizations. Binu's church is not merely Catholic, it is Malayali Catholic, and the Atlanta area's Indian American Religious and Cultural Center houses a Hindu temple. Across the cohort, with rare exceptions, research participants typically

celebrated cultural and religious events in one space. Most research participants spoke of cultural and religious gatherings and community in the same
breath, and even interchangeably;—even when describing to informal gatherings in private homes, few drew sharp lines between religious and nonreligious
gatherings. I use the term *ethnoreligious community* precisely because it acknowledges the role and social impact of religion as the community's organizing
force and the vehicle through which many "do ethnicity."[28] The word *community*, when used in this section, is shorthand for this ethnoreligious community.

Ethnoreligious community experiences were foundational in the lives of
the research participants; they played a pivotal role in providing information on
religion and culture to the second-generation Indian Americans. An ethnoreligious community was an occasional refuge where research participants encountered two phenomena available almost nowhere else: membership in the
religious and racial majority in that space, and the company of others their own
age who shared the ethnic experiences that characterized their own home
lives.[29] Through involvement in an ethnoreligious community, research participants met others who were different from the dominant society in the same way
as they were. Inasmuch as the community and its events were organized around
religious themes, it functioned in particular to affirm to the research participants
that their religion was legitimate—however unfamiliar by broader community
standards, however unlike the Christianity with which they were bombarded in
school and their neighborhoods—Some research participants especially enjoyed
attending large-scale celebrations, such as the Sikh holiday Vasaki, the Muslim
Eid al-fitr, or Hindu holidays like Diwali, Holi, and Navaratri.[30]

For the majority that reported being part of an ethnoreligious community,
exposure to cultural and religious practice gave substantive content to the individual's self-understanding as an ethnic person. Religious activities were the
major impetus for Indian American families to gather. Ethnoreligious communities provided some of the first experiences with religion outside of the home
for Hindu, Muslim, and Sikh research participants growing up in a society that
presented a competing religious worldview.[31] Community also functioned as a
forum where research participants interacted with their own peers and those of
their parents; there interactions functioned to reinforce norms of Indianness
modeled by parents in the home. Attending a function did not necessarily mean
sitting quietly or fully participating—whether the event was a performance, worship service, or banquet. Once the research participants were at the location of
the event, they could more often than not be found outside the common space,
playing or hanging out with others their own age. Nevertheless, the functions
served to socialize research participants into Indian culture. The full experience
was more than just attending a play or festival. It meant getting dressed in *kurta
pajamas* and *salwar kameez*, donning Indian jewelry, eating Indian food, seeing
the adults and hearing them speak native languages and talk about India. It

was, in short, about expressing an Indianness. In Irfan's words, community exposed the research participants to "things that just kept you aware of who you were," and as such was very important to the development of Indian American identity.

Virtually all of the research participants spoke of an Indian community—but for each, the term had a different meaning. So when Sweta spoke of an Indian community, she was referring to a predominantly Hindu community where she found herself among coethnics who were also coreligionists. When Binu used the same term, she was referring to her Malayali Catholic community. When Irfan spoke of an Indian community, he was referring to the Indian American community of his own childhood: a community where Hindus predominated that was separate from his mostly white religious community at the Catholic church. Harjit spoke not of an Indian community but of a Sikh community—his ethnoreligious community, which he understood at the time of his interview to be something distinct from Indian community as the interviewer might use that term.

Why did the immigrant generation build ethnoreligious communities? For these research participants' parents, immigrating to the United States was a "theologizing experience" (Smith 1978). The effects of personal challenges and culture shock can cause immigrants to turn to religion as a place of emotional refuge. It can provide a sense of home's remembered comforts amid the tribulations of the new home; religious belief, rituals, and structures may serve as interpretative frames addressing the hardships of immigration and oppressive conditions in the United States.[32] Saran (1985, 42) predicted: "Indian immigrants with children are particularly likely to turn to religion and religious practices since they see this as a way of raising Indian consciousness among their children." Observed fifteen years later, my research participants experiences show Saran to have been correct. Their parents used religion, largely through the vehicle of ethnoreligious community, to maintain and convey culture.[33] Moreover, they succeeded: The data reveal that ethnoreligious communities played a critical positive role in these second-generation Indian Americans' lives. They connected the second generation to coethnic peers and adults, conveyed a sense of connection to the divine through religious practice, and fostered in most the belief that such things are important. As the ultimate proof of community's importance, some second-generation adults are now attempting to reconstitute the communities, or build new ones, to convey culture and religion to their own children.

Some scholars have found that houses of worship and cultural centers serve the economic and material needs of immigrants and their children, such as by providing access to employment and capital from sympathetic coethnics (see Ebaugh and Chafetz 2000, 2002). Although that may be true of Indian American ethnoreligious communities today, the nascent communities of these second-generation Indian Americans' childhoods were themselves too young to serve such a purpose. The research participants' parents were often among the first Indian immigrants to arrive in their geographic area; they were more likely to be the benefactors than the beneficiaries of the community network.[34] The communities as they existed during most research participants' childhoods were still on the whole in the home stage—or were literally laying the foundations of a community's physical space. A few of the research participants were witnesses to the construction of the community's facilities; Seema, for example, spent many weekends "cleaning up the building, painting the walls" of what became the Hindu Temple of Nashville.[35]

The irony in the story of ethnoreligious communities is the fact although the immigrant generation turned to religion for cultural maintenance and transmission, most Indian immigrants lacked substantial religious education or training. As a result, they transmitted only whatever religious knowledge and practice they could remember and considered important.[36] Therefore the immigrant parents transmitted only a slice of the whole religious pie as it might be found in India—a particular type of culture and a limited subset of traditions, based upon whatever knowledge and familiarity they developed in their own experiences growing up within their particular geographic region, faith tradition, caste, or socioeconomic class in India (Fenton 1988; Williams 1988). This point is critical for at least two reasons. First, it shows us that any reproduction or reinvention of Indian religions in the United States will be different not only by virtue of the American milieu and the religion's minority status here but also because the practices and interpretations transmitted and propagated here can be incomplete, inaccurate, or unnuanced. Second, it introduces a point to which I will return in the next chapter: When some research participants reached college and for the first time encountered coreligionists of a different regional, linguistic, or caste background, they had the jarring experience of realizing (for example) that their Hinduism was not the only Hinduism.

As part of their attempt to pass on the key parts of their national and ethnic identity to their children through the ethnoreligious communities, Indian immigrants established regular programs, typically led by an adult in the group, to educate their children on the home language(s), culture, and religious tradition.[37] These programs were most often called Sunday school but were as likely to take place on Saturday as on Sunday. When a community center was not available, Sunday school would be held in a private home. Most research participants, across faiths, attended Sunday school.[38] There they learned about their cultural and religious heritage and in the process also formed a community of peers their own age. Harjit, a Sikh, attended classes at a gurdwara in his home town: "Every Sunday at the gurdwara, I learned a lot about my religion as well as a lot of the culture."

Sunday schools offered what might be called both conscious and unconscious learning. The *conscious learning* for Sunday school attendees involved language, religion, and culture—the elements of the curriculum their parents designed for them. One frequent focus of these Hindu Sunday schools was language—usually Hindi, unless the school served a specific population in which another language (such as Gujarati or Tamil) was heavily represented. Curricula also typically included stories from the Puranas, the *Ramayana*, and the *Mahabharata*, plus information about M. K. Gandhi and Indian history. As Anisa described, "we had prayer, we had songs, and we would sing the [Indian] national anthem." The element I call *unconscious learning* often included internalizing cultural values, behaviors, and mores. One example is the importance in Indian culture of family and of respect for one's elders. Attending Sunday school, research participants observed their peers showing respect for their parents and saw members of their parents' generation treating the "grandparents" with similar reverence. So even when they were not teaching but simply acting out their own respect for elders, the immigrant generation provided models that supported the unconscious learning process. Another way in which Sunday schools formented a sort of unconscious learning was that Hindu parents did not distinguish between Hindu and Indian traditions, ideas, and culture. The near-total conflation of Hinduness and Indianness exhibited by the Hindu research participants thus was also learned through the blending of religion and culture in the Sunday school curriculum.

Whatever expressly or implicitly didactic function parents and teachers meant Sunday school to have, its major function was to provide social space for interaction with coethnic peers. Priti, a Hindu female, offered a typical comment: "We went to Sunday school and we would learn about the different stories. I did not understand the rituals and traditions. I went mostly to see my friends." Some research participants reported being very active in their communities and seeking out even the study opportunities; others said they were passive or even unwilling participants "dragged" out by their parents.[39] Across these groups, the social effects of Sunday school could be powerful and lasting. Whether they loved it or hated it at the time, the research participants in adulthood all spoke nostalgically of their Sunday school experiences in ways that showed their emotional and social value with respect to identity development. For most, it was the only exposure to Indian culture outside the four walls of home. For some, it was the only opportunity to interact with coethnic peers.

However, it would be erroneous to characterize community as occurring anywhere coethnics or coreligionists gathered. The positive effects described above were the product of more than merely the physical and social space or the experience of hanging out with coethnics. Girish's example demonstrates that the mere presence of coethnics, without more, was not community. Girish grew up in a rural town in the South and was one of a handful of students of color at

his school. Indians from his and surrounding towns would often gather to socialize. "Growing up, we used to have this Indian Association in the next neighboring town. They used to have events there, and there were a few kids like my
age, and we used to go play football and stuff, but it wasn't anything like, you
know, like connected with Indian people. I just thought they were other people
and that was it." Girish did not feel as if he was a part of a community despite
gathering regularly with other Indian Americans to play touch football. Girish's
experience indicates that some ethnoreligious factor—such as worship, language, food, or a study program like Sunday schools—must be present in order
for the experience to serve the function of ethnoreligious community described
in this section. Without these, merely bringing together coethnics may not result in the development of the relationships that in turn lead the individual to
feel part of a community.

Across all the religious traditions represented in the cohort, ethnoreligious
communities exhibited a common theme: They were a place were a particular
Indian American norm developed and was displayed. Specifically, they were
communities created and populated by a predominantly upper-class and professional cohort of Indian Americans and their spouses—in most cases, organized and governed by men while supported by the work of their wives. This fact
does not diminish the importance of what these individuals created, and should
not be used to minimize the tremendous investment of time and energy the immigrants dedicated to this pursuit. For one thing, in their economic and professional makeup the communities simply reflected the cohort that arrived in the
early post-1965 period. Any organization or community will be built by the individuals who have the time, money, and energy to create it, sustain it, and organize its ethnic and religious events. Temples, mosques, and gurdwaras thus
became the place were the image of the upper-middle-class family becomes solidified. Most of the research participants had at least one professional parent,
if not two, who could commit resources to the ethnoreligious community. A
smaller number of research participants, like Ahalya, found that the socioeconomic situation of their family hindered their involvement with a local ethnoreligious community. Ahalya never felt attachment to an ethnoreligious
community because her parents were not professionals and worked long hours
in the restaurant business. They "were usually running the restaurant, whenever things were going on"; there was no time off, especially on weekends. Because Ahalya grew up on the periphery of her ethnoreligious community, she
now feels she grew up without basic religious instruction and that she is now
"less Indian" as a result.[40]

Another reason for not feeling attached to an ethnoreligious community
was geographic isolation. Several research participants grew up in small towns
where they were virtually the only Indian Americans. Because of physical distance from communities of size, their connection to those communities was too

sporadic and attenuated to have a meaningful positive effect.[41] These research participants experienced less ethnic attachment. As adults, having by now compared themselves to peers who did have these experiences or having had their own community experiences in later life, most expressed the sensation of having missing pieces or "holes" in their K–12 social development. The sense of disappointment at having missed out on ethnoreligious community experiences came across in their tone of voice and choice of words. Several speculated that if they had had a community they might feel a stronger sense of connection to Indian culture today, as adults.[42]

So ethnoreligious communities helped lay a foundation for the research participants—a sense of connectedness to their coethnics and a resulting sense of security despite being minorities in virtually every other social setting. This foundation serves two important functions with respect to ethnic identity and social identity more generally. First, it helps the individual develop resilience with respect to other situations—such as school and, later, the workplace—where they "don't belong" socially for reasons related to their race, ethnicity, or religion. Second, inasmuch as it represents emotionally positive reinforcement related to aspects of culture and ethnicity, it functions as a glue that helps other elements of ethnic identity stick. From the standpoint of forming a positive ethnic identity—one that offered a social and emotional buffer or fall-back position when research participants encountered racial and religious discrimination—this awareness of who you were and the chance to interact with others who were like you, was community's most important contribution in the lives of the research participants.

Community, Religion, and the Next Generation

Most of the second-generation Indian American research participants, now in their late twenties and early thirties, are exploring what they want being Indian or Indian American to mean in their lives. During adulthood, second-generation Indian Americans exhibit various levels of commitment to and involvement in the community. Many are content with consumption-oriented ethnicity/culture—characterized by enjoying the food, music, dance, art, and other popular cultural aspects, and in some cases speaking the language. A second and overlapping group is satisfied with being members of "geographies of ethnicity," for example, cultivating Indian family, friends, and other social relationships; going to temples, mosques, or other functions; and participating in community events. The third and smallest group is concerned about producing and practicing the communities—caring about the political future of their communities. For many of these individuals, working for the Indian American community entails a broader vision of social justice.

Ethnoreligious community remains vital to feeling connected to religion. It responds to a longing for *cultural recovery*—for a chance to reconnect with one's roots and the sights, smells, and activities of childhood. Even in adulthood, there is a direct correlation between the presence or absence of an ethnoreligious community and the participants' feelings of religiosity. In the adult life period, involvement and participation with an ethnoreligious community waned as compared to the K–12 and college periods. Therefore, many feel less religious despite spending more time thinking about religion. Here too the influence of family as the conduit to community (and thereby to religion) continues; the only research participants who gather regularly to worship with a religious community are those who have returned as adults to live near their parents in the community where they grew up.

For those who have moved away from their childhood home, community religious gatherings are something they do only when they go home to visit their family or when their parents visit them. Avinash, a Hindu male, is typical of this group: "When I would go home, I would take part in things with my parents, but that's about it. We would go to pujas and celebrate Diwali together, but I don't think I ever went on my own." Avinash went on to say he considers himself to be less religious as an adult because he now has less contact with his home religious community. Research participants in the adult period also distinguish between having an ethnoreligious community—apparently defined by the nature of the experience and, often, the presence of members of the immigrant generation—and the qualitatively different experience of having Indian friends.

As in college, many research participants who are not actively involved in cultural and professional organizations that cater to the second-generation population nevertheless attend events sponsored by these organizations in order to feel involved in, or at least have occasional contact with, an ethnically based community of Indian Americans.

At this point in their lives, the research participants have befriended people of many ethnic and religious backgrounds in school, the workplace, and their neighborhoods. About three-quarters of the research participants reported attending one or more events sponsored by ethnic organizations; about a quarter said they were active in social Ethnic organizations. Social organizations seem to be growing into the major venue for Indian Americans who are now in the work force to find community and "perform ethnicity." Many became accustomed to having Indian people around during college, and upon discovering less easy access to an Indian community in the workplace (with the exception of the technology firms) seek it out via attendance at organizational events. Anand, for example, has coworkers who are "Indians from India" but goes to NetSAP (Network of South Asian Professionals) events in Boston to talk with others who grew up in the United States as he did. However, these organizations are not ethnoreligious communities. Nor are the informal circles of friends that most research participants reported as their major vehicle for interacting with coethnics.

One research participant, Salim, reported being affiliated with an organization that can be described as ethnoreligious in nature. He works with other Isma'ili youth as a summer camp counselor. This community is one of Salim's top priorities these days: "I had an arrangement with my company where if I traveled for them four days a week, I would get Fridays to do my own thing, and I would use that to be involved with these youth projects. I told them that was very important to me." Other second-generation Indian Americans are creating their own communities by building cultural and social organizations around social services such as mentoring teens or support services for abused women.

One might speculate that those research participants who do not currently interact and worship with an ethnoreligious community may seek out that opportunity once they have children, as a strategy for providing religious exposure and education to the third generation. They will do so in the context of ethnoreligious communities that continue to be replenished by the ongoing influx of new immigrants from India. These communities will probably not break apart but rather develop subsets where programs and services are designed around the needs of participants. For example, programs may develop to accommodate worshipers who do not understand any Indian spoken or scriptural language, or to retain and support families formed by marriage across caste, regional, or even racial lines. Prayer books containing transliterated prayers may be printed for worshipers who cannot read Gurmukhi and Sanskrit, the traditional languages of Sikh and Hindu practice, respectively.

Whatever happens, the home religion will surely remain an ethnic and religious marker. At the same time, for many research participants, "practice" may not be a regularized phenomenon (as it often was for their parents), but rather will remain connected to events and critical incidents involving family members. Monali expresses the position of most of the research participants who have not returned to live in the vicinity of their parents:

> No, I don't [participate in religious group events]. I mean I would except that the Indian temple is outside of Boston, and I don't know those people. If I was with my family I would, but I am not. It is important to retain the rituals and traditions so that I can pass them on to my children. . . . My grandmother was a big force in my mother's eyes, so doing [the prescribed rituals on] her death anniversary is a big deal. When my grandfather passes on it will be the same thing. When my mother passes on it will be the same thing. This is a cultural identity with religion.

To a greater degree than many other research participants, Monali recognizes that participating in group practice shapes the development of religious identity, and that the religious identity aids in the maintenance of culture and tradition. She sometimes feels that from the standpoint of connection to her ethnic identity she is remaining stagnant, or even backsliding, because she is not participating in ethnoreligious community events.

In discussing their present and their future, many research participants expressed a strong desire to maintain or reestablish their connection to an ethnoreligious community. Most research participants, whatever their social experiences to date, said they wished to marry a coethnic and coreligionist, although this was by no means a universal opinion. Individuals within the second generation vary in the extent to which each has internalized "American" and "Indian" sensibilities.[43] Among the research participants in this study, this desire for ethnic recovery is coupled with nostalgia for the ethnoreligious community of their childhoods. For those who lacked such a community, ethnic discovery—the creation of a new such connection—is an oft-expressed desire.

Alongside these wishes looms a major concern for many research participants: They do not know exactly how they will achieve this cultural maintenance because they do not have a command of their home language or the knowledge necessary to engage effectively in their home religious practices. On the subject of worship, which she now considers important, Anita lamented that she did not learn the underpinnings of religious practices from her parents, "I just did them." Now, she is not sure what to do when she wants to engage in worship.

3

Facets of Lived Religion

In the preceding chapters, religion largely came to the research participants, and not the other way around. Their parents designed Sunday schools for them, their peers illustrated new ways of thinking about themselves, and the world around them simply existed as the backdrop and scenery of their lives' drama. In this chapter, we see how these forty-one second-generation Indian American research participants went to religion. The lived religion of this chapter is found in the information they sought and the conduct they aspired to, in their experience of contact with India and the sensations of private ritual practices. The four major sections of this chapter do not include all the ways religion exists in the lives of second-generation Indian Americans, but they represent common threads that were found across the range of religious affiliations and life experiences in this cohort. Whether they saw themselves as "religious" people or not, the research participants lived religion as a moral compass, as a thirst and search for knowledge, as acts of ritual practice, and through the experience of travel to India. Religion was and remains an influence on the ethnic identity development through these experiences.

Religion as a Moral Compass

If we are to concern ourselves with "what matters" in an individual's religious life, we must recognize the tensions and choices faced by the individual and acknowledge that even in breaking known religious rules, an individual may be "living religion."[1] Despite their imperfect knowledge and feelings of theological self-doubt, religion nevertheless served a profound role in the lives of nearly all the research participants: that of a moral compass, an invisible navigation device that parents placed in each research participant's pocket, to which the second generation would refer—and, in some cases, by which they would be guided—as life's choices and temptations came into view. Experiencing religion as a moral compass means ascribing religious importance to distinctions between "right" and "wrong" conduct on the basis of the home religion's rules and mores as second-generation Indian Americans have come to understand them. True north on an individual's moral compass included the set of values he or she understood to be good conduct, in accord with the rules of the home religion; examples include not eating beef (Hindus) or pork (Muslims), not drinking alcohol or engaging in premarital sex, respecting and obeying one's parents, and the like. In the words of Shiren, this facet of religious identity is about "basically you live a kind of life that if Jesus or God was sitting next to you, you would never feel ashamed. You know what I mean?" For most research participants, some version of the moral compass functioned as the measure against which they judged their own and their peers' conduct as "good" or "bad," "right" or "wrong." Importantly, the concept of the moral compass describes the beliefs and thought processes of the research participants—not necessarily their actions. Put another way, *having* a moral compass (as all research participants did) and *following* it were and are two different things.

Salim, for example, was aware of the direction his moral compass pointed but comfortably acted in a contradictory manner. "I believe very firmly in giving back to the community. . . . So the role of Islam in my life has certainly influenced that aspect, but it hasn't ever made me put down a drink." The major element of Salim's moral compass religiosity was his adulthood commitment to *sewa*, or service to the religious community. For Salim, *sewa* is the fundamental way in which he "practices" his religion today—as a participant, leader, and servant in religious youth camps, to provide South Asian Muslim youth of today peers and experiences and a sense of (ethnoreligious) community that he lacked.[2] Aziz—an Isma'ili-born Muslim who described his two conversions to Sunni Islam—also focused on *sewa*.[3] Whereas Salim's *sewa* grew from a desire to connect with his community, Aziz's grew from anger at the Isma'ili community of his childhood, which he felt was "straying and losing touch" by ignoring *sewa* and getting caught up in materialism and in competition over who gave how much money to the cultural center; in losing touch with *sewa*, Aziz felt, his community had lost their focus on God.

For many others who "veered away" (Nikhil's words) from the home religion during college or adulthood, the moral compass was experienced as a religious pang of guilt or failure. For example, Aziz, the Isma'ili-raised Muslim who twice converted to Sunni Islam in college—spoke disdainfully of how he conducted himself before his second conversion experience: "It was a repugnant time in my life. There were only six Muslims on campus and they were strong, but only a few of them were united and religious or intensive. It was my fault. . . . White women are attracted to power. . . . I would fall for that a number of times even after I converted to Islam—their advances, sexual advances. It just feeds you." Whatever else one may say about Aziz's viewpoint, it is clear that what some would consider normal collegiate behavior characterized by sexual permissiveness was profoundly troubling and led him to two points of moral crisis, each of which resulted in a conversion experience. (Since his second conversion experience, Aziz said, he has "stuck with it.") The disdain with which he spoke of his former self was as palpable during his interview as it is conspicuous in his remarks quoted above: Moral weakness and his sexual desire for white women were repugnant; to avoid these temptations and be observant was to be strong, united, and intensive.

Collegiate youth culture, of course, offers many of the temptations that a typical second-generation Indian American moral compass would instruct the research participants to eschew—particularly alcohol. As amply noted above, the college years are the first time for most of these research participants when their association with religion was voluntary rather than enforced by parents. At the same time, religion had already been infused into their lives; the formal and informal teachings they had received before college stayed with them. Across the cohort, the most common behavior that research participants described as wrong relative to their moral compass was drinking alcohol. Islam and Sikhism forbid the consumption of alcohol, and although Hinduism does not expressly forbid it, many "observant" Hindus do not drink. Of those research participants whose parents did not drink alcohol, Harjit was typical; he said that being Sikh meant "the constant reminder that I shouldn't be drinking." The other activity that was uniformly interpreted as irreligious or wrong across religious identifications was engaging in premarital sex.

Awareness of straying from a religious path by engaging in such conduct could bring on so intense a sensation of internal conflict as to compel a return to religion. Shiren, a Catholic, decided that due to "drinking and partying, I basically realized that I did need spiritual guidance." As a first-year college student, She had engaged in alcohol use, partying, and had taken up smoking, while also taking a course on the New Testament that led her to question certain tenets of her faith. She was one of several research participants who experienced moments of moral doubt or failure in college and as a result sought to reconnect to religion. Shiren talked about sitting in church at the end of her freshman year and contemplating God and the role of God in her life: "I would go to church by myself and sit down when there was no one around, and just start praying, and basically asking God to help me figure out what I really believe and why am I having all these questions, why am I having all these doubts in my mind when for so long, you know, everything just made sense." As a sophomore, Shiren reported, "the church thing didn't really work out too well"; she rarely attended because she was tired from partying on Saturday nights. "But since my parents had always said religion is something that comes from within, I didn't feel like I had to go to church." As an adult, Shiren reported, she has become a churchgoer again and now, "whenever I feel like I'm getting off track, whenever I feel like I need some sort of guidance, I always start praying again. I go to church again." She gauges her conduct against the needle of her moral compass and when she feels she is veering too far from a right course, she returns to religion as a way of modifying her conduct; prayer and ritual function as tools to reform her actions in the outside world. This illustrates the essential role of religion as a touchpoint for the moral compass among virtually all the research participants in this cohort. Inasmuch as they use religious language and metaphor as a moral reference, they feel they need to return to religion in order to return to acting morally.

Some respondents actually followed the rules of their moral compasses. Ravi attended college in California, and for him college was a time of religious self-discovery through reading and talking with his father; he reported that he did not drink alcohol in college. Nija, who went to school in up state New York, also made a conscious moral choice not to drink alcohol and not to have premarital sex. Ravi and Nija did not report feeling isolated for their beliefs; both specifically stated that they did not feel different from typical American college students.

Because of the common mental association between ritual practice and religiosity, a result of childhood observations of parental and grandparental worship practices, many research participants reported feeling a moral obligation to engage in ritual. Avya's moral compass included obligations related to both personal conduct and conscientious worship. She said being a Hindu "meant being disciplined and not eating meat. It still means constantly trying to put Hindu teachings into practice . . . not losing my temper. Chanting and keeping up with things like holidays, . . . going to ashram . . . [and] always trying to practice seeing God in everyone." For Harjit, a Sikh male, "practicing started to mean going to gurdwara every Sunday, but more than that, [it was about] applying it to my everyday life and how the beliefs reflected my everyday life."

Recall that most research participants reported feeling that they had inadequate knowledge of the home religion and that they did not practice the religion—or even were "not religious"—because they did not perform the rituals their parents or grandparents did. Many research participants disclaimed religiosity, offering instead sentiments like Priti's: "I am a spiritual person. And I am not a religious person. I don't practice. I don't attend any religious events." The moral compass may represent a manifestation of the view that parents' and grandparents' religious practice is normative and authentic. Many Hindu research participants reported having a parent or grandparent who performed a lengthy *puja* every morning and kept strict fasts on major holidays, just as one of the Sikhs in this study reported that his father abided strictly by the "five Ks."[4] Even if such research participants had a deep and abiding faith in God, prayed, or tried to live a life consistent with the tenets of the home faith (as they understood them), they might not consider themselves religious by comparison. Priti is interested in believing in a supreme being, in transcendence; however, like other individuals of her generation, Priti is not interested in identifying with a religion (Beaudoin 1998; Marler and Hadaway 2002). This illustrates the confluence of research participants' major frustrations about their home faith: a lack of clear rules, inadequate information, and a language barrier separating them from many sources of more information (since, after all, clear rules often do exist in scripture).

The frequency of remarks like Priti's, and the fact that they often arose in the context of a discussion about conduct or life choices, indicate that that research participants frequently spoke of spirituality when referring to their moral compass and its role in shaping their conduct. This choice to use language like "spirituality" and "belief" over "religiosity" or "worship" reflects the space where many second-generation Indian American are positioning themselves with respect to religion and morality, and offers the beginning of an insight into what American Sikhism, American Hinduism, and American Islam may look like in future years.

Sweta, a Hindu woman, was typical of a minority of research participants who both described a moral-compass orientation and described engaging individually in prayer or other ritual worship. In college, Sweta developed a sense of devotion with the help of a "very religious" Hindu friend, who taught her certain prayers and rituals. These prayers and rituals continue to be a comfort to her today. Yet when asked about her religiosity, she still replied promptly: "Practicing Hindu? No. I knew I was Hindu, I knew there certain things we do. . . . I don't pray everyday but I talk to God often. (*Laughs*) A little bargaining session with God! I do feel a sense of inner peace. I feel good." Here, Sweta seems to be comparing herself primarily to her friend, who "got up every morning to pray," which struck Sweta as "really strange [for] someone my age."

It is not that the second generation is rejecting the ritual practice of their parents and grandparents. Indeed, it is likely that many second-generation Indian Americans have an idealized, futuristic image of themselves rising at dawn to perform prayers and ablutions, and for Muslims, observing the *Salat*, the obligation to pray five times daily. But for now, many of the research participants particularly Hindus, Muslims, and Sikhs remain uncomfortable in the sphere of organized religion: both uncomfortable with their image of Christianity, which is associated with dogmatism, judgmentalism, and discrimination, and uncomfortable with worship in the home religion because of unfamiliarity with ritual practice and inability to fully participate because of language.[5] Nevertheless, they have internalized a moral code and see this code as being informed and fed by a theological rather than a secular wellspring. In this respect, many second-generation Indian Americans are like what Ammerman calls "Golden Rule

Christians" who "claim that the practices they put at the center of the Christian life inform their everyday economic and civic activities"—that is, that Christian principles shape their daily moral choices. Although they reject the aggressive evangelistic and political dogmatism now more and more associated with the term Christian in the public sphere, they are Christian rather than secular in orientation because they "simply see no other organization that puts caring for others so clearly at the center of its life" (Ammerman 1997, 204). Like Golden Rule Christians, second-generation Indian Americans may often skip worship services but nevertheless see themselves as members of a religious group and consider their life conduct to be guided by transcendent principles.

Moral-compass religiosity is a comfortable and appealing middle path for the second generation. Positioned between an unappealing majority religion that rejects them and a parental or grandparental measure of religiosity they cannot live up to, the second generation has formulated a conceptual connection to the home religion which they can act out through day-to-day conduct. We should not make the error of characterizing moral-compass religiosity as something less than the ritualized religious practice of the immigrant generation. Nor should moral-compass religiosity be seen as exclusive of ritual practice. Moral-compass religiosity is a major but not exclusive component of the developing American Hinduism, American Islam, and American Sikhism—of how the second generation goes about being Hindu, Muslim, or Sikh.

Another reason so many second-generation Indian Americans seem to be oriented first toward a "moral compass" religiosity is the barrier to religious practice and participation that has vexed many of them since childhood: a language barrier. Moreover, many religious rituals continue to be practiced in languages other than those spoken day-to-day by Indian American families. Pujas and other Hindu religious ceremonies are most often conducted in Sanskrit or, as noted, in a high dialect of a regional Indian language like Tamil or Gujarati. Most Indian Americans—including all the Hindus in this study—do not understand Sanskrit. Likewise, Muslim worship is often performed in Arabic, Islam's scriptural language but a language not spoken by most Indian American Muslims, or in a complex dialect of an Indian regional language. Sikhs pray in Gurumukhi, a language that is related to, but contains many words and structures that differ from, modern Punjabi, the home language of the Sikhs.[6] Even if their parents and communities performed rituals using their home language, the complexity of prayer language—its unique grammar and vocabulary—could often make it incomprehensible even to research participants who spoke or understood the vernacular home language. (Attending worship gatherings nevertheless had a language-maintenance function. When their parents gathered with other adults, research participants got to hear the native language spoken. Particularly for research participants whose parents conversed with them in English at home, this was important.)

The language barrier both explains the dearth of individual ritual practice reported by the second generation and the orientation toward moral-compass-type religiosity. Most second-generation Indian Americans do know, from a childhood of attendance at religious services and/or observations of parental practice, what to do at religious functions. But functionally, that made the research participants (as teens) passive and unknowing participants, sitting bored through prayers, wishing for the social hour to arrive—or skipping out on prayers entirely, to hang out with their friends while their parents engaged in prayer and rituals. The ritual becomes disconnected from its underlying meaning.[7] The disconnection of adult second-generation Indian Americans from ritual practice is among the lingering impacts of this reality.

It is therefore unsurprising—but important to note—that moral-compass religiosity springs from the research participants' subjective *understanding* of the rules of their home faith, and not necessarily from the actual rules or their scriptural underpinnings. When it comes to the moral compass, rules and mores that a theologian might not characterize as religious nevertheless take on religious meaning. Examples abound. For example, regardless of what scholars and critics state, it is generally accepted that Hinduism prohibits the consumption of beef. But for many research participants—particularly those who were raised in strictly vegetarian Gujarati or South Indian homes—the consumption of any meat (including fowl and fish) was seen as religiously improper. Others imbued cultural concepts or traditions with religious meaning. Reflecting the respect for scholars and for learning that is common in Indian culture, Anita said: "you'd always do a little prayer before you start a test or when you—certain things like, you know, you don't put your feet on books or anything like that. I was very, I'm very picky about certain things I do. But I didn't go to the Cleveland temple." For Aziz, believing in God meant being tolerant of people in the community at large and his own community: "It meant community and it meant justice and tolerance—like Gandhian tolerance, M.L.K. tolerance, not Malcolm X tolerance."

The moral compass was not only turned inward. Many research participants reported using their moral compass to judge another person's religiosity and moral quality on the basis of the other person's conduct or religious knowledge. Ravi, who grew more religious over the college years because of his studies and conversations with his father, did not drink alcohol. He recalled thinking ill of his Hindu peers who did drink: "It's like, 'You people consider yourselves Hindus and you're going out and getting trashed and throwing up everywhere.' I guess I thought of myself as a little more righteous than the average college student." Ravi was not alone in thinking this way. Anisa learned about Hinduism and described many of her friends as "ignorant about so much of Hinduism." In American society there is a great emphasis on conduct and formal belief of religion because Christianity places importance on rules and on intellectual and formal belief. Thus, by adopting the dominant society's tendency to look critically at those who act contrary to their own religious tenets, research participants like Ravi and Anisa could look down on their peers who were inadequate or "fallen" Hindus.

In this respect, moral-compass religiosity also represents a form of authenticity. Just as practice was often seen as authentic when it was "just like they do in India" (Binu's words), individual Indian Americans' decisions to engage in or eschew prohibited conduct became a test of authenticity in the eyes of themselves and others. Ravi and Anisa saw their friends as "less Hindu" because they drank alcohol. Other Hindu research participants reported having their religious identity (not merely their religiosity!) questioned when they were observed eating meat. Salim reported being asked whether he was "really Muslim" when he partook of daytime meals during Ramadan. Satish had been asked why he did not wear a turban, since he identified as Sikh.

Ravi's life story also illustrates (as do others') how both one's moral compass and one's decisions about whether or not to follow it—like religious and ethnic identity themselves—evolve over the life span. As an adult, Ravi did drink alcohol, eat meat, and cheat on his fiancée. The research participants' reports about their conduct and their outlook on moral issues demonstrate that both the content of and the individuals' allegiance to their moral compasses was evolutionary over the life span. In this respect, the moral compass is quintessential *lived religion*. Evolutionary, contradictory, and often "observed" by an individual as he engages in "wrong" conduct, moral-compass religiosity will remain a major element of second- and later-generation Indian American religious experience.

Transnational Experiences

The reader will recall that "authenticity"—the degree to which a practice or a person was genuinely "Indian"—involved an inevitable reference to one's understanding of how things are done in India. In addition to functioning as an emotional touchpoint for identity and authenticity, India was literally only a plane flight away, albeit an expensive one, for the second-generation Indian Americans who came of age in the 1980s and 1990s. Of the forty-one research participants in this study, thirty-nine traveled to India at least once during their K–12 years, and more than half reported going to India at least once every three years. No one ever discussed these trips as vacations. These were transnational experiences.[8] I use the term *transnational experiences* to refer specifically to experiences of travel to and in India, and the resulting personal interactions and relationships—the experiences that affect the individual's ethnic identity. They were forced family interaction at first, which often blossomed into self-discovery trips later in life.

Transnationalism for these second-generation Indian Americans is part of their experience of lived religion, both inasmuch as it informs their notions of authenticity and by virtue of the actual experiences research participants reported during travel to India.[9] Transnational experiences had an impact on the research participants that was both broad—touching language and other dimensions of culture, family relationships, and religion—and deep because of India's role as a reference point for origin and authenticity.[10]

This particular type of second-generation transnational engagement is affected primarily by the transnational experiences of the immigrant generation, and here specifically the transnational activity of the research participants' families. There is, of course, a socioeconomic element to transnationalism. The freedom to travel to India encompasses the wherewithal to pay for it, the influence to get weeks or months off from work, and the ability to stay with family in India. Transnationalism was thus affected by the wealth and wherewithal of both the family and the hosts.[11] The research participants' parents' status as professionals made these transnational experiences possible (see Vickerman 2002).

Transnational experiences exerted a strong influence on the research participants with respect to religion, particularly in adulthood. After a drop-off during the college years (when only nineteen of forty-one reported an India trip), more than three-quarters of the research participants traveled to India as adults. This independently expressed desire to reconnect with "India" itself demonstrates the importance of the transnational experience in identity development. For these research participants, the search for "roots," always an element of transnational experiences, took on a particularly religious importance. They usually discussed the trips by reference to religion, religious experiences, and feelings of religious belonging. Nikhil described his trip to India:

> I wanted to see temples, I wanted to see the Taj Mahal. I wanted to see India, and so that—I really liked that trip. We did sort of like a religious trek to all the big temples in India, and I really enjoyed it because, you know, all of a sudden you're seeing not just, you know, like five or six families getting together to do a *puja*, you're seeing thousands of people, you know, going to these temples and it's just an amazing sight. I'm still in awe of that trip. You know, seeing the Taj Mahal was amazing, but I still think that the most amazing thing was seeing the, the land, the people, and the temples. They were just amazing.

Many described "reconnecting" to their religion by going to temples and experiencing "spirituality" in the company of other coreligionists. Travel to India is seen as a way to recharge one's religious batteries. For those that made the journey, their travels reified the notion that the Hinduism or Sikhism "done" in India is the most authentic, and that participating in worship in India is therefore the best way of learning it. Some considered travel to India a pilgrammage of sorts. Few literally undertook pilgrimages to sacred sites in India, but the experience of going to India, and in particular going to gurdwaras and mandirs there, had a similar emotional effect. For some, merely standing on the street and realizing that one is in the company of hundreds of thousands of one's coreligionists—an experience virtually impossible to have in the United States—created a sense of religious belonging and strength of self. By comparison, research participants spoke of trips to India during the K–12 years mostly in terms of its effect on their ethnic identity and connection to family.

As adults, the research participants saw and treated their trips to India as opportunities for religious discovery. Reflecting the new importance placed on religion and religious identity due to their experiences to date and the life decisions that loomed before them, the research participants described their adult trips to India in heavily religious terms. (They also described them almost exclusively in positive terms—a contrast to the many research participants, described below, who did not enjoy trips to India during the K–12 period.) Many—particularly the Hindus, who continue to conflate Indianness and Hinduness—described "feeling more Indian" there. They could go to temples that in quantity, size, and intensity of simulation dwarfed what they could access in America, and they could be surrounded by coreligionists and coethnics not only there but also in the public square. Mahesh described India as a place where he reconnected to his Hindu religion because "Just in general, you feel a lot more spiritual because you realize how important it is to a lot more people. I guess I respected [religion]. No, I always respected it. But somehow, [being in India meant] having it be significant. I started taking more notice of things." It remains to be seen if this generation of individuals will participate in some of the transnational religious activities that their immigrant parents engaged in, such as donating to temples in India or seeking counseling and advice of Hindu priests (Williams 1988; Lessinger 1995).

One element of the adult focus on religion may relate to the place of religion in American life. Religion is becoming a more meaningful social identity for so many research participants because religion is becoming a more meaningful social identity for so many Americans; it is front and center on the U.S. political scene with the rise and electoral success of the "Christian right." At the same time, these second-generation Indian Americans are settling into careers and starting to think about choosing life partners, starting families, and building or joining ethnoreligious communities. India and the idea of India functions as an emotional refuge from the alienation and isolation they have experienced throughout their lives—in particular, at those moments when they encountered racial or religious discrimination in America.

The size and visibility in India of religious communities that are tiny and invisible in this country—Hindu, Sikh, Muslim, and Malayali Catholic—was an important part of the transnational experience. For those who felt marginalized, invisible, or outright rejected in the American milieu, suddenly finding oneself among multitudes of people with whom one shares attributes that make one an outcast in the United States was transformative. At the same time, the data showed distinctions among the experiences of Hindu research participants and the experience of others. All discussed going to India in religious terms, but not all the research participants experienced India and religiosity there in the same way. Transnational experiences are affected by the religious place of the research participants in both United States and Indian society: The experiences of a Catholic (part of the American majority but a small minority in India), a Hindu (an American minority but a religious majority with hegemonic cultural influence in India), and Sikhs and Muslims (an oppressed religious minority in both countries) are inherently different, and the nature and effect of the transnational ties differ as well.

Trips to India thus seem to invoke a similar depth but different emotional and political quality of transnationalism across religious affiliation. Again, the bonds between coreligionists are strengthened, and those between immigrants from different religious backgrounds are weakened. Despite national origin's status as the officially recognized criterion for "ethnicity" in the United States, the data indicate that different religious groups in fact develop substantially divergent definitions of nationality and constructions of homeland, culture, and identity. Put another way, the families of the second-generation research participants may have immigrated to the United States for similar reasons, but they may also have emigrated from India for very different reasons, because the various religious groups have a different social histories in India. For example, for many Sikhs in America the concept of a "homeland" invokes not India but specifically the Punjab region—the epicenter of the Sikh population and site of the *Darbar Sahib*, more popularly known as the Golden Temple in Amritsar.[12] By contrast, the Hindu research participants are part of the majority culture in India. So when many of the Hindu second-generation members go to India, they talk about parts of their identity being everywhere. These transnational experiences occur within a diasporic context, particularly for the Hindu and Sikh research participants. The notion of a diaspora connotes, of necessity, a homeland from which one is separated, but that one shares this separation with all other coethnics or coreligionists who are outside the homeland.[13] India appears to serve this function for Hindus, as the Punjab region does for Sikhs.[14]

Aziz's experience in India soon after finishing his undergraduate studies offers an instructive example. It solidified the bonds of his faith and led him to reach strong conclusions about religion and religiosity: "Over the summer I went to Bombay, Mumbai, as a part of [a group] who educated high school and

college, English-speaking, mostly private school kids, about AIDS and HIV. . . .
That was really eye opening. I was with all these South Asian Americans who
were trying to figure out, 'Who the hell am I as a South Asian, American, Indian?'" During this trip he encountered anti-Muslim prejudice in the form of
difficulty in getting service in stores. Aziz saw himself as in India to educate and
to help Indian young people; he had an emotional attachment to both the place
and the task. Yet his name alerted Hindu shopowners to his religion, and as a result he was made to feel unwelcome. He concluded: "That trip was quite remarkable. I realized cultural bonds are far inferior to religious bonds." The
message he received was that being of Indian lineage is not good enough for
many in India; rather, one must Hindu to be considered Indian. For Aziz this experience solidified in his mind the desire to practice and live his life, like the
British Muslim youth in Jessica Jacobson's (1997) study, with "culture free Islam,"
to which he subscribes today. Aziz very much considers himself to be part of the
ummah, the global Islamic community.

It was not only religion that could lead to a feeling of rejection where
acceptance had been expected. Many research participants of all religious
affiliations—particularly those whose trips to India were less frequent over the
life span—exhibited *emotional transnationalism*. According to Dianne Wolf, the
emotionally transnational second generation can only imagine the Home that
constitutes their parents' and grandparents' primary point of reference. This
home is morally superior to the home they now inhabit and constitutes the foundation for judging behaviors as proper, appropriate and shameful.[15] Note the
functional similarity between emotional transnationalism and moral-compass
religiosity. Both link righteousness to an imagined primordial ideal. There were
indeed research participants in this study who developed and nurtured a romanticized concept of their parents' home country as a place where they would
belong as they did not in the United States; in their minds, India would welcome
them as fully Indian people. The experience of Binita, who traveled to India in
fifth or sixth grade and then did not return until after graduating from college, is
illustrative. When she went to India in adulthood, Binita found that she was "not
accepted. I'm getting to a point where I think I'm really comfortable with who I
am and, you know, and I really appreciate my culture and then I go to India. And
I'm not Indian . . . it was kind of interesting. I think in a different kind of way, but,
you know, it makes me think, wow! I'm not, not necessarily not accepted, but I'm
not one of them, you know, I [thought] I found the group that I think I identify
with." Ravi, a Hindu male who also experienced a fifteen-year gap between childhood and adulthood trips to India, recalled feeling like "a fish out of water over
there" when he went as an adult. "I felt very American." By developing a more nuanced understanding of India and his relationship to it, Ravi has now answered
certain childhood questions he had about Hinduism and Indian culture while
also coming to consider his relatives in India some of the key people in his life.

He says "I am getting into more contact with some of my relatives in India. . . . I would not say I know them. . . . I know them somewhat." This eyes-open approach to the relationship with India is common among those research participants who have traveled there multiple times in adulthood. These research participants have reconceptualized their relationship with India, valuing what's real, identifying spiritually with the land, but also exhibiting an understanding of the limits of their own Indianness.

Maira (2002) argues that the second generation comes to see India as representing a pure and authentic formation of "Indianness." Wolf (2002) describes second-generation emotional transnationalism as an "echo [of] their parents' transnational connections."[16] These characterizations are largely accurate for emotionally transnational people like Binita, but for the research participants who went to India regularly, essentialist notions of identity were questioned and the connection was not merely derivative. Rather, their direct exposure to things Indian helped them build a more constructive, nuanced, and unromanticized notion not only of India but of their religious and ethnic identities.

Put another way, actual transnational experiences were an antidote to emotional transnationalism. The research participants who actually went to India regularly were less likely to develop idealized notions of the country and therefore less apt to experience disappointment and disillusionment there. In Girish's case, he spent his seventh-grade year at a boarding school in his mother's hometown—at his request.[17] After spending summers there, Girish wanted to experience some thing he felt he missed out on living in the United States. "My cousin was telling me about things they do in all of the holidays, like Holi and everything and how they celebrate everything. And deep down inside, [I] felt like I'll never get to see these things because there's no way I can come to India during like every holiday." After spending his seventh-grade year at his cousin's boarding school there, he said he felt "I didn't belong there either because I'm not really an Indian because I'm growing up in America and I don't share the same views, the beliefs, and the things we do, I don't do the same things. And so I always felt like I was stuck in the middle somewhere and didn't really have a place."

The 50 percent drop-off rate between research participants who traveled to India during K–12 (thirty-nine of forty-one) and during college (nineteen of forty-one) is probably the product of several factors: the need to participate in career-building or money-making summer jobs instead of "recreational" travel, the reduced family ability to pay for international travel along with hefty college tuition bills, and the greater freedom from parental edicts that characterizes the college years.[18] For those who did go to India during college, the trip was an important reexposure to the home religion and culture; asked to describe their trips, research participants often volunteered stories about going to masjid, gurdwara or mandir with grandparents and other relatives. Perhaps because of the soul-searching that is indigenous to the college years, research participants characterized these trips to India as moments of self-discovery. If K–12 trips to India had been about seeing family, then trips to India during college became more about seeking answers to introspective questions such as, "What is my attachment to this land? Do I even have one? What does it really mean for me to be from this country or my parents to be from this country?" Here then we see the beginning of the adult experiences described above: the use of India as a reference point for identity and authenticity, for things "internal" to the research participants as well as the externalities of family, food, tourism, and the like.

For most research participants, the experience of India grew on them as they matured through the K–12 period. In Harjit's words, "when I was younger, I hated going because I would just get sick and like I just thought it was boring. But after I got more mature, I realized the value of it and liked it." Anya said she always "loved going back" to Kashmir, in northern India, which had a climate similar to her home in Massachusetts; she particularly enjoyed the attention she received. "I had lots of family. You get a lot of attention, grandparents really dote on you." Several research participants reported being local celebrities when they returned home. It's important to recall that this was a period before two more modern developments, India's opening broadly to international commerce and the relative commonness of emigration to the United States. Having a relative visit from America was extremely novel at the time, and was literally in some cases an occasion to invite friends and neighbors over to look at the child. India-bound suitcases would be filled with Coca-Cola, Levi's blue jeans, and other items not then available in India—further adding to the popularity of the research participants on arrival. As a contrast to the alienation most experienced in the milieu of their American schools and neighborhoods, this celebrity was a salve for bruised egos and part of what made trips to India appealing for many.

Others did not enjoy their trips. "It was something that was done," Sarvesh deadpanned. He reported going to India every two or three years and described it as an "obligation" (read a "chore"). He and other research participants described disliking "the poverty" and "filth" they encountered in India, the "substandard living conditions" of their extended families' homes, and the common experience of getting sick with a food-borne illness or malaria. Still others recounted being miserable at the thought of going to India, but enjoying it once they arrived. Importantly, the data reveal that the distinction between those who enjoyed the trips and those who did not is *not* manifested in outcomes: Research participants across the cohort, whether they characterized during K–12 as positive or negative experiences, said they resulted in feeling more connected to and grounded in Indian culture. Asked what made him feel a connection to Indian culture, the first thing Anand volunteered was his experiences in India. Shabnam said her "thirteen or fourteen" childhood trips to India "definitely helped solidify my identity as an Indian." Several research participants, like Avinash, remarked that "going to India more than anything else" provided a sense of connection to Indian culture.

The lion's share of second-generation Indian Americans will continue to live and work in the United States. For this population, the import of continuing transnational trips will be to maintain and augment India's status as a homeland but in particular as a spiritual homeland. This generation is likely to identify more and more as American over the course of their lives, but also to maintain India's place as a spiritual homeland. India's relevance as a place of friends and family, even as a cultural source, will diminish far more quickly than the association of India with religious faith and observance. Raj's (2000) study of British Hindus of Indian origin is instructive here; he found that this population refashioned its connection to India. The connection continued to have meaning and relevance to the lives of people born and brought up in Britain—but instead of being "perpetually foreign" in Britain, connected politically or nationally to a distant homeland, they redefine themselves as British people with a *spiritual* connection to far-off India.

Positive or negative, encouraging or discouraging, research participants' experiences in India—regardless of the individual participant's religion—had a strong impact on their thinking and actions from a religious perspective. Visiting India got research participants to think about religious issues and shaped their ethnic identity development process as second-generation Indian Americans. Across life periods, the trips to India and the relationships research participants developed with relatives in India created, reinforced, and fortified a connection to Indian culture and, in particular, to a sense of connection to the home religion.[19]

Knowledge

As briefly noted above, many research participants found that observing parental religious practice and even engaging in ritual practice with an ethnoreligious community was not enough to make them feel "religious." Worship alone did not offer a sense of a relationship with God or of believing in the home religion. For these second-generation Indian Americans, the ability and knowledge to explain the home religion's rituals and tenets to themselves is fundamental to having the experience of faith, belief, and transcendence. The data reveal that an intellectual connection to the home faith's belief system can facilitate belief as such, and that the lack of such connection can make a research participant feel disconnected from the home faith despite engaging in frequent ritual practice when growing up and or even continuing to do so in the parents' company of as an adult. A majority of research participants lived their religion by studying it in the academic setting, and by doing so they increased their sense of connection to and belief in it.

Some research participants got the information they needed from Sunday schools created by parents in the ethnoreligious community. Sunday school—a term used rather consistently across the ethnoreligious communities in which the research participants were reared—did not necessarily take place on Sunday. Its size and scope depended upon the size, organization, and inclination of the ethnoreligious community that supported it. In smaller communities, and during the research participants' younger years when a physical community center was not yet available, it would be held in a private home. Many began with a single family teaching its own children, then expanded to become regularized programs of study and activity. Before their communities were large enough to support religious Sunday school of their own, Indian American Sikhs and Muslims would often attend Hindu Sunday schools.[20] (Ironically Catholic research participants who went to the "white" Catholic Sunday school faced a schedule conflict and could not attend Indian Sunday School.)

Nija studied religion and Hindi language at the Hindu temple near Pittsburgh, Pennsylvania: "I attended *Bal Vihar* classes for the children on the Indian mythologies and language. . . . We would talk about Hindu scripture, he would tell us stories. That was my exposure to Hinduism." Anisa described her weekly ritual in Burlington, Massachusetts: "On Sunday mornings, the first hour was language, the second hour was culture. As soon as we walked in we had prayer, we had songs, we would sing the national anthem and all that other stuff." As these remarks indicate, one frequent focus of these Hindu Sunday schools was language—usually Hindi, unless the school served a specific population in which another language (such as Gujarati or Tamil) predominated.[21] Curricula also typically included stories from the Puranas, the *Ramayana*, and the *Mahabharata*, plus information about Mohandas K. Gandhi and Indian history. For the Hindus in this study, this subject matter—especially the religious material—represented Indian authenticity and Indian national culture. Neither the research participants nor, apparently, their Sunday school teachers drew clear lines between secular and religious, historical and mythical.

If these subjects constituted the conscious learning that went on at Sunday school, there was another element of unconscious learning that also informed the research participants' identities. Research participants' descriptions of Sunday school show that they also picked up subtle cues from adults, internalizing cultural values such as the importance of family and of respect for one's elders.

Anisa described the Sunday school experience much as research participants described other ethnoreligious community activities: "It empowered you so you could feel more comfortable." It was when she got to spend time with people her own age of a similar cultural background that she was happiest.

Anisa's experience is also typical of Indian Americans whose families hail from the southern part of India. As the child of Telegu speakers, the Hindi Anisa learned at Sunday school was not of much use at home. Because sometimes Hindu gods are referred to by different names in the south than in the north, she also learned stories that sounded different from those her parents told her. Still, it's impossible not to hear in her words the emotional and social value of Sunday school.

From the standpoint of knowledge as an element of religious affiliation and ethnic identity, Sunday schools were not uniformly successful in giving the second generation what it needed. Even those that failed in this respect could succeed in providing a peer group for research participants—the social safe haven described in Chapter 2—and providing opportunities for the unconscious learning described above. In the words of Nija, a Hindu female, "Sunday school . . . is why I know what I know today." But many research participants said Sunday schools did not provide enough of the knowledge or context they were looking for. This often left the research participants still searching for answers and pursuing further academic study of the home religion. Harjit, for example, said: "There wasn't really a forum for me to ask questions. [There was] my parents and the Sunday school, but that wasn't really that much. My parents didn't always have the answers. My biggest question always was, 'Why do I keep my hair?' Because that was the single most differentiating item between me and my peers, and the answers that they gave me I just wasn't content with. . . . They would tell me, 'It's part of your religion. It's one of the five things that you're supposed to identify with the religion.' And I'd just say 'Why? Why?' " Harjit later gained access to answers to his religious questions thanks to a summer camp he attended during high school, which functioned like an extended and intensive Sunday school-type experience:

> When I went to Sikh camp, every day they would have like a question and answer session. It was an open discussion, no parents were allowed, so you could ask absolutely anything. There were priests and the counselors just four or five years older than us. That's where I learned the most, just being able to ask like questions like why do I do it and why am I supposed to keep my hair and stuff like that. There I got answers so that I was proud to return [home and have answers for] people when they asked me, "Why do you do it?" and "What's the significance of that?" So I think that was a key for me.

Those research participants who now have children of their own have begun to develop Sunday school programs for the third generation. In Atlanta, for example, an informal network of second-generation parents (plus a small number of young immigrant families) gathers their children periodically in private homes. The group is made up entirely of Hindus, and the curriculum includes religious stories, prayers, and the Hindi language. Despite the presence of several temples and cultural associations that could provide a venue, the group elects to meet in private homes. The curriculum is of their own design and does not draw on the resources or reflect the religious or political agenda of the Vishva Hindu Parishad, also popularly described as the Hindutva movement.[22]

Religion, the College Environment, and Academics

Fenton (1988) found that most second-generation Indian Americans had very limited knowledge about the rationale for and practice of specific rituals in the home religion. Fenton's exploratory study took place at a time when the oldest members of Atlanta's Indian American second generation were from eighteen to twenty years old: just reaching the stage of cognitive development when religious identity and questions often come to the fore, and not old enough to have pursued independently the academic study of religion.[23] Eighteen years later, my study confirms Fenton's findings: As they passed through adolescence, even those who grew up in the presence of an ethnoreligious community, a temple, or a Sunday school program felt they did not know enough about their home religion to identify with it—or, by extension, practice it independently.[24] This second generation arrived in college in the late 1980s and early 1990s still looking for answers, and they sought out courses to fill the gaps (Fenton 1992) .

In the late 1980s and early 1990s, when the research participants began their undergraduate studies, many American colleges and universities offered only a single course on an Indian religion, Indian culture, or Indian history. In the context of these slim pickings, research participants took what courses they could. Christians like Irfan reported taking classes on Hinduism; absent any other courses on India or Indian culture, a class on Hinduism at least offered Irfan a degree of exposure to Indian history and culture, to non-Western theology, and to the religion to which many of his coethnic friends subscribed. Nikhil, a Hindu, saw classes as a chance to move "towards understanding myself. . . . I wanted to explore myself. . . . I started taking a lot of different cultural classes. I took a South Asian geography course, I took a religions of the world course, I took several religion and philosophy classes, I took Ritualism in Primitive Cultures, and I really tried to explore differences in people." Although he never took a course on an Indian religion per se, Harjit used other classes, like American civilization and political science, to study Sikhism-related topics. For example, in a class on twentieth-century politics he wrote his term paper on Indian Sikhs' struggle for an independent Khalistan. He found himself in an exciting cycle of learning: "Doing research papers just increased my overall awareness, and then people began to ask more in-depth questions, which would require me to have even more in-depth answers."

Shiren, a Catholic, had begun to question her religious identity but also to develop a sense of curiosity and a desire to dig deeper than her Catholic school upbringing had allowed her to do. Shiren enrolled in an exegesis course on the New Testament in which she analyzed and compared the four Gospels. Because of her Catholic school background, she was familiar with the stories, but she said she had never really considered the differences among and complete impact of the Gospels. She recalled:

> I remember saying to myself, this is the first time that I'm not being spoon fed religion, the first time I'm not just sitting in class and hearing what people say and just taking it in. . . . I felt like I was always spoon-fed my religion. Never really questioned it. And this was the first time I'd stepped out of that and I actually said to myself, "Everything that I've learned so far up 'til now, do I really believe in it? Or am I just doing it because of what I have to do because I'm Catholic, because I've been raised Catholic?"

For Shiren, her study led to a more detailed knowledge of the scriptural underpinnings of her home religion, but also to a more complex and critical relationship with Catholicism.

> I started feeling like I don't believe in God—not that I don't believe in God, I don't agree with the views of the Catholic church. I started becoming very, just questioning a lot of my faith—you know, abortion, premarital sex, this and that. All these things that I felt so strongly about before because it—because I had to, there was just no question. You don't have sex before you're married in the Catholic church. You don't use birth control. You basically lived the kind of life—you live a kind of life that if Jesus or God was sitting next to you, you would never feel ashamed.

Like Shiren, the Hindu, Muslim, and Sikh research participants who took courses on their home religions wanted to understand their own faith and the scriptural underpinnings and theological rationales behind it. Unlike Shiren, they were also seeking to understand themselves and their religion as it existed in the context of the United States' Christian-dominated society.

Ravi and Sina, both Hindu, came from families where religion was practiced devoutly—through daily pujas and prayers before each meal—but where the religion was rarely explained to them. Sina described her father as a very religious man who taught Hinduism classes in her ethnoreligious community and loaded the family into the car for a visit to the local temple on every major holiday and whenever someone in her family had a birthday. Ravi grew up with comic books telling Hindu stories, but ultimately acknowledged that he knew little more about Hinduism than "the holidays." Both proclaimed they never really knew what Hindu meant as a religion. In college each found a different path to knowledge. Sina pursued academic coursework, while Ravi read independently about Radhakrishnan and other Hindu philosophers and engaged in long telephone conversations with his father.

Several of the Hindu research participants reported experiencing an internal conflict when they took collegiate religious studies courses focused on Hinduism: The Hinduism they were studying "doesn't look like my Hinduism." Research participants had learned, for want of a better term, a limited form of their own religion in the home; their parents couldn't always answer their questions, and if they could were followers of a particular region's or caste's version of Hindu thought and practice. In the classroom—where they had gone seeking more information about their parents' stories and beliefs—these research participants were confronted with other religious ideas and manners of practice with which they were not previously familiar and which they found jarring. This led many not to the strengthening of faith they sought but rather to another crisis of confidence in even the limited religious knowledge they had gleaned from their childhood. They also questioned the academic material, and in some cases also questioned the person teaching it: The faculty teaching Hinduism, or Indian history, were generally white and often Christian. The research participants seem to have responded by saying to themselves, "How can he possibly know my religion better than I do? Who is he to be telling me these things I've never heard before about my own religion?" Despite perceiving that the professors were misrepresenting of the subject matter, the research participants, who knew their knowledge was imperfect, did not have the confidence to challenge such authorities. In this respect, they were unlike the students described by Rudrappa (2004)—immigrants, raised in India, who positioned themselves as insiders during a lecture on Hinduism given by two white men and questioned the speakers. Raised in India's Hindu milieu, Rudrappa's subjects possessed more "religious capital" and therefore the confidence to invoke their insider status and challenge the presenters. My respondents clearly felt their insider status—hence the cognitive dissonance—but also knew they lacked religious/educational capital to challenge the professors. Some research respondents caught in this situation wrote off what their professors told them as inaccurate or flawed. Avya, for example, expressed disenchantment and frustration with her studies so extreme that she decided *not* to pursue graduate studies in religion after earning her bachelor's degree in the subject: "By the end of college that is why I quit religion, because I could not do that for a lifetime. I could not always be judging myself on these objective standards created by non-Indians or non-Hindus."

What makes all these pursuits lived religion is that they were sought out as a source for knowledge and provided a forum and impetus for second-generation Indian Americans to wrestle with religious facts and concepts. For one semester, two or three days a week, intensive exposure to the home religion was a part of their life. College coursework also sparked informal discussion among coethnics and coreligionists that gave research participants yet another forum for this grappling, struggling process of learning. Even where this learning was compared unfavorably with the ideas imparted to them as children, the process of acquiring knowledge helped many people (as they report) practice their faith and feel connected to it. The irony, of course, is that for many research participants, these studies carried greater credence and legitimacy than did their Sunday school teachings because it was received in the Western milieu of the scholarly, university setting.

The research participants reported that the knowledge they acquired through their studies, the classroom debates they had, and the reflection they did on course readings made them feel more religious or believing. The long-term fruits of these students' labor has included feeling more spiritual, having a philosophical grounding, and sensing a deeper connection to God and connection to family as compared to those who did not pursue study during the college years. Those who took courses were more likely as adults to identify themselves as religious, practicing, or as a person of faith. Harjit, a Sikh, said his studies "made me like more aware and cognizant of" his religion; by understanding his own religion "more in depth . . . I think I practiced even more." Salim, an Isma'ili Muslim who never took courses but who engaged in intensive reading, reflection, and debate on religion during his college years, remarked: "I'm more religious now, probably because I understand why the religion says to do certain things. Before, it was like, 'Don't do this, don't do that.' There was no context behind it; it was like, 'Do it because I said so.' Now, I understand the value of it, the ethics behind it." Although not all reported increased practice or religiosity like Harjit and Salim, virtually all said their academic experience had improved their respect for and sense of commitment to their home religion. The acquisition of knowledge had resulted in a better grasp of the stories, traditions, and reasons behind some of the rituals they grew up with—in Nija's words, a "basic organized groundwork in my head." As a consequence, they felt a greater sense of connection to the experience and practice of worship, if not a greater likelihood of participating. Some research participants reported other salutary benefits, such as the relationship Ravi developed with his father through their intense phone conversations about religion.

The importance of collegiate study and its effect on the lived religion of the research participants may be best illustrated by the stories and decisions of the two research participants who earned their bachelors' degrees in religion: Avya and Aziz. Avya—the Hindu woman who seriously considered pursuing a religious studies PhD but decided not to, in part because of disenchantment with the detachment of white, non-Hindu faculty—described herself as "very spiritual from a young age." In comparison to all Hindus in this research cohort, she had an atypical religious upbringing; Her ethnic life existed separately from her religious life. Her religious socialization occurred in a multiethnic ashram community in upstate New York, rather than in an ethnoreligious community.[25] As an undergraduate majoring in Religion, Avya participated in a seven-month study-abroad program in India. While in India, she researched the interaction of contemporary Hinduism with the conservative Hindu political movement represented by the likes of the Bharatiya Janata Party (BJP). She discovered that a religion she had idealized as peaceful and tolerant—the way her parents had always described it—was being used in India as a tool for political gain and discrimination against religious minorities. On the basis of several adolescent experiences with both racial and religious discrimination at the hands of white supremacists, she had come to associate the ideas of intolerance and hatred with Christianity; when her studies in India opened her eyes to similar misuse of Hinduism—her own religion—it sealed her decision not to pursue further religious study.

Aziz did follow his religious studies through graduate school, but only after a series of intense religious experiences. Raised as an Isma'ili Muslim, Aziz in college came to see Isma'ilism as not "real Islam"; he said that Isma'ilis do not pray in Arabic and "don't even use the Qur'an," focusing their worship instead on a living human being, the Aga Khan. Implying that "some people" included himself, he summarized: "Some people would describe it as a heretical branch of Islam, and other people would consider it a legitimate sect of Shi'a Islam. It depends on who you ask." Disgusted by the materialism of his upper-middle-class Isma'ili ethnoreligious community and perhaps jaded by his experience dealing illegal drugs as a teen, Aziz befriended other college students who were strict followers of Sunni Islam and went through two intense conversion experiences.[26] Of his first experience he said: "I approached the whole thing academically. [I said to myself,] 'Yes, I will convert to this and then I will have the five pillars and the Qur'an.' Because the Qur'an was never touched in the Isma'ili house, because we don't need to because the Aga Khan is the living Qur'an. . . . So I converted. I accepted that there is one God and Muhammad is his messenger. And then I fell again."

Along with his friend Samir—who told Aziz early in their friendship, "You're a sand nigger just like me. You need to face up to that situation"—he tried to organize a Muslim students' organization. Lacking institutional support, except from the Jewish students' advisor, he developed instead an informal social network of other strictly observant Muslims. He pursued graduate studies because he felt he would be "more Muslim" if he could acquire more knowledge about Islam. For Aziz, knowledge of his faith represents both authenticity and theological legitimacy. Whereas Avya's romanticized notion of Hinduism was shattered when she studied the religion in depth, Aziz reports that increasing his knowledge has consistently resulted in increased commitment and observance.

As an adult, Aziz has harsh words for the "Islamic" scholars in the American academy:

> I don't expect with my PhD from Harvard, *insha'llah*, to teach at a place like Harvard. Because they would not hire a man with a beard, a Muslim to teach religion within this institution. I really believe that, because every decision that is made in this place is political it is not based on merit. There are many Muslims in the world, especially in America who are practicing Muslims, who show their practice on their limbs, who qualify to teach at places like the Ivies, but don't get hired. Instead we have a homosexual Shi'a Muslim who shaves, teaching ulterior forms and validating them. It is very interesting. Is that discrimination? Yeah, I think so. It does not faze me anymore. 1.3 million children have been killed in Iraq since the sanctions. That is discrimination.

Religion as knowledge acquisition continues to be a major way in which the research participants live religion today as adults. Although they now lack access to academic courses, most report wanting to know still more. A few have studied independently, becoming self-taught by reading books and attending lectures by religious authorities.

Rituals

The data reveal that although many second-generation Indian Americans view religion conceptually as composed of the rituals and practices of their parents, the second generation themselves are unlikely to engage in regularized ritual observance. Whereas most research participants live religion every day as a moral compass, the compass rarely leads them to an altar or house of worship.[27] Most research participants offered one of two reasons that they did not engage in ritual practice independently of their parents or other family members: either they did not understand and could not speak the language of worship, or they did not feel they could perform the rituals "the way [their parents or grandparents] do." Whereas some described being told stories by parents or in Sunday school, none said they read scripture.

Most research participants reported attending group worship during the K–12 period, but most also reported that they were not particularly interested in the rituals that they observed and nominally participated in during that period. Rather, they were interested in the social (read "fun") parts of coming together as a community—the hanging out with peers described in the previous chapter. Sensations of believing and a desire to connect with the transcendent essence of God came later, if at all. For those who described a desire for this connection in adulthood, participating in formalized worship (such as a puja at a temple or at home) did help them feel connected to God.

Ritual practice declined dramatically when the research participants were beset with the personal freedoms of collegiate life. Only Smita reported engaging independently in a ritual worship activity while away at college. She performed *aarti*, a light offering to Hindu gods and goddesses, with a friend every week in that friend's dormitory suite. Smita described it as modeling her parents' traditions, and said she found comfort and peace in actually performing the ritual: "I definitely became more religious, and now I think I am more religious than my parents are."[28] For the other respondents who discussed it, prayer was one of the least understood and most easily left-behind aspects of their childhood religious experience. Particularly because of the language barrier, many research participants characterized prayer and chanting as merely "ritualistic" lack deeper meaning and something that was not a part of their college life.

Leela, a Hindu, grew up going to private school and by the time she reached college knew about the key tenets of Christianity and even knew information specific to denominations. She was embarrassed to find that her white friends in college knew more about Hinduism then she ever did: "A lot of my friends from out there would ask me stuff, every now and then, not like it was a constant discussion, but you get into—they're really philosophical types of people. They wanted to know more about this religion [Hinduism] that I don't even know much about it. . . . And then I started to learn." In the interview she expressed remorse about not even knowing a little bit about Hinduism. After several encounters like this, Leela took it upon herself to learn more. A cynic could point out that Leela only became interested in Hinduism when she discovered white people who found the subject interesting. There is probably an element of this, but the lasting effect on Leela was an increased level of knowledge and comfort and an increased sense of connection to Hinduism.

Even in adulthood, a relatively small number of research participants report regular involvement in ritual worship. Nikhil goes to temple, and Shiren to church, alone to pray. Smita performs *aarti* at home on a regular basis. Harjit attends weekly worship services at his local *gurdwara*, Aziz at a Sunni *masjid*, and Binu at the Malayali Catholic church where she grew up. The remainder of the research participants continue to report religious attendance as occurring primarily, if not exclusively, in the company of their parents. Alok is typical: "I don't go to temples at all unless my parents come to see me."

Across life periods, by far the most important role and function served by religious ritual was to make research participants spend time with and feel connected to their parents and extended family. Listen to Vishali's description of when and why ritual practice was meaningful to her:

> There is something beautiful about taking an *aarti* dish and going like that to a persons face. It even feels good when someone does it to you. I noticed that when I went to Kentucky a few years back; my cousins came

[to the United States] only ten years ago and they still have a lot of the traditions. My aunt is very much into it. It was a Maharastran holiday, *Bhoulbis*, it is a lot like [the Gujarati holiday] *Rakhdi*: you tie a string to your brother. It was nice because I sat down and my aunt did the *aarti* on me and then I did it to my two brothers. I felt very loved. There is an aura there that is created. And it is created not because of the ritual but the meaning behind the ritual, and when that sincerity is there it really does come across. . . . When I was little I had this thing done to me [at a temple]. And so I have no sincerity attached to that. When I see that being done to other people, I am like "oh, whatever," and when the priest does it to me I am like "whatever." Yet when my aunt does it to me and her own sons it means a great deal.

Rituals take on meaning when—often only when—they are performed by and in the presence of family. One might call this a familial adaptation of the concept of *satsang*—the unique power of religious ritual when experienced and performed in the company of other believers. Notice as well the ways Vishali distances herself from the idea of ritual practice: Her aunt engages in practice because she "is very much into it," and her cousins "still have a lot of the traditions" because they came to the United States "only ten years ago." As a second-generation Indian American who feels no nonfamilial pull toward ritual, Vishali illustrates the essentiality of family as a conduit to and reason for engaging in religious practice.

Put simply, the research participants live religious ritual first and foremost as a connection to family. A large number of research participants, when asked about ritual practice, volunteered a specific type of description; they described going to the house of worship either with their parents or when they came home from college. Two types of emotional tie, to their parents and to the divine, had begun to take on the particular meaning that they do in college. At the same time, for the first time in their lives, the research participants are away from their parents for months at a time.[29] Likewise, Jayenta "would not say I am a practicing Hindu, I would say it is more like I go to temple with my parents and I would fully participate with my parents. It is only something I do with them."

Even in adulthood, the connection to family continues to be the pitch at which ritual resonates with the second generation. Consider this description of worship by Binita, a Hindu female: "I like doing puja. . . . It's not something that I do every day personally, but when I do it . . . I feel connected to my family, and so it may not be a religious or spiritual connection . . . but it's a connection, it's a bond that says, you know, 'Hey, my mom and dad used to do this and I feel like I'm doing it as well.'"

Scholars agree that religious rituals provide ties to tradition, help in the reproduction of ethnic cultures (Ebaugh and Chafetz 2000), and help individuals engage in the production of meaning. Yet most of the research participants in this study—and virtually all of the Hindus, Sikhs, and Muslims—said they really never knew what their respective faiths really meant and what the rituals were all about. For the vast majority of research participants, this activity and meaning is not only found primarily in the company of their parents; it is the company of their parents, as much as a connection to God or gods, that provided the research participants' impetus to engage in ritual at all.

As an adult, Nikhil's understanding of and engagement with religion is very important to him. Although he attends religious functions less frequently than when in college, he reports making a concerted effort to participate regularly. He and his wife have *pujas* at home. Being Hindu is a central part of Nikhil's ethnic identity. Indeed, his religious identity is not a separate identity, but part of being Indian. He associates going to the temple with the cultural aspect of Hinduism. By contrast, religion is a matter of daily reflection and thought. "Everything we do, every big transition in our life, I feel that God has given me this opportunity, whereas I never felt that way before. I think that every time I make a decision, I sort of take time and reflect, and I think that's a lot of religion in that reflection."

Conclusion

Religion exists in multiple forms in the lives of the second-generation research participants, whether they consider themselves to be religious or not. The list of forms in this chapter are by no means an exhaustive set. Just by way of example, religion may also exist as a political viewpoint or affiliation. Aziz described how understanding himself as part of the *ummah*—the global community of Muslims—shaped his views on Russian president Vladimir Putin. Aziz was visibly angry when he discussed Putin's handling of the separatist movement in Muslim-majority Chechnya: "I am my community. My community is me. Like what is happening in Chechnya, Putin has his hands colored in blood." Aziz identifies his anger at Putin not on abstract principles of human rights or self-determination, but specifically with his status as part of the *ummah*.

It is interesting to note that the only two research participants to draw connections between religion and politics were Aziz, a Muslim who is pursuing a PhD in religious studies with a focus on Islam, and Avya, a Hindu who earned a bachelor's degree in religion and decided not to pursue further religious studies when she saw how Hinduism was used in India to organize acts of political repression of non-Hindus.

As we enter what appears to be an era of increasing interpenetration between political and religious movements in the United States and abroad, it is not surprising to observe that Hindutva—what Vinay Lal identifies as "a Hinduism stripped to its imagined essences and purportedly reinvigorated by arming it with attributes commonly thought to belong to the more masculine faiths Christianity, Islam, and Judaism" (Lal 1999, 148)—is receiving increased popular and scholarly attention. If one were to rely on the information now available in scholarly journals and books, one could believe incorrectly that the only form of diasporic Hinduism that exists today is Hindutva. The reflexive tendency to immediately invoke Hindutva when discussing second-generation Indian American Hindus is not supported by the experiences of the research participants in this study.[30] None of the research participants mentioned any of the bodies associated with Hindutva such Vishva Hindu Parishad (VHP) and the Hindu Students Council (HSC), because most of them were growing up and attending college at a time when neither organization had much of an impact. Campus student organizations had not shifted from broad-based groups bringing together all Indian or even South Asian students to the narrower sectarian groups now becoming common. Also, groups like HSC, which was created in 1987, were still developing and had not yet achieved the degree of organization and resources that allows them now to distribute Hindutva-oriented "cultural information packages" broadly (see Prashad 2000).

All that said, it seems likely that Hindutva's influence will grow as Second Generation B reaches college. Given the ascendancy of aggressive and politicized evangelical Christianity, and the model it offers of a hierarchical and dogmatic approach to religion, Second Generation B will probably be looking for just the "reinvigorated" and "masculine" Hinduism Hindutva offers. Indeed, the more oppressed and alienated that younger second- and even third-generation American Hindus feel, the more likely that Hindutva will grow in popularity. Considered against the backdrop of this cohort's wish for a "Ten Commandments of Hinduism," described in chapter 1, Hindutva ascendancy seems likely indeed.

Whatever the future holds for this cohort or the younger generation rising behind it, the experience of these research participants reveals not only what the different manifestations of lived religion looks like over the life span for the research participants but also how the meaning attached to the experience changes across the life span and varies from participant to participant.[31]

4

What Does Race Have to Do with Religion?

This is a book about religion and its myriad impacts on the lives of second-generation Indian Americans, an inherently dynamic phenomenon, lived religion must be situated within the whole life of the individual. As we explore religion's role in second-generation Indian American ethnic identity development, we must also recognize religion's intersections with other social identities such as gender, sexual orientation, socioeconomic class, and race. The swirling patterns that created these identities are themselves part of the story of lived religion. In particular, race, recognized as the preeminent social organizing principle of American society, is an essential element of the equation for a nonwhite population such as Indian Americans.[1]

Race and experiences related to race affect the way Indian Americans experience religion. For example, the racialization of religion—a phenomenon discussed at length below—influences the way in which individuals approach their faith and connect with it. Racialization affects the formation of religious communities (see Iwamura and Spickard 2003). Racial discrimination leads ethnic groups to create communities that are inherently monoracial. Thus, for example, Sikhs who gather with other Sikhs for worship and ethnic performance do so in the unmixed social company of other Indian American Sikhs. Indian American Christians and Muslims break away from pan ethnic communities when they can. Priti, a female Hindu, tells a story that illustrates how the monoethnic experience was in fact, at some level, what Indian Americans were seeking:

> During freshman year, because I was so used to going to pujas and
> things . . . I looked in the paper and saw there was a puja going on at
> the multicultural, multireligious center for Hindus. And I went. All the
> other people there were—oh, what are the white people who believe in

Hinduism called?—the Hare Krishnas. They were all Hare Krishnas and I was the only Indian person there. I stayed for a little while and I remember feeling so uncomfortable. And I remember thinking that even though the people were Hindu as well, and they we singing the same *bhajans* I grew up singing, this is not where I belong at all.

The monoethnic character of the ethnoreligious community was an essential part of the element of social safety it provided. Priti did not feel at ease among Hindus who were not also Indian—or, perhaps more to the point, who were white. Broadly speaking, she understood Hindu religious practice as something done in a context that was Indian American as well as Hindu, and without that context she could not feel engaged in a spiritual act. Having grown up, like most research participants, with an ethnoreligious social safe haven counterpoised against sometimes upsetting experiences in a white-majority K–12 school environment, Priti was also particularly uncomfortable engaging in religious practice in the company of whites.

Alongside this unease runs another trend that makes race relevant to religion: the Asian American image as the model minority and the idea advanced by some that Asian Americans are poised to "become white." In this schema, whiteness connotes economic success, which Second Generation A achieved thanks to their parents' professional status. Thus, for example, Nikhil commented that he "thought of myself more as white" early in life. Twine (1997) theorizes that "the back door to whiteness" is open to Indian Americans and other Asian Americans, because they are not black. Twine's theory ignores the centuries-old symbiotic relationship between whiteness and Christianity in America. Although the back door to whiteness may be open, the aspirant must show a Christian ID card to enter.[2] Neoconservative commentators like Dinesh D'Sousa, a Catholic, point to the historical examples of Jews "becoming white" by dint of hard work and economic success, while ignoring the crucial distinction: Jews, although seen as racially different upon arrival in the United States, are ultimately meltable rather than unmeltable ethnics. If the door were really open, would Shiren—a Christian—have experienced racialized religious discrimination as described later in this chapter?[3] Shiren is a member of the Christian majority except for her race, and that, it turned out, made all the difference. Although one can predict that race's role in their lives many change—its impact may be felt differently, its "flavor" may change, or the color lines that demarcate racial groups' access to relative privilege in the United States may shift—race will remain significant for second-generation Indian Americans and probably for their progeny as well. Twine's fictional door will remain closed.

The intimate embrace of whiteness and Christianity in America stretches back to the first ethnoreligious group to step off a boat, the Puritans. The Puritans were Anglo-Saxon and Protestant, and their encounter with Native Americans made them white as well.[4] The historic echoes of the Puritan norm, as influenced by the social importance of black slavery and the influx of Eastern European Jewish immigrants in the late nineteenth and early twentieth centuries, created a uniquely American religious dialogue in which two dichotomies are set up: the Christian and the black, and the Christian and the Jew. Racism interacted with Christian supremacy as both causes and characteristics of the slave trade: Africans were "beings apart" because they were not black, they were black *and* heathen (Lincoln 1999). Non-Christian Africans' "depraved condition"—a condition that their enslavement both rescued them from and condemned them to—thereby explained their place in society as slaves. As slaves converted to Christianity, whites used purportedly Christian doctrines to rationalize slavery by describing their slave status to Christian blacks as the "curse of Ham," the destiny God intended for them (see Fredrickson 2002). Jews were defined as "not white" upon arrival because of the conflation of Christianity and whiteness (Brodkin 1998). The legacy of these dichotomies continues to reverberate in scholarly work, where blacks remain the quintessential other of racial studies and Jews the quintessential religious other.[5] Set against these modes of thought, Indian American Hindus, Sikhs, and Muslims are the other other—brown-skinned non-Christians who are therefore doubly foreign. With a facile, second-grade art-class kind of logic, Indian Americans have been put between blacks and whites on the American color spectrum. But just as the utility of the black-white binary and the position of Indian Americans in that binary is contested, we must ask: In a pluralistic America where Christianity is the privileged faith, what is our new image of the relationships—theological, social, geographical—among different faiths and their adherents?

For each of these reasons, race is both an essential element and a unique challenge in the study of Indian American populations. The scholarly theory that the importance of race for many of the post-1965 immigrants will fade over time (Ebaugh and Chafetz 2000; Warner 1998), like the theory that economically successful nonblacks can "become white," springs from flawed assumptions. First is the wishful idea that U.S. society is moving toward the multicultural ideal that will soon render race obsolete. Second, these scholars' theory relies heavily on the experiences of early-twentieth-century white ethnics, who despite their Catholic and Jewish religious identities had substantially melted into the dominant white milieu by the third generation. Just as recent scholarship has shown that concepts of race were significant for white immigrant groups of the past two centuries, and has illustrated the shortfalls of earlier work on Catholic and Jewish American populations that failed to account for race as such (see Roediger 2002; Jacobson 1998), so I believe this and future works will illustrate the theoretical flaw in these scholars' work. Race is too irreducible, and the arc of multiculturalism's rise in society too long, to support the theory of race's growing irrelevance in the near term.

Race, Indians, and American History

Race is a social construction by which phenotype comes to serve as a visible touchstone for a deep societal story about origin, privilege, and destiny. But who or what are Indian Americans, racially speaking? It really depends on who you ask. If you ask the majority of research participants, they respond "Indian" or "Indian American," indicating that in their minds the idea of race connotes cultural identity and not just skin color.[6] If you ask the United States Census Bureau, the answer would be "Asian"—at least after 1980. If you ask many white folks, they may look at you quizzically and say, "I don't know, I haven't given it much thought. But I know they aren't white." If you ask a black person, he might say, "I'm not sure, but they are not black." Ask a Hispanic, and you might hear "brown like me"—or, "brown, but not like me."

What these responses tell us is that the racial identity and status of Indian Americans in the United States in contemporary society is ambiguous. Describing racial identity is a little like trying to hold water in your hands: It is unwieldy, moves when you move, changes shape, and ultimately is impossible to entirely hold onto. To quote Higginbotham, "When we talk about the concept of race, most people believe that they know it when they see it but arrive at nothing short of confusion when pressed to define it" (Higginbotham 1992, 252). Indeed, it is the very historical ambiguity of Indian Americans as a "racial" group that makes them such a good example of how race is a social construction. The racial designation of Indians has changed over time in American history, bending to the prevailing winds of popular thought. Indian Americans today are racially classified by the United States government as Asians or Asian Americans, but this is a relatively new development that made its first appearance on U.S. census forms in 1980. Before that Indian Americans had been labeled Other, White, and Hindu (Koshy 1998). The Hindus, Muslims, Sikhs, and Christians in this study trace their lineage to India and for this reason belong to a phenotype that is not "white" as that term is traditionally understood. Yet they have at times in American been considered white by some.[7] The bipolar American race schema of black and white renders Indian American ambiguous, and social factors—particularly the first-wave Indian Americans' relative privilege with respect to socioeconomic class, but also a degree of academic success and political conservatism not typically associated with communities of color in the American mind—help perpetuate this ambiguity into the present day.

The story of the uncertain and shifting nature of Indian Americans' racial status begins when immigrants from India first arrived on American shores in 1790. Although allowed to enter the United States, their brown skin dictated

their legal rights and social access; they were denied citizenship and the economic opportunity that came with it. The religious makeup of this group mat-
tered only secondarily; it was the visible element of racial difference that
categorized them as nonwhite. These Indian Americans—a predominantly Sikh,
predominantly male group of immigrant laborers—were known as "hindoos."
The word (spelled either with a final "u" or "oo") functioned as what Haney-
López (1996, 88). calls "a racial appellation of difference, its use of obscure but
certain origins in the Western colonial discourse of race, culture, civilization,
and empire." By 1910, there were between 5,000 and 10,000 Indians in the
United States.[8] The majority were Sikh and fully another one-third were Muslim,
yet they were all called Hindus by government agencies and the popular media.

Between 1907 and 1923, approximately seventy individuals, all of them educated professionals, successfully applied for—in some cases even sued for—U.S.
citizenship on the grounds that they were members of the Aryan race and as
such were of white or Caucasian origin. This distinguished Indian Americans
from "Asiatic" or "Mongoloid" groups like the Chinese and Japanese (Jensen
1988; Takaki 1989). In fighting against this trend, the Asiatic Exclusion League
argued that although Hindus (Indians) may once have been "members of the
same family as Americans of European ancestry," the distinction was that the
"forefathers" of white Americans "pressed to the west, in the ever marching of
conquest, progress and civilization; . . . the forefathers of the Hindus went east
and became enslaved, effeminate, caste-ridden and degraded. . . . And now we
the people of the United States are asked to receive these members of a degraded race on terms of equality" (Takaki 1989, 298). What would become of the
United States, the League asked, "if this horde of fanatics should be received in
our midst?" (Takaki 1989, 298). In 1910 and 1913, two separate federal courts
ruled that Indians were Caucasians and hence entitled to be considered "white
persons" eligible under the Naturalization Law of 1790.

A decade later, in 1923, the U.S. Supreme Court in *U.S. v. Bhagat Singh Thind*
concluded that although Indians were "classified by certain scientific authorities as of the Caucasian or Aryan race," they were in fact nonwhite according to
"the understanding of the common man."[9] The nation's highest court wrote,

> the term "race" . . . must be applied to a group of living persons now pos-
> sessing in common the requisite characteristics, not to groups of persons
> who are supposed to be or really are descended from some remote, com-
> mon ancestor. . . . It may be true that the blond Scandinavian and the
> brown Hindu have a common ancestor in the dim reaches of antiquity,
> but the average man knows perfectly well that there are unmistakable
> and profound differences between them today.

The "privilege of American citizenship," the Court concluded, was meant by the
framers to be conveyed upon "only the type of man who they knew as white."

That group of people "was almost exclusively from the British Isles and North-western Europe," the Court wrote; while it might include "the Slavs and the dark-eyed, swarthy people of Alpine and Mediterranean stock," it clearly did not include "people of Primarily Asiatic stock." Because of those differences, Indians in the United States were ineligible for the privileges of white status, such as the acquisition of citizenship and with it the right to own land. With the question of Indian Americans' whiteness resolved, the question remained of precisely who or what Indian Americans were as nonwhites.[10]

The racial ambiguity of Indian Americans raises the question: What is whiteness? Although my intention here is not to discuss whiteness per se, it is critical to this discussion to note that groups that are white today such as the Irish, Italians, and East European Jews, were not always white. Whiteness has been a shifting designation that is affected by social class and religion. For example, as Karen Brodkin argues in her book *How Jews Became White Folks and What That Says about Race in America* (1998), at times Jews have been white and at other times they have been "not quite white," and the entitlements of whiteness are extended to specific groups at specific moments (see also Ignatiev 1995; Orsi 1992).

The application of Brodkin's analysis to the nuances of Indian Americans' racial status in the United States is illustrated in two anecdotes from my own life. When I was in middle school, I was kept inside by the teachers during recess one day while all my classmates were allowed to go outside and play. I later learned that they had kept me indoors because a Ku Klux Klan rally was taking place across the street and they felt that I would be in danger if allowed outside to play. My white teachers understood a world where the line of color—and with it personal safety—was drawn between white and "not white," and that my white classmates would be safe outside on a day when I would not be. Twenty years later, I was leading a workshop for teachers in South Carolina. The class was about evenly divided between black and white teachers, and in the course of our conversations about race it became clear to me that the black teachers viewed me as white. One teacher actually made the comment, "If you're not black, you're white." Here, informed by the teachers' Jim Crow understanding of racism and perhaps by their own assumptions about Asian Americans and so-cioeconomic class, a color line had again been drawn—but this time I was on the white side of the line.

Of course, the very concept of a single color line implies bipolarity—one either is or is not on a given side of the line. And indeed, one of the fundamental dynamics of race in the United States has been the dichotomous scheme of white and nonwhite based loosely on skin color (Lee 1994; Root 1996).[11] The post-1965 immigration waves, including not only Asian Americans but also Latinos/as, Arab Americans, and others, have strained this schema to its breaking point, and yet it remains the paradigm of choice. Society's vocabulary and political attitudes on race have not kept pace with our changing demographics, and for the time being the "black/white" paradigm remains the underpinning of the American dialogue on race. It is appealing and appalling in its simplicity; it permits facile distinctions—white and black, powerful and powerless, rich and poor. But second-generation Indian Americans are a visibly nonwhite population in a nation which, more often than not, either miscategorizes them or ignores them entirely. Even within the developing dialogue on Asian America, Indian Americans are the other, often invisible or marginalized because of the widespread popular understanding of the term "Asian American" to refer primarily or even exclusively to East Asian Americans.[12]

The Racialization of Religion

We have established that racism exists in and affects the lives of second-generation Indian Americans. In the next chapter, we will examine experiences of religious oppression and how they affected the research participants' ethnic identity. There is a third element, at the crossroads of race and religion, that has a particularly dramatic effect on the lives of Indian American Hindus, Sikhs, and Muslims because of their status as racial *and* religious minorities and that also affected Indian American Christians. It is the racialization of religion. Omi and Winant (1994) characterize racialization as an ideological process shaped by history, prejudice, and the human tendency to use conceptual categories to simplify their ascription of meaning to nonidentical experiences. Among other things, racialization involves the attribution of undifferentiated identities, cultures, and behaviors to individuals on the basis of their membership in a racialized group. While the characteristics so attributed are not always negative—take, for example, the association of Asian Americans with academic success—they are pernicious in that they replace individual uniqueness with facile assumptions about motives, background, conduct, and interests. The racialization of religion is a process whereby a specific religion becomes identified by a direct or indirect reference to a real or imagined physical appearance or ethnic/racial characteristic. Certain phenotypical features associated with a group and attached to race in popular discourse become associated with a particular religion or religions. Race thereby becomes a proxy for religious affiliation in the American visual library. Although the racialization of religion is not a new phenomenon (Barot and Bird 2001), it has taken on new meaning—and particular salience for Indian Americans—in our post-9/11 world.

Racial difference as such is not at the root of racialization. As described in the preceeding section, human beings ascribe social meaning to certain biological characteristics within the unique context of their own time and place in order to differentiate, exclude, and dominate (Said 1978; Miles 1989). Reinventing the ideation of "race," individuals create a racialized other and simultaneously racialize themselves. This process occurs not in a vacuum but in the context of the historical moment, social values, and political assumptions connected to the racialized object. Racialization is most obvious when its effect is directed at groups that are clearly—that is, visibly—phenotypically different from others, but "invisible" minorities are equally vulnerable to being racialized. The racist imagination views their nonvisibility as the proof of their "essential" but concealed difference; this difference is then signified by a socially imposed mark like, for example, the elaborate system of color-coded patches developed by Nazi officials to make visible "invisible" Jewishness and homosexuality.

Today Indian Americans are assumed to be of a certain faith (Hindu) because of their "skin the color of mocha."[13] Although the mere assumption of religious identity may seem an innocuous error to the casual reader, repeated experiences of religious misidentification is experienced by many Christian, Muslim, and Sikh Indian Americans as a negation of their religious identity. (The effects of such negation, and the other ways in which it is manifest in contemporary American society, are addressed in chapter 5.) The conflation of race and religion, when religion is racialized, results in a one-dimensional identity that is as likely to be inaccurate as accurate. With race and religion as proxies for each other, Indianness in the cultural, geographic, or linguistic sense—which is shared by Indian Christians, Jews, and atheists as well as by Hindus, Sikhs, Muslims, and others—becomes part of an indistinguishable mix colored by an assumed association with Hinduism. Distinction, like nuance, is lost.

For example, Shiren's school friends—who apparently learned everything they knew about Hinduism from *Indiana Jones and the Temple of Doom*—asked her whether she and her family ate monkey brains at home.[14] Shiren's experience shows just how much religion is racialized. Shiren is Catholic, and attended a Catholic school. Those who asked the questions were her Catholic classmates. Yet it was her brown skin that rendered her different, and its association with what they understood to be "Hindu cuisine" was what resulted in the questioning. Value-laden characterizations of Hindu images as absurd or evil abound in society and the media; *Indiana Jones* was just one example popular during the research participants' preteen and adolescent years. To the extent that the research participants' classmates were aware of Hinduism at all—since the religion was, and remains, largely invisible to mainstream America—they knew it as bizarre and evil.

The ascription of religious identity to a racial or phenotypic feature occurs but within a context of time and place that renders the distinctions relevant and drives people to ascribe social meaning to biological characteristics. Of all social factors present in the current historical moment, the United States has, since the oil shock of 1973 and the Iran hostage crisis of 1979, been confronting "enemies" in the developing world whose ideological identity is intimately linked to their interpretation and use of Islam. As this theology/ideology is racialized, and America's attention is repeatedly focused on these particular rivals, brown-skinned non-Christian Americans become more (or less) than just an other within the society; they become an other that is associated in the American mind with a foreign enemy. They go from merely being a minority to being viewed as a potential fifth column due to their presumed connection with and loyalty to this enemy.[15]

Indeed, in our current sociopolitical climate and historical moment, the most conspicuous example of how Indian American religions are racialized is probably not through association with Hinduism but through the American tendency to assume that people with brown skin are Muslim. Islam is a global religion; there are not only Arab and South Asian Muslims but also black (African and African American) and white (Albanian, Bosnian) Muslims. Yet brown skin equals Islam in the American mind. How do we know this? First, Hindus, Muslims, Sikhs, and even South Asian American Christians have become backlash targets because their race connotes an assumed religious identity—a racialized identity in the United States. For example, Balbar Singh Sodhi, a fifty-one-year-old Sikh gas station attendant in Mesa, Arizona, was killed on September 15, 2001 by a man police described as angry about the September 11, 2001 attacks in New York City and Washington, D.C. As there was no money stolen from the cash register, people have surmised that this was a hate crime, though law enforcement officials initially refused to classify it as such (Sikh Mediawatch and Resource Task Force [SMART] 2001). Second, black and white Muslims have not been the targets of violence in the so-called post-September 11 backlash.[16] A final a sign of the perceived tie between religion and race is the surprise expressed by the media and commentators upon the capture of Al Qaeda members John Walker Lindh (the white "American Taliban") and José Padilla (a Latino who converted to Islam). We also know religion is racialized because of how the phenomenon uniquely impacts people of color. Despite the Oklahoma City bombing in 1995, the U.S. government does not go looking for skinny white guys when an act of terrorism occurs. That brown-skinned Americans are targeted for 9/11 backlash attacks even though they are Sikh, Hindu, or even Christian shows how the racialization of religion has not only normative meanings but also concrete—sometimes life-and-death—implications for South Asian Americans (see Singh 2002).

Although it is critical to identify and consider the distinctions between religious and racial oppression, we must also acknowledge that at times the line between them blurs to the point of vanishing. Consider, for example, the struggle that Sikhs have faced in community after community when they seek to construct sacred sites in which to peacefully worship and practice their religious and cultural heritage (Singh 2003). The building proposed is different in many ways from houses of worship as the American Christian mind understands them: architecturally (how they look, particularly with respect to statuary), the-ologically (what is taught there), and racially (who worships there). Does the un-ease of white- and Christian-majority zoning boards spring from discomfort with Sikh theology? Or with the image of many brown-skinned people wearing turbans and saris and kirpans—a foreign other—congregating and organizing? Do Indian American Sikhs trigger thoughts of terrorism in the same way that black populations trigger thoughts of crime? The real answer is probably "yes" to all three questions, but it is clear that the racial element, and the resulting the-ological misimpressions described above, is a major aggravating factor. This contemporary theological redlining is just one example of how the racialization of religion affects South Asian Americans at the individual and policy levels.[17]

When a religion becomes identified by its association with a real or imag-ined phenotypical characteristic, and vice versa, the oppression of the minority is aggravated. Yet at the same time, the essential nature of the discrimination—racial or religious—becomes disguised or lost entirely. The racialization of reli-gion thus exacerbates the "othering" of a religious group. Here context is important: Race has become a proxy for religion in a country where most peo-ple believe the bromides about religious freedom, where religious intolerance and discrimination are deemed unacceptable but racial discrimination, while frowned upon, retains a certain degree of acceptability and historical cachet. Members of the Christian majority are thus able to act out religious animus by using better-accepted racial terms and images. The racialization of religion also allows the outsider to downplay the emotional impact of religious discrimina-tion, and allows the wider culture to ignore the continuing (some would say growing) presence of religion-based prejudice and violence in the United States. Acts of oppression that are fairly clearly religious in nature (such as harassment of a Sikh man for wearing a turban) come to be seen as race-based, and the uniquely powerful importance for the target for religious discrimination is dis-regarded.

Second-Generation Indian Americans' Encounters with Race and Racism

Race, as a dimension of human representation and an element of social struc-ture, carries no inherent negative or positive weight; it marks some individuals as different from others in U.S. society (Omi and Winant 1997). But what about racism? Here, racism means substantially more than the preference for one complexion over another (cf. Ignatiev 1995). Rather, racism describes the struc-tures, policies, and individual acts whereby privilege, access, and opportunities that are otherwise unrelated to a person's skin color are in fact meted out or withheld on the basis of skin color. Racism is ascription of moral or social value to differences of appearance. Individuals may manifest its patterns of thought in the form of discrimination, such as when research participants discussed en-countering individual acts of racial harassment in their schools, communities, and in their extended families. Racism also exists as a societywide system of ad-vantages for white people, of norms and social mores that convey or withhold social capital based upon skin color. At the institutional level, racism describes how institutions, including the state, discriminate directly or indirectly, inten-tionally or unintentionally, through their structures, organizations, and policies to support or maintain differences of access, privilege, and opportunity based upon race (Fredrickson 2002).

In current society, whites are unequivocally in power at the institutional and societal level, and Indian Americans and have been the targets of racism. At the individual level, the concept of racism enters a much grayer area. It is no longer merely a white-on-other phenomenon. Indeed, several research partici-pants reported experiencing racial discrimination where the agent or "oppres-sor" was another person of color. Racism at the individual level involves specific acts and behavior by individuals or groups of individuals, such as the use of racial slurs and other language and expressions that are offensive, degrading, intimidating, or embarrassing. It may escalate into physical intimidation and violence. Indian Americans can be the agents as well as the targets of racism at the individual level; some research participants reported their parents express-ing views about other minority groups that made Indian Americans the agent and others the target. Whereas discrimination at the institutional and cultural levels still clearly involves the power of white norms and privileges, as against the relative powerlessness of communities of color, at the individual level one's status as white or nonwhite does not necessarily determine whether one will be the agent or the target in a given interaction.[18]

When addressing identity development, we must measure racism by its ef-fects and "outcomes for people of color, rather than its intentions" (Derman-Sparks and Phillips 1997, 22). Whereas a lawyer might inquire first into the intent of the actor, if we wish to understand race and its relationship to ethnicity and religion in the lives of these second-generation Indian Americans, we must do so by focusing on how research participants understood and were affected by race and racism. Our task is made more difficult because most second-generation Indian Americans and most people in general only see the racism that occurs at the individual level. For example, only four of forty-one research participants made mention at any point during their interviews of the existence of any socie-tal or institutional racism. (Indeed, some of them do not even acknowledge individual racism.) When racism is perceived as existing only at the level of individual interactions, even negative race-based experiences can be rational-ized as being external to the victim's own identity. People of color who retain this worldview successfully rationalize efforts on the part of others to change their consciousness. Even people of color who experience an urge to question their

current status may find themselves seduced into remaining in place by the rewards offered from the dominant white society. The popular understanding of
racism as a phenomenon of acts rather than of structures results in a belief arguably shared by most Americans—the idea that the individual level is the only
place where racism "happens." This understanding is largely uncontradicted in
the lives of these research participants: Their educational system did not reveal
it to them, their socioeconomic class status shields many of them from its starkest effects, and their racial ambiguity (in particular, their status as nonblacks)
masks certain shades of prejudice that were difficult to understand by mere reference to the concept of racism as popularly understood (Mazumdar 1989b).

Influence of Parents' Outlook

Inasmuch as the second generation's understanding of the phenomena of race
and racism will shape the effect these phenomena have on their identity development, the experiences and viewpoints of their immigrant parents—the
source, initially at least, of the information the second generation uses to process its experiences—is perhaps the most influential factor, along with their
own experiences of discrimination and marginalization based on race during
their K–12 education. Indian immigrants brought their views of white and black
to this country, as guided by their socialization process in India.[19] Upon entry in
the United States, Indian immigrants quickly learned one of the rules for gain-
ing success: not aligning themselves with blacks and positioning themselves as
nearly white as possible on the racial spectrum between black and white in the
United States. The first wave of post-1965 Indian immigrants—the parents of the
research participants in this cohort—were aided in this quest by their status as
professionals and by the economic privileges resulting from this status (Steinberg 1989).

Indian immigrants are similar in this respect to other immigrants, including twentieth-century European immigrants. As Robert Orsi (1992, 315) notes,
immigrants from Italy learned that "achievement in their new environment
meant successfully differentiating themselves from the dark-skinned other."
Amritjit Singh (1996) acknowledges that it is understandable that Indian immigrants choose to align themselves with WASP culture and distance themselves
from African Americans—after all, most left homes and family in India to provide their children with the best opportunities possible, which includes being
financially successful. These individuals are going to take the path of least resistance and, from their perception, this meant aligning with whites and distancing themselves from blacks.

What Indian immigrants often don't understand and sometimes don't want
to understand is that their politics of alignment with the white community contributes to the perpetuation of the cycle of oppression of African Americans in
the United States. Prashad (2000) aptly points out that whereas blacks are

racialized as the "problem" in American society, Indian Americans are racialized—and often proudly racialize themselves—as the "solution," a model minority programmed for success and privilege. Their native conceptions of race may provide a frame of reference for Indian immigrants which allows them to resist the dominant society's racial thinking. Mazumdar (1989a and 1989b) and Kibria (1998) argue that Indian immigrants perpetuate the group's racial ambiguity because of their efforts to ignore or bypass the issues of Indian racial status in United States society, Prashad (2000) has further noted, many Indian Americans actively disengage themselves from the "discussion."

Although a few of the research participants reported their parents describing the racial discrimination faced in the workplace, the majority had parents like Vinay's, who were unwilling even to entertain the idea that they or their children had been targeted racially. Vinay described an incident during the high school years when he told his parents that he believed his teacher was treating him unfairly because he was Indian. His description is illustrative of the attitude many research participants reported their parents exhibited when it came to race and discrimination:

> I remember a couple of times coming back and saying something to my parents about, you know, "The teacher gave me a B because I'm Indian." And my parents have always been the antivictim attitude type of people. They said, "We don't have that attitude. If you're the best there is, nobody can take anything away from you." So whenever I complained about something [because of unfair treatment] because I was Indian . . . they'd ask, "Were you the best you could be? If not, then I don't want to hear it." They said, "If you didn't get a 100 on the test, then you can't complain about getting an 80." It's like, "When there's no room for improvement, then, then come talk to me and say somebody's holding you back."

Although Vinay may have been engaging in shenanigans in wanting to blame his B grade on somebody else, this is not the main lesson to be drawn from his experience. Rather, note his parents' reaction: Failures to achieve are blamed on the laziness of the victim rather than on the prejudice of the person in power—here, a teacher. Perhaps they did not even want to consider that their son might be the victim of racial discrimination, which would connote an undesirable connection to American blacks. Whether or not they bear animus against blacks, they may want to avoid association with blacks. In doing so they have internalized just enough of the American race schema to understand that color can be a barrier to achievement; denying their and their community's non-whiteness is both a response ("Vinay, do better") and a way of copying with their dismay at not having escaped the race trap. Indian American parents even push their children to adopt certain distancing strategies, such as by emphasizing cultural and religious rather than racial affiliation. In this respect, Indian American immigrants are like Afro-Caribbean immigrants, who invoke accents or other references to French or British colonial culture to differentiate themselves from American-born blacks and thereby avoid the stigma of blackness (Waters 1994). Or perhaps Vinay's parents' reaction had nothing at all to do with race. Respect for the teacher is a foundational principle in Indian culture; Vinay could have been experiencing parental respect for the teacher being taken out on the child in the form of disbelief or punishment.

Indian American parents may also refuse to acknowledge to their children the racism they themselves faced. Jyoti's parents, for example, left her to surmise what was going on in her mother's professional life: "My mom used to work in this department store—I think it was hard on her. I think she was discriminated against in her job. I remember she finally quit when somebody who was the same level as her got promoted and she didn't. My parents did not talk about it front of me. I just knew they were always upset." Immigrants are less likely than U.S. born people of color to report experiences of discrimination, and Indian immigrants' awareness of the disfavored status of blacks made reportage of racial discrimination particularly unlikely (Mazumdar 1989a). Most research participants' parents, as first-wave professionals, had the resources to negotiate a certain degree of immunity from the worst effects of American racism. In this sense, economic privilege brought access to safe neighbors and good schools populated predominantly by whites—a blessing and a curse that shaped their children's experiences.

Second-Generation Views on Race and Racism

Raised and socialized in the United States, second-generation Indian Americans are nevertheless separated from their nonimmigrant peers by the racial identity society ascribes to them as well as by Indian culture, by a sense of ethnic identity, and by their intense emotional involvement with and loyalty to their families (Lessinger 1995). Notwithstanding the views and hopes of many in the immigrant generation, the second generation, raised in the United States, have become racialized and now find themselves as entries in the American "race library"—grouped, categorized, and placed in juxtaposition with other racial groups. Although Maira (2002) found many second-generation Indian Americans to be aligning themselves consciously with blacks, this is inconsistent with the findings of my study and may be unique to the cohort of second-generation Indian Americans Maira interviewed: college-aged residents of New York City who were attracted to hip-hop youth culture. Likewise, the second generation members in Min and Kim's book (1999) identified more with African Americans and Latinos than with whites but, as the researches indicated, they were a self-selecting group who had given the subject and their own experiences a degree of thought and reflection atypical of the second generation as a whole.[20] In fact, most of the research participants in this study aligned themselves with reference to whiteness and the suburban professional aspirations associated with whiteness in the common mind. Although some understood that they encountered racial discrimination, they were not politicized by it. Perhaps because they were more likely to encounter religious discrimination than racial discrimination, they did not generally see themselves as having common cause with African Americans, Hispanics, or other Asian American groups.[21]

Every research participant in this study reported thoughts and experiences that dealt with racial identity. Such acts and statements might be overt—the obvious and caustic discrimination most associated with the historic experiences of African Americans—or they might constitute covert, "modern" racism disguised and rationalized with nonracial explanations.[22] Race also existed in the lives of the research participants as a set of thought processes. Raised in the American milieu—indeed, in the case of more than half of the research participants, raised in the American South where racial divisions are part of the well-known history and social fabric of the region—the research participants were familiar with race and, with some exceptions, were aware of their status as nonwhites. Even in the absence of a specific identifiable race-based experience, overt or covert, the research participants reported thinking about race and racial difference. These thoughts were shaped by social influences at the societal level (such as the historical racial ambiguity of Indians Americans) and at the individual level (particularly in the case of parental influence).

Just as with lived religion, a person may report race-related views and experiences that appear contradictory. For example, a research participant can freely admit to being nonwhite while denying the existence of racism, as Neha did. She can simultaneously conclude that a sorority's decision not to admit her "must have been discriminatory" and still have a "philosophy . . . that I don't really focus on those things," as Binita did. A research participant can both reject parents' racist views against blacks and engage in a self-orientation toward whiteness and its benefits, as Vinay did. Certainly, research participants can at various life stages change their viewpoint on race, or become aware of racism in their own past that was not recognized at the time, which is why it is particularly useful to think about race and racism in the context of identity development.

The data and analysis presented here offer insight into how different research participants viewed race and understood race and racism, and how they then expressed these understandings in their identities and their actions. Returning to these same research participants today would result in different data, different viewpoints, different orientations toward an individuals' racial identity. Certainly many research participants' viewpoints would have been changed by the experience of September 11 and the post-9/11 backlash that often targeted the brown-skinned. This subject matter is discussed much more thoroughly in chapter 5 and the Epilogue, but one vignette is illustrative here of how a single critical incident—even one involving allies—can change a second-generation Indian American's entire viewpoint on race. During the 2001–2002 academic year, I taught Asian American Studies at Columbia University in New York City. Class was canceled on September 12, 2001, but when we met on September 17 one of my students shared this story: She had grown up in the Northeast and had never thought about her race or considered herself to have been discriminated against; it would be fair to say that although she was self-aware as a nonwhite, she didn't appreciate that that meant being seen differently by others. On September 11 and 12, this student's white roommates would not let her leave the dormitory suite because they feared she would be targeted for a backlash attack. This experience stunned and upset the student by reminding her of what her race connotes in some others' minds and by showing her that even to her closest friends her race was noticed and made her different. It became clear over the course of the semester that this experience had changed permanently the way in which see sees her self.

"No Problem"

A small number of research participants reported experiencing no racism, even to the point of denying its existence even in theory. Neha, for example, explained away the very idea of racism by reference to nothing but her own personal experiences: "Like, I got into every college I applied [to]. I got into every law school. I got the law firm job I wanted, so as far as any sort of indication [of discrimination, there has been] none that I really know of." Because she did not face racism, Neha maintains, racism does not exist—or, at least, does not victimize Indian Americans. Neha's comment is an extreme example of the phenomenon described above: an inability to understand American racism as both structural and individual. If pressed, Neha might admit that individuals can make inappropriate race-based comments and take illegal actions based on race; but as her comment indicates, she would be unable to identify or acknowledge the existence of institutional or societal racism.

A major trend among research participants involved admitting experiences of race-based incidents or remarks but attributing them not to racism but to other factors—to anything but racism. The thoughts of this group of research participants offer insight on the broad range of ways research participants perceived (or failed to perceive) and understood incidents that occurred as result of their racial identity. For example, Irfan claimed not to have experienced racism in the K–12 period, but promptly went on to describe certain experiences that might be described as equivocal, or worse: "Raleigh, North Carolina, the Research Triangle area, is a pretty, it's honestly a pretty northern city when you look at demographics . . . and lots of university professors, lots of educated

professionals . . . maybe a couple of times at the beach we got funny stares . . .
maybe we weren't served first at a restaurant." Irfan described being stared at
and getting poor service at restaurants, but noted two reasons why his experiences had not been racism: his hometown is "a pretty northern city" and it is
populated by "a lot of educated professionals." Rudeness, inappropriate attention, condescension—all could be written off as something besides racism for
people like Anita, who said, "They're going to be rude, regardless of whether
you're white or Indian and what. . . . I view somebody who's been that way as
just rude versus discriminatory."

Most of the research participants who described experiences of racism but
never labeled them such seemed to have accepted several ideas about racism
from the dominant white society. For Irfan, getting funny stares and not being
served first become something he notices but dismisses as a quirk of life rather
than as an individual or systemic manifestation of racism. He does not deny that
racism exists, as Neha did, but argues that racism might exist in a southern city;
his hometown is "a northern city"—Irfan's proxy image for the idea of "no
racism here." Irfan's excuse-making was not uncommon. From the perspective
of these Indian Americans, since they did not encounter racism, it does not exists. It is just that simple.

One of the motives at work here is a desire not to be "raced" (see Dhingra
2003). This "anything but racism" way of thinking about negative experiences
in school, the workplace, and society springs from a variety of factors, most of
them amply described above. It may even fuel an increased attention to ethnicity as a nonracial way of identifying. The research participants who subscribe to
this philosophy of "anything but racism" have accepted, tacitly or expressly, the
dominant society's messages about the inferiority of target groups and cultures.
They seem to have adopted their parents' reticence about so much as forming a
mental association between themselves and disadvantaged American racial
groups, particularly African Americans. In so doing, they limit their own ability
and inclination to think about the nature and cause of certain negative life
experiences.

The Impact of Stereotypes

Some research participants balanced their own negative experiences against
more positive messages about their social group—often the so-called model
minority myth of Indian Americans' (and other Asian Americans') innate intelligence and drive.[23] This comfortable stereotype, of course, allows Indian Americans further to rationalize their own distancing behavior vis-à-vis African
Americans and allows them to suppress or deny the resulting cognitive dissonance. According to the model minority myth, Asians and Asian Americans
are innately high-performing, intelligent, and driven to succeed. The myth is
perpetuated by teachers, by the media, by the parental generation of Indian

Americans, and by second-generation Indian Americans themselves. For society, the myth is a tool that allows it to blame American blacks for their social, academic, and economic plight; it allows society to say, "see, *those* people of color succeed," thereby implying that there is no longer a color barrier to success and generating a mirror-image effect implying that if Asians are innately successful then perhaps blacks are just as innately low-performing. As many other scholars have acknowledged, since its invention in the 1960s, the model minority myth has been used as a hegemonic device to maintain the dominance of whites.[24]

For most research participants, the image of the model minority was a source of pride. It offered an emotional buffer for some research participants, who could respond to experiences of discrimination and exclusion at the hands of their peers by thinking, in effect, "well, at least I'm smart [because I'm Indian]."

For others, the myth was a source of anguish as they sought to live up to it. The implication that success was her genetic destiny was a tremendous frustration to Vishali:

> When I was a freshman [in high school], the senior class valedictorian was Indian, so people assumed I would be the valedictorian of my school. It was as if she was looked upon as the model Asian. And I was like, "What the fuck? That was so unfair!" All the Indian people and Chinese people were lumped into one category and were supposed to do really well. And she [the Indian valedictorian] grew up in a different household than me. Her parents were more supportive and much more loving. I grew up in a house with huge domestic violence issues. If I got anywhere it was because of what I did, not because my father created a wonderful environment. I would actually have to sneak out of the house to study because I could not concentrate 'cause I would get beat up. It was really unfair that [they thought] I would be valedictorian. I mean she had it really easy. . . . I was always expected to work up to some level.

Vishali experienced frustration and alienation, feeling she had to live up to teacher and peer expectations based on her race and without regard to who she was or what she was dealing with (see Asher 2002) . Vishali's candid remarks differed from most other second generation members' outlook on the model minority stereotype. Like Vyas (2001), I found some Indian Americans felt flattered by and therefore sought to fulfill the stereotype of being academic high achievers. It is not unreasonable for Vishali, who is burdened by these expectations, to become resentful because she sees others around her without the same combination of phenotypical expectations and real-life restraints she experienced. The model minority myth is discriminatory, harmful, and insidious; it imposes a categorical label on all Asian Americans. Lee stresses how the myth "silences the multiple voices of Asian Americans . . . creating a monolithic monotone." As Vishali's story graphically illustrates, the label erases "ethnic, cultural, social-class, gender, language, sexual, generational, achievement, and other differences" (Lee 1996, 6). It transforms individuals with individual needs and unique interests into bundles of usually inaccurate assumptions—which, as Vishali's story indicates, is particularly problematic when it comes to teacher perceptions and assumptions.

Nikhil's story presents a different way the model minority myth rears its ugly head. Nikhil did well academically, but said he felt he didn't always deserve the A's he received. He felt that particularly in the later years of high school he got his grades because the teachers just assumed he did well, because he did do well at times and his older sister had been a high achiever.

> My sister was very smart and I think there was one other Indian person that went through and that person was very smart. . . . Everyone believed because of that I was supposed to be smart. Sometimes I believed that it didn't matter what I wrote on my essay, what I put down for my answers, I always got an A. And, you know, sometimes I'm like, "This didn't deserve an A," and it still would be an A. And, if I ever cut up or acted like people around me, the teachers would single me out as being a disappointment because I should set an example because I was smarter—or they just assumed it.

Nikhil considered himself to be benefiting unfairly from the assumption that, as an Indian American, he would do well as his older sister had—getting A grades even when he didn't earn them. This is another negative effect of the model minority myth: Achievements are most meaningful when they are earned, and the pride in and value of those achievements can be diminished when they are (or feel) unearned. If Nikhil felt he was getting good grades because of an ethnic assumption rather than the actual quality of his work, this may have made him value the achievements less. It may have felt, in effect, like cheating.

Unfortunately, both Vishali's and Nikhil's experiences are all too consistent with my own experience teaching educators. For eight years I have worked with teachers as a faculty member in schools of education. I have never gotten through a semester without hearing one of my students—an in-service or preservice teacher—gush about how Asian kids are so bright, so good at obeying the rules, and so skilled with math and the sciences. This prejudice, however positive, affects these teachers' ability to see, diagnose, and respond to situations like Vishali's, or the differing needs of today's cohort of working-class and limited-English-speaking students, or simply the interests of an Indian American student who hates science and has a passion for poetry. The model minority myth is alive and well in the faculty lounge, and it's harming students in the classroom.

Racial Outsiders, Looking In

Just as the reader should not assume that denials of racism encompass a denial of race, or of the respondent's status as a nonwhite, neither should the reader assume that every person confronted with a racist act will react vociferously. Many research participants reported encountering racism and recognizing it as such, but making a conscious decision not to react or fight back against the perpetrator. Some research participants simply encountered racism at an age when they were not prepared to fully understand it, much less respond. For example, Nikhil described a childhood experience that made him feel he was "a nobody":

> I remember clearly there was a time in third grade where they were doing a survey. I'm not sure exactly what it was for, but they wanted to make sure that they had accounted for all the racial percentages in the classroom. So what they did was they asked everyone to stand up if they were white and they counted the number of heads, and then they asked everybody who was black to stand and they counted the number of heads, and that was it. And I never stood up, so I raised my hand and I said, "Well, when am I supposed to stand up?" And the teacher looked at me and she scratched her head, and she goes, "I don't know, I guess I'll just put you down with the blacks." And that was the first time I ever realized there was—I think it's the first time it dawned upon me that people took note of racial differences. . . . And it was the first time I ever think that someone that counted making a distinction between white and black and others. But even at that point, I was the only one there not being accounted for.

Nikhil was placed in an undifferentiated category of nonwhites that bore no relationship to his Indianness. Nikhil's experience vividly illustrates the sensations that many research participants had: that they were racially different, but that race was about being black or white. For the individual, this is not just a question of color. It's a question of meaning: Nikhil saw that he "didn't count" because he was neither black nor white—and, by extension, he came to understand that being Indian "didn't count" in the American social context. The impact of the experience was magnified by the fact that the comment came from a white teacher, a person in a position of power who represented the American cultural norm. This point cannot be overemphasized. Teachers are students' source of information on how the world is—not only on math and science and English but on the way things are and the way Americans think. For a teacher to deny Nikhil's ethnic and racial identity was to say to him, "society does not see you."

Whether or not they had any experiences like those above, many research participants described a constant feeling that they did not belong. This was particularly true of those who grew up in "*very* white" (a phrase used by nearly a quarter of the research participants) towns, but even those who grew up in diverse communities reported feeling different from their non-Indian peers. Whether at school, in the neighborhood, at the store, or hanging out with friends, there was a sense of alienation and solitude. When they were little, some research participants said, they couldn't even give a name to this feeling— but they felt it. Jaya and three other research participants reported constantly feeling different because their skin was neither "black" nor "white." Vishali said she was "always a brown girl in a white community. The way I saw it I was a chocolate chip in this big white-ass cookie."

Feeling like an outsider led many research participants to wish they could be insiders.[25] Some research participants who felt alienated and isolated due to skin color wished they were white. Anisa, for example, described a memory of feeling different as a very young child. Although she could not recount an experience with "racism" during her childhood, Anisa described the following exchange with her father: "I hated it [being brown-skinned]. I was five years old and my father was having a beer with a colleague and I went up to him and said, 'Daddy can you paint me white?' he said 'Anisa, why do you want me to paint you white?' And I said, 'Everyone else is white. I want to be white too.'" In the social context of an American school and of American society more broadly, the research participants thought that looking like everyone else would enable them to fit in in a way (they felt) their brown skin otherwise prevented. Most of these second-generation Indian Americans wanted to be white at some point in their childhood or, more often, adolescence. They had learned and accepted messages about the inferiority of people of color and their cultures without being sufficiently exposed to countervailing opportunities (which often also had to come from the dominant culture) to live out their ethnicity in a positive and respected manner. Girish said: "I hated it [being of Indian origin]. I wish I was an American. I mean I wish I was a white person. I always used to think I wish I was a white person; my life would be so much simpler, I wouldn't have all these problems." Smita said she thought "all the time" that "it would be so much easier . . . for the color of my skin to be like everybody else's." She said she never wished "not to be Indian American, I just wished I wasn't brown." In fact, most of the research participants who said they'd wished to be white also added that they still wanted to be Indian from a cultural standpoint—they just wished they could shed their brown skin. In the minds of these research participants, skin color was the manifestation of all that was different as they struggled to navigate the two worlds of home and school; it was the barrier that prohibited them from being completely part of the white-dominated social world. For females in this group, the issue of fitting in applied as well to beauty aesthetics. Many discussed their skin color and appearance in context of never being asked out on a date, or of wishing they could be attractive to men; this issue diminished for most when they reached college.

Wanting to be white can also be understood if we understand the role that internalized racism can play in the lives of second-generation Indian Americans.

Indian Americans exhibit internalized racism when they collude with the racist ideas of the dominant white society and adopt, consciously or subconsciously, the notion that white is right (see Hardiman and Jackson 1997; Tatum 1997). In response, they have developed an internal ideology of racial subordination and ethnic inferiority and embraced it in a way that is manifested as a rejection of nonwhite characteristics. (Paradoxically, these negative ideations may be held simultaneously with and despite the existence of more positive ideas and feelings about their racial and ethnic group.) This ideology can manifest in what some call the "acting white stage" of ethnic identity development; this stage involves denial of one's racial and ethnic background, and even conflict with other members of one's family or racial group. Among children and adolescents, feelings associated with acting white often involve embarrassment about the Indian American's ethnic, racial, or religious background and about parents as a representation thereof. For example, Mahesh reported hating trips to the mall with his mother, who wore a sari and spoke with a thick Indian accent; he said he avoided walking close to her, and he cringed when she spoke to him in Gujarati because he was afraid one of his school friends might hear. In the immigrant context, as the analysis earlier in this chapter should make clear, acting white may evoke ideations about acting—and thereby becoming—American. The ambition of the immigrant encounters the overlapping divides of race and class in the United States and the conclusion is that the desirable life—becoming American as the immigrant dreamed it—is found in the white direction.

The Perpetual Foreigner

The notion of the perpetual foreigner is a major theme across the research participants' life spans. One of the more common experiences reported by a substantial proportion of research participants was the assumption that they were from another country. The vast majority of the research participants were born in the United States; at the very least, all were educated here for all or most of the K–12 period. Virtually everyone faced remarks and questions like the ubiquitous, "Where are you from? No, where are you *really* from?" Such inquiries turn the only visible difference between the research participant and the speaker—the participant's brown skin—into something that renders the former less American.[26] The aforementioned factors combined with nativism and the stigma of foreignness further compound the racial marginalization of Indian Americans. Anila's childhood experience is particularly poignant. Of her classmates during the K–12 period, she said: "I thought people were hypocritical. They would say, "go back to where you came from." I felt like that statement did not even apply to me because I came from here. So I always felt it put me in an awkward position. At least my parents did come from somewhere. I mean, this was my home, and I was often made to feel like this was not my home. That bothered me." Imagine now how it felt for many of the research participants to have the same experience in

India. As discussed in the section on transnational experience in chapter 3, many research participants when confronted with social exclusion in school idealized India as a place of refuge and acceptance. Those that then went to India heard from their Indian cousins effectively the same thing they heard from their white classmates: You're not one of us. The experience of realizing that one can fit in in neither locale was devastating to many research participants and often led to a serious sense of crisis about identity: Do I belong anywhere? Some research participants—particularly during the K–12 life period, when acceptance is paramount and the idea of eventual escape to college or adulthood seems far off—manifested varying degrees of social withdrawal in response.

Anila's classmates were white, and therefore part of the normative majority in American culture. But the presumption of foreignness is not limited to white viewers. Shabnam described an incident when, seeing her brown skin, a black woman assumed she was a foreigner: "I was volunteering for Raksha [a social service organization] then. My cousin and I were helping out at the Super Bowl, and a black woman was directing us around, and she meanly said, 'Do you guys speak English?' We both looked at her—I was about to get really angry—and we were like, 'What the hell?' . . . She was saying we were basically a fresh off the boat immigrant and that kind of irritated me." The fact that the agent in Shabnam's experience was African American demonstrates one of the unique aspects of the perpetual foreigner phenomenon.[27] Instead of drawing a line between white and nonwhite, it separates people presumed to be American from those presumed to be "not from here" on the basis of physical appearance. Although experiences like the ones described above depart farther and farther from what might traditionally be described as racism, they remain race-based experiences involving attention or inattention resulting from the research participants' physical features. Even before the tragic events of September 11 and the ensuing backlash, Indian Americans were perceived to be foreigners, no matter how good their English skills and no matter if the person had been born and bred in the United States (Feagin 1997). Shabnam's anecdote is a perfect example of why we need to extend our conversations about racism beyond the white/black or white/"of color" dichotomy. In Shabnam's case, an African American was the one entertaining and perpetuating the notion of Indian Americans (and probably Asian Americans in general) as perpetual foreigners. Even though the "us" in this dichotomy encompasses both blacks and whites, it is still fundamentally a story about hegemony.

Waters (1999) offers an instructive analogy in her study of Haitian immigrants. Waters found that immigrants and their offspring resisted the ascription of "black" or "African American" to themselves. Waters's Haitian Americans reported checking the "Other" box on official forms that inquired about race and seeking other ways to emphasis their ethnicity, as opposed to their race. The distinction between Waters's respondents and Indian Americans is that the immigrant status of the former is invisible; put simply, they look black. For Indian Americans, like other Asian Americans, the opposite is true: Even American-born Asians regularly encounter an assumption that they are foreign-born.

Unfair Treatment, but That's Different from "Real Racism"

Approximately one-third of the research participants experienced racial discrimination and identified it as such. What is interesting about this group is that even among those who identified discrimination and recognized its racial component, a substantial minority did not consider their experiences to have been experiences of "real racism." These research participants characterize "real racism" by reference to the African American experience: "Real racism," it seems, involves lynchings, whites-only facilities, and other images associated with the American South before (and to some extent after) the Civil Rights era. This way of thinking is hampered not merely by its failure to recognize covert racism, but by its failure to recognize individual race-based acts that don't rise to the level of physical exclusions or violence as racism. Very few research participants, even among those who experienced racial discrimination and recognized it as such, were comfortable calling an experience racism or racist. It often took blatant, Jim Crow-style racist attacks, such as being called "nigger" and "sand nigger" or being targeted with threats and vandalism by members of the Aryan Nation, as Avya was, for research participants to use the word *racism*. Indeed, even some who were called "nigger" referred to their attackers as ignorant rather than racist. Here again, we see echoes of parental distancing on issues of race, an unease with positioning oneself as a racial minority—as "functionally black" (Haney-López 2003).

As the first Indian in his fraternity, Alok suffered the lion's share of hazing among his pledge class. "It was rough. I got hazed more than any other person. . . . It was outright racist." By contrast, Binita—who was excluded from a sorority, she believes, because of her racial background—called her experience merely "discriminatory." Sororities and fraternities—the "Greek system"—are collegiate student-run institutions that often have histories and traditions as long and deep as that of the college itself. To join a sorority or fraternity, students must take part in "rush" activities, including parties and interviews. Rushing enables sorority and fraternity members to evaluate the candidates through social events and interviews; it is, fundamentally, about fitting in. For Binita, this meant being asked many questions relating to her ethnic and racial background: "The interviewer questioned me about my culture and [asked questions] like, 'tell me where you are from.' "[28] After the rush period was over and she was not given a bid to join the sorority, she wondered whether it was her race and ethnicity that made her unwelcome, so she compared notes with a white friend who was admitted to the sorority. Even though she finally concluded that "it must have been discriminatory, because my friend didn't get asked these kinds of questions about her culture or where she's from," Binita interpreted the whole experience in a way that typifies the outlook of many in this research cohort: "Personally, my philosophy or my way of doing things is that I don't really focus on those things. So even if I was discriminated against, I think I probably would have overlooked something like that. . . . I mean, these are blatant things that I'm telling you about. If something was pretty subtle, I wouldn't have noticed it."

Here again we see echoes of the black-white racial paradigm, and the extreme nature of white discrimination against blacks over the course of American history. Racism is in their minds limited to the harsh, direct, old-fashioned discrimination of the Jim Crow-era South. By contrast, being treated like a foreigner, shut out of a sorority, or hazed in a fraternity—even when such treatment was clearly race-based or conspicuously discriminatory—often did not earn the label "racism" in the eyes and minds of these Indian American research participants. Yet they are also people of color in a country where whiteness connotes privilege and racial minority status always results in some form and degree of victimization. It was this second fact—the "but" in the Indian American story of achievement and affluence—that many research participants could not or would not see. Alok was thus out of the ordinary.

Unfortunately, teachers are similarly hamstrung when it comes to seeing and intervening to prevent modern-day racism. As Peter Kiang indicates, "Educational practitioners and policy makers must not only develop timely measures to respond to specific anti-Asian incidents, but, more importantly, must address the underlying causes of violence and establish alternative environments characterized by respect and cooperation" (Kiang 2002, 35). Unfortunately, this is not occurring. One of the common themes linking all of the stories of in-school discrimination told by my forty-one research participants was this: There was no interruption of prejudicial behavior or statements by teachers. Girish's words were typical: "the teachers would hear and do nothing."[29] (Indeed, as chapter 5 reveals, acts of religious discrimination were often perpetrated by teachers and other authority figures.) All forms of racism are harmful to students who have to deal with them—whether they are manifested in physical injuries or in the "hidden injuries of racism" (Kailin 2002). Educators must be prepared, by their own studies and continuing education programs and by common sense, to recognize and respond to modern forms of racism. This is particularly important because peer-on-peer discrimination is the most common way racism is experienced by Asian American youth.[30]

During their K–12 years, the second-generation Indian American research participants reported, they faced an array of negative, overt racial experiences. A quarter of the women and men in this study reported being called "nigger" or "sand nigger" at some point in their lives, most often by schoolmates but sometimes by strangers. "Sand nigger" is a term of unknown origin, perhaps reflecting the fairer skin color of those nonwhites who are not as dark as African

Americans, or perhaps evoking the desert from which all non-Europeans some-times seem assumed to have arisen. All of those who had the epithets "nigger" and "sand nigger" hurled at them—Anand, Girish, Aziz, and Vinay—were men who grew up in the South. This story told by Girish, a male research participant, was typical of such experiences: "One specific event stands out. We were in the cafeteria and I don't remember what we were doing, but we made a mess or something, and this one kid looks over at me, directly at me, and says, 'Hey, nig-ger, you need to clean this up.'" Likewise, Manish—a Floridian who is Sikh, but who keeps his hair short and does not wear a turban—was on several occasions in his childhood called a "towel-head." Other research participants described having the name Gandhi used against them in a derogatory manner. Said Ma-hesh, who grew up in the greater Boston area, "One person in high school who was just ignorant and got under my skin. He was a bully to everyone. He would call me Gandhi, and you know how he meant it." This appellation was extremely troubling to those against whom it was used, because they were taught at home and in Sunday school that Gandhi was among the most admirable men in the world and was an Indian figure who should inspire pride. Instead, Gandhi's name became a slur of its own.

Here the research participants' experiences can easily be labeled as overt or old-fashioned racism, which is a public, conscious act intended to harm or dam-age a person or a group of people of another race specifically because of the race of the victimized person or group. Of his experience being called nigger, Girish reported that the childhood experience had this immediate and lasting effect: "It really made me notice, or made it stand out to me more, that I was different from everybody." Girish also described going into some of the local stores: "Peo-ple were very rude. [At a time when the population was] basically all white peo-ple, they would say, 'Well, we don't have anything for you,' or 'we don't have this,' or 'are you sure you should be here? Do you think you can you afford this?' And all these little things like that. Those were some of the experiences I had."

Although Nikhil was never called nigger, he had the jarring experience of multiple face-to-face encounters with hooded Klansmen in his North Carolina high school lobby: "The KKK would come into our high school and stage their protest and sit in the front lobby with their hoods and gowns. They'd just sit there. . . . I would come out [of the office they would be] like right there in your face and I was scared. I mean literally, you know, because they'd come in with guns. They had guns in their hands. I don't know if they were loaded or not, but . . . just the physical presence [was threatening]." Although some other stu-dents were angry about the Klan's appearances in the lobby, other "kids my age were like, 'Yeah, it's very important that we white people stick together.'" There were "people in my classes who thought that, and that made me mad and made me upset. . . . There's still an element of fear every time you encounter that, be-cause you don't know when or if it will ever turn personal or physical even."

Although he never had a verbal or physical altercation with the Klansmen in the lobby, Nikhil was again receiving a stark and unequivocal message that he was unwelcome. Even if the Klan's primary targets were the school's blacks, Nikhil knew that the people under the hoods didn't look like him. These encounters with the Ku Klux Klan, in conjunction with those other experiences, led him toward a defensive posture where knowledge of and comfort in his ethnic and religious identity was something he sought as a way of protecting himself from white society.

The cumulative effects of all these experiences solidified in Nikhil's mind the message that Girish and others received when they were targeted with racial slurs: a feeling of being shut out from and unwelcome in mainstream society. The lingering impact of such experiences can be substantial as demonstrated by the vividness with which research participants recounted experiences they had years or decades earlier. The message racial epithets convey to the target is "We're different: You're different and worse, and I'm different and better." For some research participants, that has become the primary message they associate with white people. Girish and Nikhil followed the natural human tendency, to develop a thick skin (my words) with respect to interactions with whites. The result in adulthood has been that he and other research participants with similar experiences report not engaging with the dominant white community any more than is necessary to function professionally and economically.

There were a few research participants who experienced racial discrimination and then not only took action in response to a particular experience but also became engaged in fighting racism. Avya was one such person. Avya grew up in central Florida and attended a predominantly white elementary schools and a much more diverse middle school. The diversity was a result of a desegregation order, and Avya was bussed to a middle school twenty-five minutes away. Due to the new mix, racial and religious tensions were very apparent in middle school through high school. Avya said the Aryan Nation, a white supremacist group, was recruiting in her area and that students in her school had gotten involved. There were racial graffiti—"swastikas all over the school"—and fights would erupt; "people from school were expelled." Avya became the editor of the school newspaper and, as a response, began to write "scathing editorials" about the situation.

Conclusion

The experiences of the research participants discussed here show us a range of the types of racial exclusion Indian Americans encounter. As noted in the introductory paragraphs of this chapter, considering the Indian American experience with race invites us to embrace the complexity of the "racial" Indian

American—who and what *is* an Indian American? What is he or she not? It also compels us to consider the internal contradictions in how experiences are dealt with and processed by second-generation Indian Americans. Some Indian Americans of the second generation turn to the ideology of their parents, that they are a model minority destined for greatness—and, perhaps, by extension, whiteness. At the other end of the spectrum, some are like Avya and Nikhil, who both recognize and respond to individual and systemic racism. In between lie the lion's share of second-generation Indian Americans: often victimized, but just as often unwilling to call racism by its name, and sometimes unable to see discrimination as racism because their experiences seem equivocal or mild by comparison to the historical plight of black Americans.

The comparison to American blacks—both by similarities and dissimilarities to the situation of Indian Americans—is instructive also when we examine the outlook of Indian Americans themselves. Rajagopal (1995) notes that Indian Americans quickly picked up on cultural representations of blacks, compared them to those of whites, and realized they were "better Hindu than black." Why did Rajgopal choose the word "Hindu" rather than the word "brown"? After all, one could fairly argue that brown is also "better . . . than black" in the American racial system. What can be said of the second generation is that they are to a substantial degree participating in the movement now afoot in America to emphasize their religious label (Hindu, Sikh, etc.) over labels connoting national origin (Indian) or racial minority status (Asian).[31] For Hindus and Sikhs, this has the "advantage" of distinguishing them not only from blacks but also from Muslims, a religious group associated in the American mind with terrorism. (A great deal more will be said about this subject in chapter 5 and the Epilogue.) In so identifying, Hindus are aided by current positive perceptions of Hinduism in popular culture; their "peaceful," "exotic" religion is all the rage these days, from henna tattoos and "Om" T-shirts to images of deities sold as home decor. The Hindu label establishes criteria for exclusion and represents a rejection of the various alternative identities available to immigrant and second-generation Indian Americans.

Even more, others' lack of knowledge about India functioned to minimize Indianness, demonstrating to research participants that their country of origin was so insignificant, so not a part of non-Indians' lives, that some did not even know what or where India is. This last message, of course, could have a profound effect on how research participants thought of themselves not only racially but also ethnically and religiously. In tandem with the invisibility of Indian religions and the omnipresence and normative influence of Christianity in society, the message of Indian irrelevance further bolstered feelings not only of differentness but also of self-doubt, of irrelevance, and of a desire to assimilate rather than stand out.

The great mishap of this generation was treating racist incidents as ignorance. Treating racial discrimination as merely ignorance defangs racism; it removes the malice behind the act, disguising meanness and hatred as stupidity. In doing so, it protects these research participants from facing the most painful truths behind racist incidents: the malice that animates them, and the fact that they will always be as inescapable as the respondent's own skin. But it also empowers teachers, parents, and others to continue ignoring the racial victimization of this population.

Indian Americans' experiences also demonstrate the artificiality of the line I have drawn between racial and religious oppression. Sometimes more important than this line is the association made in the mind of the individual Indian American. More than half of the research participant cohort grew up in the South. Their experiences with race occurred in a physical space where they saw megachurches (a uniquely southern phenomenon) everywhere and encountered vocal Southern Baptists and other evangelicals on a day-to-day basis, including some of their teachers. Taken in conjunction with the research participants' religious minority status, this association often caused racial discrimination to take on religious import in the minds of the research participant. By contrast, their only regular encounters with groups of coethnics most often took place in the context of the temple, masjid, or gurdwara. As a result, representations of religion came to be colored by race. When congregating for religious purposes was the research participants' opportunity to connect with other brown-skinned social outcasts, the conflation was virtually inevitable.

The flip side of that coin is the racialization of religion, through an association between real or imagined phenotypical characteristics, whereby race becomes a proxy for a presumed belief system. The process is both enabled and aggravated by the presence of a white and Christian norm in American society. While racialization results in the mingling of religious and racial bigotry, at the same time, from the standpoint of who encounters discrimination, experiences can be decidedly religious or obviously racial.

For Indian Americans, as religious minorities and "unmeltable" ethnics, the phenomenon went further: In their own minds and in the American mind, race became a proxy for religion and vice versa. This will be the subject matter of chapter 5. Ironically, at the same time, and also because of race, Indian Americans are seen as having a one-dimensional identity. Because of the automatic American mental ascription of race to ideas of social difference, the "religion piece" goes unseen, undiscussed, and unresponded to. This happens with particular frequency when it comes to discrimination; acts of religious bigotry are frequently categorized as racism. The rationale for the association is clear: Race was why bad things happened to blacks and Native Americans over the course of history. Most important, it is the single element of difference that is immediately visible and apparent to the otherwise uninformed observer.[32]

5

Religious Oppression

Religious discrimination in the United States of America is not a post-9/11 phenomenon. Indeed, it is not even a twentieth-century phenomenon, nor has it been limited to non-Christian faiths. The United States has a history of religious intolerance from its beginnings. Native Americans, Catholics, Quakers, Mennonites, and Eastern Orthodox Christians faced religious persecution in seventeenth-, eighteenth- and nineteenth-century America. Antisemitism, in its turn, took root on American shores from xenophobic seeds brought from Europe, and in some forms continues to have a place in American culture. Today, the followers of Sikhism, Islam, Hinduism, and other non-Western faith traditions encounter prejudice and discrimination because of their religion.[1] Although the racialization of religion exacerbates the discrimination faced by Indian American adherents of these religions, it alone does not explain the discrimination. Nor does the excuse that the faiths are Eastern; Islam, like Christianity and Judaism, is an Abrahamic faith with adherents of all ethnicities—yet Muslims in America face perhaps the most pervasive religious discrimination of the day.

Religious affiliation, like race, has been the basis for exclusion and discrimination throughout American history. The real story of religion, oppression, and privilege in America is as long as American history itself and has touched the experiences of each successive wave of immigrants to arrive on these shores (as well as the experiences of those who were here before the first European trod the land). A detailed discussion of the history is unnecessary here; a brief review shows important parallels between the significance of racial difference and that of religious difference. In the colonial era, Virginia, the Carolinas, Maryland, and Georgia all required taxpayers to contribute money to the Church of England. The Puritan religious establishment restricted dissenters' civil rights, including their right to vote. Laws were enacted to compel church attendance, impose religious oaths as an obligation for public office, and punish "blasphemy" harshly. The cultural power of Puritanism resulted in suppression and persecution of people with differing religious beliefs (see Ahlstrom 1972; Gaustad and Schmidt 2002). Massachusetts expelled religious dissenters, banishing or executing defiant Quakers and Catholics.[2] And even as tolerance among the various Protestant denominations grew during the eighteenth and nineteenth centuries, Catholics, Jews, and other religious minorities remained subject to officially sanctioned discrimination (Moore 1986; M. F. Jacobson 1998). Legal structures were put into place to ensure the continued dominance of Protestant Christianity.[3] In addition to such state-sanctioned discrimination, provisions of the federal Civilization Act of 1819 provided U.S. government funds to subsidize Protestant missionary educators (Spring 2003).

The surge of immigration in the middle to late 1800s led Protestants to worry that Catholicism would undermine the Protestant Puritanism on which the nation had constructed its moral and political identity (Prewitt 2004). The National Origins Act of 1924, also known as the Johnson-Reed Act, effectively functioned to prevent non-Protestants from immigrating to the United States. With the support of nativist organizations like the Ku Klux Klan and the American Protective Association as well as individuals, including Protestant professionals and clergy, the act restricted immigration rights almost exclusively to northwestern Europeans in order to "protect our values . . . [as] a Western Christian civilization" (Feagin 1997, 35).[4] In doing so, it closed off large swaths of geography where the world's Jews, Muslims, Hindus, Sikhs, Buddhists, animists, and others resided. Was excluding non-Christians an aim of the act? Was it something the act's advocates saw as even a salutary advantage of their plan? We cannot say for sure. The politicians who led the charge to enact the act denied that they were out to exclude Jews—but then, they also denied that they were racists.

Religious oppression did not disappear in the decades that followed the 1965 Immigration Act's passage, and the reader is left to consider whether and to what extent the beliefs that animated Congress in 1924 continue to exist today. The discrimination that one faces for being Hindu, Muslim, or Sikh is another way religion is by second-generation Indian Americans. In many respects, this chapter continues the discussion of lived religion begun in chapter 3 by discussing in detail religious discrimination and, more broadly, religious oppression. Nearly half of the research participants described at least one experience they perceived as religious discrimination. These experiences took many forms and had substantial effects on the ethnic identity development of these second-generation Indian Americans. In exploring the experiences of religious discrimination, the intent of the actor, although it might be of paramount relevance in a legal case, is not my concern (see T. Yang 1997). When Harjit, a Sikh who wears the turban, was harassed at a local pub, did his attackers target him because he is brown-skinned or because he is a turban-wearing Sikh? This text is not concerned with this question; rather, this text is concerned with how he experienced the attack.

Just as religion affects ethnic identity development in a variety of ways, depending on the research participant's exposure and experiences at various life periods, religious oppression has a similar range of effects. Sometimes these effects are highly visible, such as Nikhil's pursuit of religious practice as an adult, despite his discomfort with it earlier in life; religious oppression was a substantial part of what pushed him toward studying and practicing Hinduism. But not everything about religion is visible to the eye. As Idinopolous (1998) states, "There is another dimension called the nonobservable, which is the source of religion's purpose and meaning." The nonobservable effects of religious oppression can include changes in how the individual thinks about or relates to religion, even if there is no clear behavioral manifestation of such change. The effects of religious oppression on second-generation Indian Americans shape how many of these individuals negotiate religion in their lives and by so doing, impact ethnic identity development.

Religious Oppression's Twenty-First-Century Transformation

In the United States, we have freedom of religion, the right to choose and practice the faith we hold dear. But having a choice is not the same as having that choice accepted and supported rather than ignored, marginalized, exoticized, or demonized. Notwithstanding the United States' history of having minority religions present and the nation's self-image as a haven for those fleeing religious oppression, the reality of life in America for a follower of a non-Western faith is one of misunderstanding, missed opportunities, and outright abuse.

The issue is particularly salient because so many of these religious minorities are also members of visible racial and ethnic minority groups; they are people of color. These double minorities, such as Indian Americans, encounter discrimination on both racial and religious levels. At the societal and institutional level, these groups are subject to oppression and face conflict on the basis of injustices that spring from their racial status, their religious status, or from the combination of the two. They may also find that their religions have been racialized. As discussed in the preceding chapter, the racialization of religion can render religious oppression both invisible and acceptable. As phenotype becomes a proxy for religious identity, a visible attribute, race, generates a presumption about religious identity. We must be particularly careful not to conflate the two in our analysis, because the data reveal that experiences of religious discrimination are qualitatively different from those of racial discrimination. Teasing apart the religious warp from the racial woof of oppression's fabric is essential if we are to meaningfully examine, diagnose, and perhaps salve the oppression experiences of Indian Americans.

Religious Oppression and Where It Exists

Hindu, Muslim, and Sikh research participants encountered religious oppression along two dimensions of religion: their actual or presumed religious beliefs; and manifestations of their belief through worship, ritual, and other practices. Religious oppression was thus both about who they prayed to (and who they did not) and about how they prayed (and how they did not). The religious discrimination experienced by the research participants is embedded in the systemic dominance and privilege Christianity enjoys at all levels of U.S. society. In other words, religious discrimination is an element of religious oppression. Identifying a social phenomenon as oppression "emphasizes the pervasive nature of the social inequity woven throughout social institutions as well as embedded within individual consciousness" (Bell 1997, 4). Identifying religious oppression recognizes that the disadvantages of non-Christians are played out not merely at the individual level, in one-on-one encounters, but that these disadvantages also exist at a societal and institutional level where individuals are socialized, punished, rewarded, and guided in ways that maintain and perpetuate oppressive structures (see Hardiman and Jackson 1997). This subordination is a product of power and of the unequal power relationships among religious groups within American society; it is supported by the actions of individuals (religious discrimination), cultural norms and values, institutional structures, and societal practices. Through religious oppression, Christianity and its cultural manifestations function to marginalize, exclude, and deny the members and institutions of Hindu, Muslim, and Sikh religious groups in society the privileges and access that accompany a Christian affiliation.[5]

The government, media, and the educational system are some of the institutional structures that manufacture and maintain religious oppression. As with other types of oppression, religious oppression is more than an ideology that asserts superiority, and more than a "a condition of being, a particular stance one is forced to assume with respect to oneself" (Goldenberg 1978, 23). It is a pervasive social creation, involving what Paulo Freire (1996) called the oppressor and the oppressed. The product is an individual (or a community) who is in fact alienated, isolated, and insulated from the society of which he or she nominally remains a member. In the context of America's racial schema, religious oppression sets up a dichotomy between that which is privileged and normative—whiteness and Christianity—and that which is not: dark skin and non-Christianness.

The norms and practices of religious oppression at the societal or cultural level are the most ubiquitous and yet the most difficult to describe. The level of society and culture is where our society's norms are "perpetuate[d as] implicit and explicit values that bind institutions and individuals" (Bell 1997, 19). A norm, of course, is illustrated also by its opposite: the other. The process of "othering" entails a dialectic of inclusion and exclusion, simultaneously (Pharr 1988; Said 1978). By comparison with the norm, which encompasses everything from theological "truth" to manners and customs of practice, the non-Christian "other" religions come to be seen as evil, wrongful, deviant, or sick.[6] That which is associated with the Christian norm is considered religious or spiritual, while that which is not is rendered exotic and illegitimate, and relegated to cult status. By attributing to a population certain characteristics in order to categorize and differentiate it as an other, those who do so also establish criteria by which they themselves are represented (Said 1978; Miles 1989). In the act of defining Hinduism, Islam, and Sikhism as deviant, and thereby excluding them from society, American Christians represent themselves as good, normal, and righteous. Moreover, by using the process of racialization further to exclude and make these groups inferior, that same discourse, but with inverted meanings, serves to include and make superior a particular group—the white Christians.

As oppression imposes the dominant group's cultural perspective on institutions and individuals, that perspective becomes the societal norm that is written into laws and inscribed on the daily thought patterns of the populace. Christian holidays—"holy days"—are given institutional endorsement by their inclusion on a calendar designed around the convenience and priorities of Christians. Individuals within these institutions act upon the presumed righteousness of Christianity and express the implied illegitimacy of other faiths. The mindset of rightness and privilege is manifested in the treatment of religious minorities by members of the majority—whether that treatment is meant to harm, threaten, or "save" the target person. These attitudes and behaviors, whether conscious or not, function to maintain systematized religious oppression. The paramount institution in the lives of these research participants to date has been school, and Priti described how holidays made her feel excluded: "In grade school on many occasions, when we would celebrate Christian holidays, I definitely remember feeling that I was not a part of that celebration. I mean every holiday—Easter, Thanksgiving, Christmas."

Socioeconomic class plays a role in all types of oppression because the oppressors—whites, men, and so on, perpetuate their economically advantaged status by perpetuating the oppression. Can the same be said of religious oppression? One could argue, by way of example, that the Christian prayer meetings held at the U.S. Department of Justice provided Christian attorneys with career-advancing social access to then-Attorney General John Ashcroft that was not similarly available to non-Christians. Likewise, business deals can be made in the church pew, as they are on the golf course. But at the societal level, what is the economic advantage for Christians of marginalizing Muslims, Hindus, or other Indian American religions? In Palos Heights, Illinois, the city gave $200,000 to a Muslim organization in exchange for the group agreeing to build its mosque elsewhere—a cost to taxpayers that they would not have borne if they were willing to have Muslims in their midst.[7] Here, the city perpetuates the economic advantage of its predominantly white, Christian residents by using a relatively small amount of money to avoid what it expects will be a larger economic impact if Muslims are allowed to build their masjid—the decline in property values that would result from the presence of an undesirable population.

Let me be clear. I am not saying that Christianity, as a faith or a belief system, is to be held accountable for religious oppression; that would be a theological argument and therefore beyond the scope of this book. Nor am I saying that all Christians consciously or purposely oppress non-Christians. What I am saying is that Christianity and a Christian identity in the United States are used as tools of oppression because Christian hegemony is created and perpetuated. The issue at hand here is not one of guilt but one of effect on religious minorities in our pluralistic society. *Hegemony* (Gramsci 1971) describes the ways in which a socially dominant group promulgates and spreads its philosophies and social structures, and how these ideas thereby come to be accepted as universal and commonsensical. The ideas of the hegemonic group—here, Christians—take on such an air of normalcy that they come to be seen as representing the natural order of things, and are accepted and perpetuated even by members of the groups they marginalize and render invisible (Tong 1989).

Religious oppression manifests the majority's belief in the superiority of Christianity and the inferiority of Hinduism, Islam, and Sikhism and the oppressors' desire for a homogeneous nation. Because these particular other religious are made visible by Indian Americans' racial minority status, the issue of homogeneity illustrates the indistinct and sometimes permeable line between racial and religious oppression. Religious oppression even impacted those who no longer subscribed to their home religions. Anand, an atheist raised by Hindu parents, took the criticism of Christians "personally. . . . Even though I wasn't religious, I still get angry when I think about . . . people telling me I'm going to hell because I worship idols."[8]

Religious oppression in the United States exists and is perpetuated by and through a specific combination of facts and acts, each building upon its precedent: first, one particular religious group, Christians, has the power to define normalcy; second, the histories and belief systems of Hinduism, Islam, and Sikhism are misrepresented and/or discounted; third, harassment, discrimination, and other forms of differential treatment toward non-Christians are institutionalized; and fourth, religious oppression is manifested through violence or the threat of violence. I shall discuss each of these in turn.

Christian Groups Have the Power to Define Normalcy

To be nominally Christian requires no conscious thought or effort on the part of the Christian American; "business as usual" follows their schedule and reflects their theological understandings. In other words, Christianity is the privileged religion in the United States because Christian groups, people, and organizations have—and have always had—the power to define normalcy. Norms, of course, connote comfort and propriety as well as similarity. Thus, that which is not Christian is not merely different; it is different in a way that diminishes the non-Christian faiths. Social norms and rituals, language, and institutional rules and rewards all assume the existence of an exclusively Christian sociopolitical history and a current Christian sociocultural context (see Cromwell 1997; Beaman 2003). America's linguistic and symbolic vocabulary of faith, practice, prayer, belief, house of worship, and history largely ignore the existence of other religions, many of which are older than Christianity.

How can we prove Christianity's normative nature?[9] At the institutional level, we look at the words and deeds of federal, state and even local governments. Although the First Amendment requires the government to allow and sometimes even accommodate individuals' religious practices and forbids the government to show hostility toward any particular religion, we must look at which religion is accommodated and which religions in fact are not. The United States Senate and House of Representatives each employs a chaplain whose salary is paid by all U.S. taxpayers; both are Christian and always have been.[10] The traditional "days off" for virtually all public school systems are structured around Christian holidays, particularly Christmas and Easter. For example, spring break could be placed anywhere in the March or April calendar, yet is often made the week between Palm Sunday and Easter. Policies like these permit Christian children to accompany their parents to worship and participate in the festivities leading up to each holiday without missing school or having to make up work. Yet in stark contrast to these generous accommodations, observant Muslim students' need to pray during the school day—part of the *salah* (daily prayer) obligation— may become the subject of controversy or even obstruction (Nimer 2001). In many states and municipalities, so-called "blue laws" regulate the conduct of business on Sundays; historically, some types of business—such as the sale of alcohol—were forbidden on Sundays. Islam forbids the consumption of alcohol and recognizes Friday as its day of prayer; so why don't American blue laws restrict the sale of alcohol on Fridays?[11] We see Christianity's normative nature also in the invocation of New Testament scripture in speeches by U.S. presidents and other public officials of both major political parties, even when those speeches are unrelated to the subject of religion.[12] Against this backdrop, it becomes abundantly clear *whose* God is referred to on U.S. currency and in the Pledge of Allegiance. It is interesting to note, however, that both of these nominally nonsectarian invocations are relatively recent developments; the words "under God" were added to the Pledge of Allegiance and the words "In God We Trust" returned to the face of U.S. currency in the 1950s as a pointed response to "Godless Communism."[13] These are just a few of many examples of Christianity's privileged institutional place as among the diverse American religions.[14]

Christian hegemony at the societal level is maintained in American society through our daily practices and via the exercise of Christian privilege. Having privilege with respect to a particular social identity means that the individual does not—need not—question "the assumptions underlying institutional rules and the collective consequences of following those rules" (Young 1990, 41). Discussing the parallel concept of white privilege, Peggy McIntosh writes that it is "an invisible package of unearned assets," a "weightless knapsack of special provisions, maps, passports, codebooks, visas, clothes, tools, and blank checks" (McIntosh 1998, 79). White privilege, she continues, means having and using these "unearned assets" every day and yet remaining oblivious to them all the while. In the United States, Christian privilege, like white privilege, is a phenomenon that denies or protects, marginalizes or embraces, on the basis of religion. Christian privilege, like white privilege, exists through the cultural power of the norm; by extension, everything not adhering to the way religion is understood, taught, and practiced by Christians is abnormal (see also Blumenfeld forthcoming). Some examples of Christian privilege are:

- Worship as place and group practice: the idea that real worship occurs in a church and in the company of a member of the clergy. Here, the church represents both a place outside the home to go and pray, and the more fundamental phenomenon of congregationalism—the idea that prayer, properly performed, is done in groups and led by a person imbued by an institution with special theological authority.

- Images of god. All of the traditional American images of god derive from Western (that is, Christian) art and literature. This god is anthropomorphized in a particular manner: he is singular, male, white, often elderly, and usually bearded, with two arms and two legs.

- Architectural norms relating to houses of worship follow Christian models: A steeple is normal; a minaret is something foreign.

- Norms of prayer. The American image of prayer—the mental picture that that very word conjures—is similarly Christian. "Prayer" is an act of worship performed in a seated or kneeling position, in silence, and with crossed hands. That which is different is not "prayer"—or, perhaps, is not the sort of prayer God would hear.

- Believable stories.[15] In American society, Judeo-Christians stories, however fantastic, are considered credible. The stories told in other faiths, which are no more fantastic, are seen as impossible myths.

- State and federal holidays—including the position of the weekend on Saturday and Sunday—structured around the Christian calendar.

- At least with respect to white Christians, the privilege of being able to pray safely without fear of violence.

- The privilege of being able to build a house of worship without opposition from neighbors and local authorities.

These different facets of privilege are possessed by Christians, knowingly or unknowingly. They result in exploitation and the reaping of unfair advantages as compared to Hindu, Muslim, and Sikh members of society. There does not even have to be conscious thought or effort by Christians. Indeed, Christian privilege benefits not only people who identify with Christianity or consider themselves religious but also those "cradle Christians" who do not.[16] Christian privilege is something Christians have whether they want it or not, and whether they know it or not. It is an unearned perquisite of their birth. Even people who renounce the Christianity they were raised with as too institutional or too intolerant, or who lament the Southern Baptist demonization of Hindus or Hollywood's fixation with the Muslim terrorist, still live in a society that is familiar to them (and with them) as people raised with the Christian ethos. They can live their lives unaware of the daily exclusions, insults, assaults endured by those who are those who are of Hindu, Muslim, and Sikh backgrounds. This is Christian privilege.

Contrariwise, non-Christians find themselves forced to explain their religions not in their own terms but by reference to a Christian vocabulary: "What is your church like? What is your Bible? When is your Christmas?" By inevitable comparison, the non-Western religions are cultish and exotic; they are thought and spoken of in caricature, preached about as false paths, or coopted to sell candles and perfume. The conveniences of life as a Christian are lost to the Hindu who must leave work to observe a Hindu New Year or the Muslim student who must participate in gym class while fasting for Ramadan.[17] The opportunity to organize and build houses of worship is too often denied, as it was for Sikhs in California (Singh 2003) and Muslims in Illinois (Edwards 2000).

Hinduism, Islam, and Sikhism Are Delegitimized, Misrepresented, and/or Discounted

By exacerbating the otherness of Indian American Hindus, Muslims, and Sikhs, the racialization of religion contributes to the delegitimization of these three faiths through the following process. First, in social dialogue and thought on theological topics, the Christian norm is applied. Second, Hinduism, Islam, and Sikhism are then compared to this norm. Third, differences, real or imagined, from the Christian norm are found with respect to the Indian American religions' theology and manners of practice. For example, the Christian image of prayer—kneeling, with the fingers of both hands interlaced—is compared to Muslim bowing eastward or to Hindu *aarti* (fire offering) or *pradakshina* (worshipful circumambulation[18] of an image of the deity). "Real" myths such as the virgin birth or the Assumption are compared to "false" myths such as Mohammed's midnight flight to heaven or Vishnu's periodic visitation upon earth under different guises such as Rama and Krishna. Fourth, the comparison of the Christian norm, which is associated by the Christian majority with the idea of "goodness" or righteousness, with the differentness of these other faiths, fosters the belief that the latter are illegitimate.

This illegitimacy is acted out in ignorance of, contempt for, and mischaracterization of Hinduism, Islam, and Sikhism by the mass media, the government, and individuals. Its effect is felt most dramatically by children and adolescents, whose home belief systems are invalidated, ignored, and even actively contested by educators, other adults, and peers. As Salim stated many times during his interview, many Indian Americans believe that mainstream American culture has shown disinterest in and disrespect for fundamental pieces of their identity, particularly their religious identity. Disinterest may be manifested in the absence of news coverage or the congratulatory public service announcements aired around Christmas, Easter, Hannukah, and other "recognized" holidays. Disrespect is shown by the commodification of holy images and prayers. Images of Hindu gods have been printed onto miniskirts and shoes. A particularly abhorrent example is the toilet seat images of Ganesh and Kali made by a U.S.-based company called Sittin' Pretty. In addition to the pop merchandise, there are less tangible forms of this particular type of appropriation. In Stanley Kubrick's film *Eyes Wide Shut*, for example, verses from the *Bhagavad Gita* were recited during the infamous orgy scene. Kubrick takes religious scripture describing Hindu teachings on human virtue and overlays it upon a graphic sexual fantasy otherwise unrelated to religion or South Asian culture. Madonna's pop-rock *Ray of Light* album features the song "Shanti Ashtangi," which is an adapted version of a Sanskrit prayer. She takes a Hindu prayer not because it is religious but because it is exotic, markets it, and thereby robs it of its spiritual meaning; for Madonna, Hinduism is something to be adopted at her convenience, run through secular sieve, and sold to the masses alongside songs about adolescent crushes and self-gratification.

As troubling as it might be in one respect to see the holy symbol "om" stretched across a woman's chest on a T-shirt, it also provides a certain degree of satisfaction for some Indian Americans who grew up seeing nothing in stores or on television that reflected or affirmed their identity. Binita expressed pleasure that "the mainstream Americans have started recognizing the influence of Indian culture . . . like Madonna using henna . . . tattoos." Binita is typical of many Indian American who are consumers of Indo-chic and see its popularity as a point of pride (see Maira 2000; Sandhu 2004). Whether or not they should feel this way or engage in such consumption is a matter for debate, but also beyond the scope of this book.[19]

Islam is delegitimized and misrepresented as monolithic, fundamentalist, and violent. Long before the attacks on the United States on September 11, 2001, the impression of Islam as a terrorist religion affected the lives of Indian American adolescents in middle and high school. Such stereotypes about Muslims and the racialization of Islam as a brown-skinned religion resulted in research participants' being victimized by classmates and even teachers. Although Aziz, an Isma'ili who later converted to Sunni Islam, had been witness to racist attitudes against other groups ("My peers . . . would always make fun of black people by using the n-word"), it was not until first Gulf War in 1990 and 1991 that he had racial and religious epithets hurled at him. "Ninth grade was very difficult. It would take forms of like verbal and physical assaults," he said. Aziz was called "camel jockey," "sand nigger," and other slurs typically associated with Arabs and Muslims.

Salim, another Muslim male, also dealt with comments from peers, but also faced public humiliation because of his high school teachers' stereotypes about Muslims. Salim was made very uncomfortable by his ninth-grade homeroom teacher, one of the most popular teachers in the school; the teacher frequently "joked" with him as he walked into the room, asking: "You don't have a bomb in the backpack, do you?" Even though he laughed with the others, Salim recalled, "it made me really uncomfortable." His teacher's discrimination legitimized the view of Islam as terrorist in the eyes of an entire classroom and made Salim feel singled out for opprobrium by an authority figure (and a popular one at that).[20] Fourteen years old and unsure of himself, Salim said, "I don't know that I understood enough to go say anything to him [the teacher] about it." Nor should he have been expected to. Moreover, the teacher's comments built on negative ideations about Islam that Salim had been absorbing since "when I was six or seven . . . with a lot of what happened with the Iran hostages." With parents who were observant but never educated Salim about the religion, he had no information to counter the anti-Muslim stereotypes in the media. Although the Iranian hostage crisis was precipitated by a variety of political and diplomatic issues between the United States and Iran, Salim felt the media reported the crisis as a "Muslim thing. . . . I just knew that everything I heard about Muslim was bad."

During the First Gulf War—which occurred during Salim's senior year of high school—he again felt "really challenged about my religion." He spent a great deal of time contemplating whether he identified with the Americans or the Iraqis in that conflict. The reason for this inner conflict was how he felt this heavily publicized war was characterized by American media and political leaders. Salim wondered "which side of the coin I really belonged to." Through the years of teasing—and of learning "what I could" about Islam—he had begun to develop a sense of self-confidence about and closeness to his identity as a Muslim. And then "all of a sudden," having developed that nascent pride, he was confronted with how America dealt with and understood the First Gulf War. He said "I had to really reconcile in my heart whether, whether I believed that we, that America, was right in what they were doing," or whether Iraq was right. He reported his classmates talking "about 'Muslim' and 'Muslim terrorists' and 'Muslim bombers' instead of Iraqi leaders, Iraqi bombers, Iraqi terrorists." The result for Salim was "a stinging every time somebody said that." If America's rhetorical treatment of Muslims exacerbates the ill social effects of its military conflicts with Muslim adversaries, oughtn't that in itself be cause for concern to policy makers? Salim's story shines a light on the artificiality of the division between international and domestic—between how we treat those beyond our borders and how we treat their American kith and kin. Salim felt attacked not because of any innate affinity he feels toward Iraqis. Rather, he took his classmates' remarks personally because they did not limit them to Iraqis: They imply that because of the Iraq conflict, Muslims at large are the enemy. What are today's Muslim American adolescents feeling, and how should that inform our social policy, our foreign policy, and our pedagogy?

For Aziz and Salim, epithets that could easily be described as racist, like "sand nigger," were experienced and taken as insults about their home religions as much as religious epithets were. This illustrates how religion and culture are conflated while also being wrapped up in a self-appellation (usually "Indian") that evokes national origin and race. The particular comments made by Aziz's and Salim's classmates showed that religion and culture were often conflated in the minds of the perpetrators as well. The media, acting out its own ignorance and laziness, made no distinction between Arabs (or Persians) and Muslims—which might have protected, to some extent, these two Indian American Muslims. Nor did the media distinguish between the political and social causes of Iran's and Iraq's actions and the coincidence that each country had a Muslim majority. As a result, the concept of American "enemy" status came to encompass Aziz, Salim, and their families. Adolescence is a time of social insecurity for all people. These two young men, like many Muslim adolescents today, went through that life stage at a time when they had the additional burden of dealing with being Muslim in a Christian world that distorts, misrepresents, and fears Islam. We can see in Salim's story that the pride he developed in his religious identity was not enough to counter the effects of the media and the school environment.

Journalists and government actors have done little to ameliorate and much to exacerbate the distortion of religions beyond the Judeo-Christian. These outlets—the news media, the government, and popular movies and television— have always been the source of what most Americans know about religions and cultures of the non-Western world (Shaheen 1984, 2001). From the direct association of Islam with terrorism in movies like *Executive Decision* and *The Siege* and television series like *24* and *The Grid* to news coverage of the Persian Gulf Wars, the dominant American culture has shown disinterest in and disrespect for fundamental pieces of their religious identity—and by extension, their ethnic identity. From the oil crunch of 1973 through the post-September 11 era, the focus of America's popular ire has been a succession of Arab and Persian regimes and political movements. But given the vividly expressed attitudes of government spokesmen and the unenlightened coverage by the news media, evident to this day, it is a short step to the notion of all brown-skinned Muslims as the enemy (see Akram 2002; K. Moore 2002).[21]

Whereas Islam is "terrorized," Hinduism is exotified or treated as cultish. It is known only in caricature, with particular attention given to those attributes which mark it as most different from Christianity. Accuracy is rare. Nikhil's classmates taunted him for being "reincarnated from a dog." By reference to Christianity's normative images of God, images of Hindu gods—with their colorful clothing and multiarmed bodies—come to be seen as weird and cultic. Value-laden characterizations of Hindu images as absurd or evil abound in society and the media; *Indiana Jones and the Temple of Doom* was just one example popular during the research participants' preteen and adolescent years. To the extent the research participants' classmates were aware of Hinduism at all—since the religion was, and remains, largely invisible to mainstream America—they knew it as bizarre. More recently, individuals and organizations with substantial public influence have joined and escalated the attack. In 1995, self-proclaimed Christian leader Pat Robertson called Hinduism "demonic" (Rajan 1995). Four years later, the Southern Baptist Convention put out a pamphlet that described Hindus as "lost in the hopeless darkness of Hinduism" (International Mission Board 1999).

Along with the misrepresentation often comes theological conflation of Hinduism, Islam, and Sikhism. Because of their shared association with the brown-skinned East, Hinduism, Islam, and Sikhism have been called derivative of each other, or seen as different sects of one religion. Hinduism, Sikhism, and Islam are assumed to be theologically similar because their adherents are racially similar. The ascription of X racial features to the tenets of religion Y leads to the presumption that all people who look like X share a belief in Y. The South Asian religions are lumped into one general-purpose, brown religion. Perhaps the most conspicuous example of this phenomenon of late has been the assumption that Sikhism is theologically similar—words like "offshoot" and "sect" are often used—to Islam or Hinduism. In months after September 11, 2001, media images of Osama Bin Laden and Taliban leader Mullah Mohammed Omar—two Muslims who wear a turban, as is customary in Afghan culture—resulted in the assumption that Sikh men were in some respect Muslim. In reporting on the issue, the *Seattle Times* described Sikhism as a type of Islam. In an ironic attempt to correct its misstatement, the *Times* then reported that Sikhism was a Hindu sect (Dickie 2001). Neither is true. Sikhism is a revealed monotheistic religion founded in the late fifteenth century by Guru Nanak. The theological conflation of Indian American religions contributes to misunderstandings about theology and culture that affect the lives of individual South Asian Americans in a variety of ways, from the mere frustration of being misidentified to a lack of services (or the provision of inappropriate services) in contexts such as the public school system and commercial transactions.

It is important to note that the delegitimization of South Asian religions is largely a cultural rather than a religious phenomenon. Notwithstanding the exclusionary "one true faith" language of the Christian Bible, the process described above springs not from Christian scripture but from American culture and the privilege and cultural sway enjoyed by its Christian majority. This is to a certain extent a matter of cultural priority-setting: The difference between Catholics and Protestants, or between Baptists and Southern Baptists, is seen as salient. Americans feel no similar cultural need to know the difference between Hindus and Muslims, or between a Sikh's *dastaar* and the turbans worn by Afghanis (who are Muslim). Part of the way Indian Americans live religion is with the knowledge that beyond their families and ethnoreligious communities, their religions exist only in that dark area outside the borders of what is important, known, and welcome.

Harassment, Discrimination, and Other Forms of Differential Treatment

Another product of Christian privilege is demarcated by the important social line between the legal freedom to practice their religions and the social moment of having one's faith accepted, respected, or even visible in the various segments of American life. Christians are made confident, comfortable, and oblivious because of the omnipresence of Christianity in the American design, other religious groups are made unsure, uncomfortable, and alienated. Being Christian protects one from many kinds of hostility, distress, and violence, which—even when subtle—are part of daily life for people of Hindu, Sikh, Muslim, and other non-Western religious backgrounds. Although society's endorsement may be tacit, and even invisible to the Christian eye, it is conspicuous and visible to these religious minorities. They are aware of their difference even when their Christian classmates do not seem to be, and they are affected by experiences that clearly constitute religious discrimination and by those which may be seen as objectively equivocal but have a religious impact on the Indian American target.

RELIGIOUS OPPRESSION AND EDUCATION. Even in the public school context, the difference between being a Christian—and therefore privileged—and being a non-Christian could be as stark as the line between the classroom and the hallway. Feeling excluded for her religious beliefs took on literal meaning for Vishali, a Hindu woman raised in New England. She was literally made an outsider by her public school teacher because she was not Christian:

> I remember in second grade . . . they recited the Lord's Prayer at the
> beginning of class. And I remember that I was the only non-Christian

person who knew the prayer. Another week into the program, the teacher announced that if there was anyone who did not want to say it they were welcomed to go outside. They did not have to be a part of it. So I remember feeling strange. I remember saying that I would like to go outside. I remember going outside and being with two kids who were Jewish . . . and another Indian kid. We were put out in the hall and we were all alone. That should not have happened. There was no reason that we should have been sent out.

The nature of the oppression may not be immediately apparent to the teacher or Christian students. They are carrying out "business as usual," enjoying the Christian privilege of not having to be singled out and segregated based upon their beliefs. (Indeed, the teacher may have applauded herself, or even considered herself progressive or her actions legal, for allowing the non-Christian students the "choice" to opt out of school prayer.) Vishali, because she identified with her Hindu faith, was left literally on the outside looking in.

Some research participants' religious minority status had a tangible, and in at least one case financial, impact on their well-being. Several reported being denied certain academic privileges or awards for religious reasons. Satish, a Sikh male who grew up in Florida, applied for a major college scholarship sponsored by the local Veterans of Foreign Wars (VFW) lodge. Satish was one four area young people to reach the final round of the competition. Another second-generation Indian American Sikh was also a finalist, along with two white Christian boys. During the interview, Satish said he was asked what religion he identified with and responded that he was Sikh. Later in the interview, Satish was asked if he "had any plans" to convert to Christianity, and he replied that he did not: "The veterans were these five white guys and they each took each of us separately and interviewed us. . . . When they interviewed me, they asked me, 'What religion are you?' I said, 'I'm Sikh,' and they said, 'What is that type of thing?' 'Oh, so you're not Christian.' . . . I said, 'No.' They asked, 'Do you see yourself at any point converting to Christianity?' . . . I said 'no.' . . . And I think I was, for a lack of a better word, a wimp, so I was really polite and said, 'No, I don't think I am going to do that.' " When he learned that the scholarship had gone to one of his Christian classmates, Satish believed that his Sikh identity—particularly not being Christian—was the reason he did not receive the scholarship.

Satish's reaction to this experience—and his failure to react earlier—are typical of second-generation Indian Americans. As a Sikh who does not wear the *dastaar* (turban), Satish had experienced subtle racial and religious discrimination throughout his K–12 experience, and had for the most part dismissed "things here and there" as products of rudeness rather than prejudice. He convinced himself that such experiences were not discrimination by reasoning that the experiences, however unpleasant, were not getting in the way of achieving academically. It was only when discrimination actually blocked a path to success as it had been defined for him by his parents—academic success, winning awards, and getting a good education—that Satish was moved to respond. After learning that he had been denied the scholarship, he wanted to write a letter to the local newspaper and even considered legal action. But his parents—particularly his father, a physician who "told [me] he had a lot of patients in town"—discouraged him from responding, and so Satish remained silent once again.

It is virtually impossible to prove that Satish was denied a scholarship because of his religion. The Christian boy who got the scholarship might have been the academically superior candidate. But that is precisely where privilege comes in. Because of the questions he was asked, the issue of his religious differentness from the interviewers came into play—and may have become part of their evaluation of him as a candidate for a scholarship that was not supposed to be religious in nature. As a result, whenever he thinks back to that episode, Satish will always ask himself "what if": What if I wasn't Sikh? What if I'd said I would convert? What if I'd put up a fight? Whatever the truth is, he will always think he was denied an opportunity because of his religious identity. And this will shape his relationship to his Sikhism, to Christianity, and to the wider society. By contrast, will the other white boy, who also didn't get the VFW scholarship, go through life wondering whether he was denied opportunity because he was white and Christian? Certainly not.

Religion oppression, and a lack of access to the privileges of the Christian majority, inflicted other forms of personal harm on research participants, as well. Despite his athletic prowess, Nikhil was denied the chance to start on his North Carolina public school's soccer team because he refused to join the coach and his teammates in Christian prayer:

> Every time, [before] we played a game, the coach would made us recite the Lord's Prayer. At a certain point, I stopped doing it, and I said, "I'm not going to do it," and I would walk away. And he would yell at me to get back in the group because, you know, "you're breaking up team spirit," yadda, yadda. I said, "No, I'm not going to do it, I'm not going to be there." So I got benched and I was benched for the rest of the season, sat on the bench, and I would always come in within like two minutes, but he wouldn't start me because I wouldn't ever be in the huddle for the Lord's Prayer.

He let the coach know that he thought he was being unfair. The coach said to him: "'If you want to be an individual, you be an individual and you can think about it for the first part of the game, and when you're ready, when I think you're ready to be a team player, I'll put you in the game.'" For Nikhil's coach, the only way to be a "team player" was to pray like a Christian, in the company of other Christians. The result for Nikhil—by his account "the best player on the team"—was having to start every game on the bench.

Athletics, as an extracurricular activity, is supposed to create a space where students can have fun and enjoy team spirit and in some cases find a refuge from the academic frustrations of the classroom. Nikhil had grown up feeling aware of himself as a racial other, having been "put with the blacks" by his third-grade teacher and experienced the menacing presence of armed and hooded Ku Klux Klan members in his high-school lobby. Soccer, as a game Nikhil enjoyed and was good at, could have been a refuge from that. Instead, his coach made it yet another space where he felt like an unwelcome outsider.

When Nikhil was a senior, being Hindu meant not just getting benched by his coach but being denied an academic honor he'd earned. He recounted: "I got kicked out of the National Honor Society [NHS] because once a month on a Sunday they went to different churches so that you could have a diversity of experience with different religions. That was the purpose behind it. . . . I told them that we should go to one of the Hindu services, and they [his fellow students and the club's advisor, a teacher] said, 'No, no, we're not going to do that.'" After experiencing such a stark and direct rejection of his religious identity, Nikhil no longer wanted to go to the Church services: "I was like, 'Then I'm not going to these religious things.' . . . They didn't say anything, but when I fell out of the participation because I didn't go to the religious things, they kicked me out of the Honor Society." This discriminatory act had academic ramifications for Nikhil, who felt out of place at his own high school graduation as a result: "I was very, very mad because I was graduating in the top five in my class. Everybody around me had the Honor stole on except for me, and I was upset because the only reason I didn't have the Honor stole was because I refused to go to church on one Sunday out of the month." A listener can still hear the anger in Nikhil's voice when he describes how he was kicked out of NHS. Nikhil had undertaken a rather remarkable effort for research participants in this study: to bring his two social worlds together, to let his schoolmates get a glimpse of his ethnoreligious community. He had gone to church with his fellow NHS members, had experienced "different religions"—that is, different denominations of Christianity—as his NHS advisor had called on him to do. Until he suggested going to the temple, these experiences didn't trouble him. But the negative reaction from a club he was honored to be a member of, and into which he had earned entry by hard work, represented to Nikhil a rejection of who he was. A place of value to him was valueless to his peers, because that place was not Christian. And it was not just his peers. Peer-to-peer harassment is one thing. Religious oppression carried out by teachers, coaches, and other authority figures is entirely another. What does it say when a schoolteacher—someone charged with helping young people learn and prepare for the world beyond graduation—rejects the very idea of even encountering Hinduism?

In conjunction with other life experiences, including other experiences of marginalization, the overt religious discrimination Nikhil faced in school led him to stand up for himself as a member of a religious minority. In addition to the immediate consequences that affected Nikhil in high school, there are also lasting emotional consequences. When he spoke about these experiences nearly fifteen years after they occurred, his voice still quivered with anger. He was angry at the individuals who did him wrong, but also at the society and school culture that permitted it. As a young person, he was angry also at the happenstance of his birth: "Why me? . . . Wouldn't life be easier if I weren't Indian?" Being discriminated against led him to wanting to know more about his faith, and as a result in college he sought out courses on Hinduism. He gained confidence in his knowledge of Hinduism and became more religious. Nikhil is relatively unusual among the research participants in this study in that he goes to temple alone, when it is empty and no ethnoreligious celebration is going on. He goes simply to pray and meditate, and says he is "stronger in Hinduism" than ever before.

Nikhil's experiences also illustrate an important fact about the freedom of religion ensconced in the Establishment Clause of the First Amendment to the U.S. Constitution: Just because conduct is illegal doesn't mean it doesn't occur. The actions of both his National Honor Society advisor and his soccer coach were patently illegal; each individual, paid with taxpayer dollars, was engaging in the explicit endorsement and promulgation of Christianity and Christianity alone. The Constitution does not forbid schools from teaching about religion, but the use of public resources to promote one religion over another is illegal. But for the participation requirement, the NHS program of going to local religious services was not necessarily illegal until the moment when the NHS supervisor determined that only churches—and not mandirs, mosques, or synagogues—would be visited by the students. Likewise, coercing players into praying as the price of starting the game on the field was a Constitutional violation.[22] Hindu, Sikh, Muslim, and Jewish young people today are probably still having experiences like Nikhil's, stuck in a devil's choice between allowing their rights to be violated and inviting the opprobrium they would face if they mounted a legal challenge.

These data also illustrate another barrier to action and response in the lives of Indian American young people who have been discriminated against: lack of parental support. Both Nikhil and Satish reported that their parents urged them to keep quiet about the official discrimination they faced, and both continue to express visible, palpable anger over events that happened years ago. If they had the opportunity to do it again, both would confront their oppressors. Satish's ultimate inability or unwillingness to take action concerning a clearly discriminatory act with economic impact on his family was a product—at least in part—of not having his parents' support. Some parents denied the existence of discrimination. Even where parents acknowledged that discrimination had occurred, Satish and other research participants reported being encouraged to remain silent, ignore it, or not rock the boat. Unfortunately, the parental resistance to making waves influences not only the child's immediate reaction to prejudice, but also the way in which experiences of prejudice affect ethnic identity later in life.[23] Knowing that they were discriminated against affects how they view their place in society, which is itself an element of their ethnic identity. Right or wrong, it has also caused both men to cast a continuing critical eye on their parents: Why wouldn't they stand up for themselves, and for their sons?

SOCIETAL: PROSELYTIZATION AS HARASSMENT BY CHRISTIANS. "There was a family across the street that always wanted to convert my parents. Nice family . . . they just would always say to us, 'You should come to church, you need to be saved.'" Anisa, a Hindu female who identifies as a religious person, found it offensive that Christians wanted to "save" Hindus. Although I did not ask any of the research participants questions about Christian proselytization (see the Appendix), nearly half of the research participants offered stories about being urged to convert or being threatened with eternal damnation by Christians. Anisa's comment above, for example, was in response to a question that asked her to identify significant positive or negative experiences regarding race, religion, or ethnicity. Other research participants offered stories of proselytization when asked what made them "feel different" at various life stages.

Proselytization must be identified as a form or religious oppression whenever the person being proselytized views it as an act of harassment. Proselytization is taken as an assault on the legitimacy of the research participants' home religions. The not-so-hidden message for Anisa and others was that "my way is better than your way," and more powerfully, "my religion is better than yours." Whether or not it is an assault, some Christians' approach to Indian American religions is surely an insult: In 1999, the year before these data were collected, the Southern Baptist Convention released a special prayer book and urged its members to pursue the conversion of Hindus. Distributed on the eve of Diwali, Hinduism's festival of lights celebrating Lord Rama's return from exile as told in the *Ramayana*, the pamphlet read in part: "More than 900 million people are lost in the hopeless darkness of Hinduism. . . . Pray that Hindus who celebrate the festival of lights would become aware of the darkness in their hearts that no lamp can dispel" (International Mission Board 1999).

Religious oppression through proselytization could be experienced as deeply personal even when it wasn't personal at all—when it was part of undirected, wholesale Christian outreach. Saleena, a Hindu female, described encounters with a preacher who distributed Bibles outside her college dormitory: "There was a minister and he was really pushy, he just kept on and he would not let up about the Bible and all that. And that made me really angry, because someone was pushing something at me and trying to make me think that my religion wasn't good." The campus preacher is a fixture of the American college experience, at least in the South. For Muslims, Sikhs, and Hindus he was a visible and audible daily reminder of the message they had been receiving all their lives: that to many Americans, their faiths are illegitimate and God does not hear their prayers. For these research participants in adulthood, when a missionary knocks on the door it is like society coming up and saying, "Just in case you forgot, you're not like us, you're not good enough, and we think even God rejects you the way you are."

Irfan, a male Catholic, was bothered when he frequently encountered a preacher on campus during his college years.

> I would get into fierce discussions with a preacher in this area of Carolina called the Pit. The Pit is an area, it's like an open-air brick courtyard where students would hang out, and he was called the Pit preacher. And this guy was just a complete redneck Southern idiot. And this guy would, you know, it was fire and brimstone, thumping on his Bible whenever a group of Indians, we would walk by him, or even any other ethnic [group], he would point to us and he would say, you know, you're all going to hell, you're not baptized, you're this and that. I would tell him look, you know, you've made a judgment. I am baptized but none of my other friends here are, and my father isn't baptized, I don't think my father's going to hell because he's not baptized Christian.

Irfan was bothered that his Indian Hindu friends had to put up with this treatment, because he saw it as an attack on them and to some extent as a vicarious attack on him. He also takes it personally as an attack on his father, a Muslim. He felt embarrassed as a Christian—albeit a Catholic, not an evangelical—because he knows the preacher's harassment will shape how his Indian Hindu friends see Christianity. Like Binu and other Christian research participants, Irfan has at times found his Indian authenticity questioned by Hindu and Muslim coethnics; he could easily have seen the ire they felt in response to the preacher's abuses as putting his friendships with them at risk.

Proselytization was taken as religious oppression even by someone who considered himself nonreligious. An atheist since early in his college years, Anand nevertheless spoke at length about how he took offense at the barrage of proselytizing and conversation attempts to which he was subjected. Although he is not a religious believer, he says he has always considered Hinduism to be part of his cultural identity and was deeply angered by Christians who would push Christianity on him. Like Anisa, Anand said Christian evangelism often seemed to argue the illegitimacy of Hinduism as a religion:

> I had so many conversations . . . about Jesus Christ and the Bible. Everyone says, "Jesus Christ will save you." . . . It was just annoying because they would just never stop. Every day it's the same. And my response to

that was, "There's freedom to practice religion in America." I've had the conversations where someone will say, "In Hinduism, you worship idols, and according to the Bible, if you practice idol worship, you will go to hell."[24] [My response was,] "Don't talk to me about going to hell." Even though I wasn't religious, I still sort of get angry when I think about [the way they talked about] Indian gods like Krishna and things like that. So it's personal.

For Anand, an assault on Hinduism was an assault on his family. Although he identifies as an atheist, Anand said, "Religion is personal." Even in the years since he stopped believing in Hinduism, he said he becomes very defensive and sometimes even vocally combative when confronted with religious oppression, because religion is something sacred for those he is closest to: his family and friends.

It should be remembered, of course, that in the minds of many devout Christians, spreading the Gospel or "Good News" is an expectation—even an obligation—of their faith. The fact that it was perceived as harassment and discrimination by its targets may or may not invalidate the supposed Biblical mandate behind it. Regardless, the research participants' experiences touch a fundamental question in our pluralistic society: Can Americans practice the faiths of their choice while being respectful others' right to do the same without being judged or told to convert?[25] The research participants' reported responses to proselytization should give some Christians pause: The lion's share of those who reported being oppressed through proselytization said it strengthened their connection to their home faith. The proselytization experience was often part of what pushed research participants to pursue more knowledge of their home religion, and led far more often than not to the development of a defensive identity characterized by a stronger sense of adherence to the home faith.

Violence and the Threat of Violence

Recall Avya's experiences when the Aryan Nation came recruiting in her high school, described in the preceding chapter. In her life, violence and the threat of violence came about on the basis of what she perceived to be religious as well as racial oppression. That she fought back against religious abuse surely made her even more of a target: "In high school religion became a hot issue. In our area, the Aryan Nation was recruiting. People from school were expelled. There were [neo-Nazi] swastikas all over the school. I was editor of the school paper, and I would write scathing editorials. I started getting a name for that." Because she lived in central Florida and went to school in a predominantly white community that included a large number of fundamentalist born-again Christians, these experiences were part of a swirling mix of racial and religious oppression.

The constant "you're going to hell" was a very big theme. It was a very ostracizing atmosphere for those of us who weren't Christian. There were a lot of questions about hell and burning hell in elementary school and that was scary. In high school I would get hate mail at the newspaper saying that I was a dirty Hindu and was going to hell and things like that. I once came out to my car and found lipstick all over my car saying "You're going to hell." Once the air had been let out of the tires and the car had been keyed. I was alone. It was scary. Another time I was driving home late, and in the car behind there were skinheads hanging out the window yelling. I didn't go home because I did not want them to know where I lived. I was driving around the neighborhood until I could lose them.

Although she never suffered direct physical violence, Avya often was fearful it. For Avya, these attacks, occurring amid the social confluence of fundamentalist Christianity and neo-Nazism, took on religious salience. Note how easily her description of being proselytized and ostracized because she was not Christian flowed into a recounting of vandalism and the experience of being chased through her neighborhood by neo-Nazi skinheads. Like many Indian Americans, Avya was a "double minority," nonwhite and non-Christian, confronted with verbal attacks and physical threats from people who were both white and Christian. Among her high-school experiences the lipstick incident was objectively religious in nature and the others arguably ambiguous, but what matters most is that all of the attacks were taken as religious by Avya, whether they were intended that way or not by the perpetrators. These experiences were among those that led Avya to consider pursuing an academic career in the field of religious studies as described in Chapter 3.

Avya was one of only two research participants, out of forty-one people, who reported experiencing threats of violence. The same might not be true today, after the post-9/11 backlash. In the three months following September 11, 2001, two South Asian Americans were killed in backlash attacks and at least another 250 bias-motivated incidents targeting South Asians were reported to National Asian Pacific American Legal Consortium (NAPALC).[26] By comparison, NAPALAC reported four to five hundred incidents per year against all Asian and Pacific American groups combined prior to September 11.[27] A majority of the post-9/11 incidents involved Sikh Americans—specifically, turban-wearing Sikh men. Of the two men killed, Balbir Singh Sodhi, a Sikh gas station owner in Arizona, was the first. The second was a Pakistani Muslim businessman in Texas, Waquar Hasan.[28] Both were shot and killed by white men angered by and seeking revenge for the September 11 attacks.

Brown-skinned Americans were targets of hate crimes after September 11 largely because religion is racialized. Many of those attacked were not Muslim but Hindu or, Sikh. For reasons discussed in chapter 4, however, skin color became a proxy for a presumed affiliation with a religion already associated in the American mind with terrorism and anti-Americanism. It is impossible to say for sure, but I would venture that few African American Muslims or white Muslims were attacked during the post-9/11 backlash.[29] For Sikh Americans, their race combined with their wearing of the *dastaar* (turban) combined to result in mistaken identity; they were erroneously presumed to be Muslim. But knowing they are being wrongly attacked does not reduce the religious meaning of the attack in the eyes of Sikhs. First, they are being attacked for religious reasons (albeit in a flawed effort to target Islam). Second, like Harjit, they are being attacked for visibly engaging in religious activity in the wearing of the *dastaar*. Living "with the knowledge that they must fear random, unprovoked attacks on their persons or property" (Young 1990, 61) is part of living religion for Sikhs in America. The attacks have led to a resurgence of Sikh attention to matters of faith, by promoting the formation of ethnoreligious organizations and communities that in turn provide venues for living religion, even if the purpose of the coming together is ostensibly political or policy-oriented rather than religious.[30] At the individual level, it has surely also resulted in the greater focus and care often given to one's targeted identity.

For Muslims, all of these attacks—including those on Sikhs, as Muslims are aware of them as "anti-Muslim" attacks—may be taken as direct attacks on the faith. Whereas Sikhism as a belief system is not being attacked, Islam as a belief system *is* being attacked on the basis of the popular American understanding of Islam as an antidemocratic and anti-American theology of murder and mayhem. The Muslim experience goes beyond the Hindu or Sikh experience because the faiths are not merely ridiculed, marginalized, or rendered invisible. Islam is treated and spoken of as a source of evil in the world—America's "post-Soviet devil" (Said 1996, 28).[31] That this uncivil consensus is played out in violence against brown-skinned people of all faiths is everyone's tragedy.

The experiences described in the preceding pages are some of the most striking of those experienced by the research participants, but they are consistent in substance with experiences and feelings described by virtually all the research participants. One research participant (and arguably a second) reported threats of physical violence; more than half reported at least one incident of religious discrimination, and nearly all the non-Christians described feeling different in the American Christian milieu. In many cases, this difference took on an expressly religious tenor, such as when research participants were proselytized, felt their faiths being marginalized or ignored, or faced the uncomfortable experience of explaining on the first day of school in January why they did not have an answer for the teacher's question, "So, what did you get for Christmas?"

The Gray Area between Religious and Racial Discrimination

By now the reader has ample evidence of racial and religious discrimination aimed at Indian Americans. Many of these experiences beg the question: What kind of discrimination was that, racial or religious? Let's return to Harjit's experience in nightclubs: "I went to Dartmouth once and we were trying to get a drink there and the bartender was like, 'Sorry, we don't serve turbans,' or something like that. Also, people would grab my turban on the dance floor, or if we go out, people would just say stuff in passing that they wouldn't think I'd hear, like, 'what is that thing anyway?'" However inappropriate their behavior, we must acknowledge that the bartender and dancers of Harjit's story may not have been aware that the turban is a religious item or that his insult was directed at an element of Harjit's religious belief system. It is fair to ask, "So is this *religious* discrimination?" Whereas the courts will look to the perpetrator's intent to answer this question, that is the wrong vantage point for examining the impact of religious oppression on ethnic identity. Rather, we must consider how the experience affects Harjit. What matters in this context is that Harjit experienced these individuals' remarks as religious discrimination. The expression indicating that his turban was unfamiliar became a message that he was religiously different and unwelcome.[32] The poking or tugging at his turban on the dance floor was a physical attack on his religion—from his vantage point it showed disrespect for a symbol of faith. If for no other reason, it was religious oppression because Harjit took it that way.

We can understand why this is true by stepping back and considering Sikhism's place as an element of Harjit's ethnic identity. The non-South Asians' reactions to Harjit's turban were probably a mix of racial and religious discrimination, ignorance, and curiosity—but to Harjit, anything said or done to his turban took on religious significance because keeping the turban is a religious matter. Another person could see the bartender's and party-goers' actions as racially prejudiced. For many other research participants—and, one might guess, for their attackers—the line between race and religion was narrow when it existed at all. Because Harjit identifies as a religious person, and because his turban is part of his religious identity, the impact on him of people messing with or commenting on his turban is that of a religiously discriminatory act.

Just as insiders might not agree on the nature of oppression, outsiders also may not. In the late 1980s, a group of young toughs calling themselves the "dotbusters" attacked and intimidated Indian Americans in northern New Jersey, killing at least one person and leaving another with permanent brain damage. The *Bergen Record* (1993) called the attacks "racial beatings," the *New York Times* (Sengupta 1998a and 1998b) called them "attacks on South Asians," and the *Christian Science Monitor* (Lampman 1998) called them attacks on "the Hindu community." Eck (2001, 305) states that "the attacks had nothing to do with

Hinduism as a religion," but the theory ignores the fact that the "dot" or *bindi* is a symbol worn by Hindu women, not all Indians. As Harjit's comments indicate, the fact that the killers announced themselves as "dot-busters" likely gave the attacks religious resonance in the eyes of some Indian Americans.[33]

One major reason for the existence of a gray area, of course, is the racialization of religion. As religion and race become proxies for each other, even to a limited extent, the nature of the oppression becomes obscured. The oppressive act's impact on the target may also be less clear: When is a racist act taken religiously by its target? It is now clear that the answer to this question is frequently.

The concept of *targeted identity* explains why one or another element of ethnic identity seems to come to the fore at certain times and under certain circumstances (see Hardiman and Jackson 1997). When an act of discrimination is equivocal, the targeted identity is the identity that the subject perceives as being the object of attention or attack. For these research participants, religion's particular importance makes it likely to be the targeted identity in equivocal situations. As a result, even when an ethnic artifact such as cuisine or language was targeted, the attack could take on religious overtones in the mind of the research participants because of how religion and culture were affiliated in their mind, or simply because religion was the foremost element of their ethnic identity (which also incorporated dimensions of culture). When racial or religious oppression occurred in ways that made it difficult to say whether it was the research participants' religion or their ethnicity that was under attack the attack could be taken as religious by the research participant. Indeed, when religion represented all that it did in terms of identity and authenticity for this population, virtually any attack grounded in Indian Americans' status as a minority in American society could take on religious overtones.

Some research participants understood racial and religions oppression as indistinguishable phenomena carried out against them by society's overlapping majorities: whites and Christians. Indian American Hindus, Muslims, and Sikhs are targeted both as people of color and religious minorities by people who are neither. An Indian American may experience racial oppression, and later imbue that experience with religious meaning or vice-versa. Because of Avya's high school experiences of being targeted for violence by the Aryan Nation and for proselytization or abuse by her Christian classmates, Christianity and Christian proselytizing became associated with white supremacy in her mind.

Religious oppression is not the same as racism, but sometimes those second-generation Indian Americans who conflate race and religion may fail to see the difference. Oppression experiences may lead to feeling religiously targeted even for these research participants, because for some experiences of racism will push them toward a stronger sense of connection to ethnicity. This in turn can bring religion to the fore because of its unique position with respect to authenticity and family. Again, an exception can prove the rule: Those research participants who dismissed "race" and denied experiencing racism were generally those least connected to religion and those with a conceptualization of ethnic identity that was less emotional, more matter-of-fact, and often predominantly national origin-oriented.

The research participants' experiences of religious oppression have proved to have dramatic and sometimes lasting effects on their identities. Comparing the way in which research participants described attacks perceived as racial and those taken as religious reveals that the latter were felt more intensely, often at the time of the incident, and almost always by the time of the interview.[34] Whereas racial experiences were sometimes described with less emotion by research participants, religious oppression seemed more often to strike a deeper emotional chord. Some research participants would laugh off racism—defanging it by calling it ignorance, or disregarding it entirely despite describing experiences that were at times quite unequivocally racist—but none used minimizing language when describing attacks they took as religious. In addition to their profundity, experiences of religious oppression also seem to be more lasting in their effect. Of research participants who described thinking about experiences of oppression after the fact, more said they thought about religious incidents than racial ones; this indicates that the religious experiences caused the research participants to reflect on their identity, a step in the process of identity development.

For those who participated in an ethnoreligious community, religious oppression struck at the very social pillar around which their "weekend" communities were built, and therefore rang as a rejection not only of them as individual religious minorities but of the community of which they were a part. This was particularly true of those experiences that were had in college and the adult years. Collegiate experiences of religious oppression, although no more or less frequent than attacks during other life periods, had a particularly profound effect on these second-generation Indian Americans' self-image. In a way they had not as children, adolescent and collegiate research participants offered a clear sense that their experiences with religious oppression were important because they dealt with God, the spiritual, and the transcendent.[35] During childhood, the research participants were more likely to take religious oppression as an undifferentiated experience of being different from their white, Christian peers.[36]

Feeling excluded or targeted for religious reasons is qualitatively different from feeling discriminated against racially or feeling different because of cuisine or other dimensions of culture. Over the course of her interview, Anisa described feeling isolated and looked down upon by her classmates during their "constant" discussions in school about going to church. Anisa also described feeling isolated because she was not invited to parties or, if invited, was not allowed to attend by her parents. Her descriptions of these two types of experiences were qualitatively different in language and affect. Religious isolation and discrimination simply cut deeper. The difference may lie in religion's evocation of and relationship to the transcendent, to a God-figure (or figures), or in the way that relationship is valued and acted out by the second generation's familial role models. Religion, in Anisa's words, "is the thing your parents and other people you respect hold so true, and you believe it too because that's what you've been exposed to."

Whatever the research participants actually believe (or disbelieve) theologically, and whatever they know (or do not know) about their religion's history, traditions, and rituals, they have an understanding of and connection to religion as something sacred and particularly personal. Again, this is lived religion—and lived religion for the research participants was qualitatively different from lived race, lived culture, or the lived experience of any other element of their ethnic identity. When Aziz, a Muslim, remarked that "religious bonds are stronger than cultural bonds," or when Anand, an atheist raised by Hindu parents, said that "religion is personal," they were expressing a sentiment that could also be heard in the voices of many other research participants. The impact of religious oppression takes on religious dimensions, arising from the belief in religion as something especially profound and eternal. Religious oppression caused many research participants to learn more about and identify more closely with their home religion, magnifying religion's role as a factor in the overall experience of ethnic identity development and in some cases even increasing the likelihood that the research participant will identify as "religious" and engage in worship, ritual, and religious study in adulthood.

It is for this reason that we must continue and develop the scholarship that examines religion's role, and religious oppression's role, in ethnic identity development; as part of this effort, we must as much as possible separate religious oppression from other forms of oppression in order to understand it. By arguing religion's uniqueness, I am not at all trying to distance Indian American Hindus, Muslims, and Sikhs from seeing and responding to the implications of racial discrimination. My main interest here is to show that discrimination based on religion is a uniquely formidable force in the ethnic identity development process for second-generation Indian Americans. The implications of this for the fields of ethnic studies and sociology are striking: We must stop ignoring religion or treating it as a cultural relic, as an immigrant tool, or as merely nostalgia. The implications for school policy are even more profound. We must begin by recognizing that religion is always, has always been, and will always be in American schools. It exists there through Christian privilege, religious harassment (peer-on-peer and teacher-on-student), and in the very structure of the school week and school year. We must develop culturally relevant pedagogy that sees to it that Christianity is joined in the classroom by Hinduism, Sikhism and Islam, and that teachers and administrators are trained to deal with religious teasing as swiftly and surely as they would racial violence.

6

Case Studies

What follows are three case studies. As described in the Introduction, these case studies are for the reader's use in applying and interpreting the material in the first five chapters of the book. Each one presents the experiences of a single research participant across his or her lifespan to date, drawing heavily on the individual's own voice. The reader should bear in mind that the interview was not contemporaneous with the incidents described. Rather, the research participant's viewpoint is retrospective; it is the view of the research participant at the particular moment of the interview.

Questions to Consider

1. Neha and Salim described being aware and resentful of Christian teachers' injection of their religious beliefs into the classroom. What explains the divergent paths each has taken in adulthood with respect to his or her home religion?

2. Consider Binu's experience in high school as compared to Salim's—what explains the differing outcomes for their ethnic and religious identities?

Binu

Binu, a female Catholic, was born in Metro Atlanta and has spent her entire life there, with the exception of one year of graduate school in Tennessee. Her parents, Malayali Catholics, emigrated from Kerala and arrived in the United States in 1973, before she was born.[1] Her family, like many other Malayali Catholic families immigrated after the passage of the 1965 Immigration and Naturalization Act; Binu's mother was part of the large number of nurses hired from India (particularly from southern India) and other countries. She arrived first and later sponsored the rest of her family. Binu's father worked for an airline company.

Binu is the elder child and has one brother. She described growing up in a middle-class neighborhood that was predominantly white. She described her private Catholic school K–12 experience in much the same way, adding that there were "a few blacks." Everyone at her school was Catholic, as the school only began admitting non-Catholics during her senior year of high school. She attended a historically black women's college for one year, then transferred to an urban commuter university. Immediately after finishing her undergraduate studies, she enrolled in a one-year program and earned her Master of Public Health degree. When she was interviewed, she was working for a health insurance company and was making preparations for her upcoming wedding.

Growing up, Binu attended Mass every Sunday at a local Malayali Catholic church. In college, once a month she attended Mass at the same Malayali church she attended growing up. She and her family have been very involved with the Malayali Catholic community in her town. Binu grew up identifying very strongly with being Malyali (an Indian regional identity, centered in the state of Kerala, which has the highest concentration of Christians, mostly Catholics, in India); she spoke the language at home and traveled almost yearly "back to Kerala."

Binu's Experiences in K–12

Binu attended Catholic schools for all of her K–12 education. She reported having both African American and Caucasian friends at school, adding that she never felt "shunned or anything," but that she became "aware of differentness from my Caucasian friends" in the third and forth grade. She said she didn't feel different from her classmates, but also recalled noticing differences between herself and her classmates. She was very surprised when her classmates asked her questions about India, *saris*, or *bindis*: "That made me realize . . . I always thought everyone knew about that kind of stuff. . . . I just assumed everyone knew." There was only one time, in fifth grade, that she was taunted by classmates because of her ethnic differences: "At one point with their curiosity and everything, they would make fun of Indian women, like they would say 'why don't you wear your *bindi*,' or something." Despite the few taunts, she said, she felt love and admiration for Indian culture while growing up. She did not recall ever being embarrassed or wanting to shun Indian culture during her K–12 years. "I never minded wearing *salvars*. I would wear them to Indian parties and was fine with it, like even if afterwards some of us went to the mall or whatever. I didn't mind. I was not self-conscious of it or anything."

Binu said she always felt connected to her Indian heritage. All throughout her elementary and secondary education, she traveled to India. She said that her

> trips back to India were big. That really helped. My father worked for the airlines, so that helped because we got to go everywhere for free. Staying there for a month or two really helped. . . . I have always been close my

Indian heritage. I have been going back to India every two years. So I have been back a lot. The language is spoken at home, Malayalam. I have always been closed my culture and traditions, even as far as the foods I eat. And we are a very close-knit family. So I think all of that has led me to be Indian and to say proudly that I am Indian. I have never wanted to deny being Indian. Even during those fourth- and fifth-grade periods when people were making fun of me and things, I never, never denied it.

Although proud to be Indian, Binu, like most adolescents, had conflicts with parents because her parents would not let her go spend the night at the home of some of her non-Malayali friends or even hang out at the mall. "Like a lot of my friends would invite me over for 'spend-the-nights' and I was never allowed to go. Like even in seventh or eighth grade, I was not always allowed to go to the malls with my friends. I could spend the night at my Malayali friends' houses. (I did not have any north Indian friends at the time.) . . . That was not a problem. But it was not allowed at my American friends' houses."

Although popular among her peers, she often felt different because of the conflicts with her parents. She developed a very strong relationship with one of her teachers, which really helped her.

A key person was the religion teacher back in high school, and we formed an extremely close bond come tenth grade. I mean she was almost like a second mother to me. . . . I would tell her the struggles and, you know, things that I would not be allowed to do, and she never said anything bad about my parents. She would just sit and understand. She would just listen. But I think that—and that was back at high school, and it just felt good to talk to someone about, you know, not being able to go to homecoming or not being able to go out or not being able to go to parties. She was an older woman. . . .

Although Catholicism was addressed in school, Binu does not "ever remember learning about Catholicism in India or Catholicism in Africa. . . . We had one course that was like Christianity in the World . . . but I don't think specifically that it was ever mentioned that there were Catholics in India." Binu was involved with many extracurricular activities in high school, including some religious activities where the students went on retreats. Binu was encouraged to share her experiences of being Indian and being Catholic at these retreats.

There was a lot of religious activities in high school that I was involved in, . . . we had these religious retreats for the weekends, so I would always go and speak at these retreats and I would talk about would be basically the struggles of growing up Indian and being Catholic, as well . . . I don't know how much these Caucasian kids understood, you know, because I would really be talking from the heart. But I found later . . . at the end of the retreat, they would write me letters and that kind of stuff and I really found they were very impressed, you know, that I was here as an Indian living in America . . . and really trying to keep a close tie between both cultures and being very interested in both cultures. So, I think that helped me a lot, too.

She also had opportunities to express herself culturally at school within the school-day structure. As she got older, she and the few other Malayali Catholics at her school "were always trying to promote Indian things in high school. We had an India day for two years in a row. We brought food and I did a dance at school." She said she was "friends with the popular crowd. I used my difference to my advantage. I was in pageants and doing modeling. I was never shunned in high school."

Although Binu reported experiencing no discrimination, she said that her parents faced discrimination in their workplaces and they discussed the matters with her. They would also ask her if she had faced any discrimination in school. "I think my parents did [face discrimination] because of their accents. I think they both have in that manner. I remember my mom telling me stories about the workplace. She would tell me that they assumed she would be doing more work than other people. And with my father same kind of thing. . . . They would ask me if anything like that had ever happened in school."

Binu's ethnoreligious community was a Malayali Catholic community, and it was not until her last two years of high school and going into college that Binu realized she was different from most other Indians in terms of the interaction of her religion and her ethnicity. For her, being Malayali is her ethnic identity. "Everything comes back to junior year . . . because then I was having to explain my practices, or I was having to explain parts of my Mass, or I was having to explain the reasons for Communion or, or whatnot because my Indian friends would ask me. But all, up until that point, I, it was just something that was always done. I understood, of course, but I had never had to tell other people about it."

College

Binu attended a historically black women's college for one year, during which she had an Indian Muslim roommate. After the year, she transferred to an urban commuter university. In college, Binu said she identified as Indian, though she quickly added that this depended on who asked the question and what they were asking. Although she had formed friendships with north Indians during her last few years of high school, college was the first time that Binu spent time with non-Catholics, immersing herself in a non-Catholic "north Indian" community.

Being Catholic I never had a problem, I mean I knew there were other Indians, Hindus and Muslims, it never really hit me until college, because

I had always been in a Catholic atmosphere up until that point. So as a freshman in college, my roommate was a Muslim girl and that was the first time that it really hit me, like oh my goodness people are really shocked when they hear that I am Christian. They just have never comprehended the fact that there are Indians who are Christian. We had numerous discussions. . . . I had never been so close to someone who was not Catholic. Like all my friends are Catholics. . . . At school it was 100 percent Catholic. . . . And so that was very different. It was really me getting used to the fact that I was Christian. I mean I always wear a cross and Indian people would always ask me why I am wearing a cross.

Binu stated that her knowledge of Catholic tenets and rituals increased during college:

I think my level of knowledge increased because that's when I had to use it. Um, in my grade school years, I have never had to use my religion, obviously because I was in Catholic schools. . . . I never really had to use my religion or my knowledge of my religion, until about junior/senior year when I started associating with other people who were not Catholic . . . and then I found that I was pulling stuff that I had learned . . . it was amazing. I actually then started being more aware of my Catholic, or Christianity because I was having to explain it.

Binu enjoyed being asked questions about being Indian and Catholic. "I loved it! I don't get offended . . . especially because I think there are so many ignorant people, American and Indians. I would just explain the whole history of St. Thomas coming to Kerala and to Goa and the Portuguese." However, she also reported that being asked these questions was one thing that made her feel that perhaps she is "less Indian" or more Caucasian.

[Late in college] is when I realized that being Catholic and being Indian is very different. I knew it was rare, but I guess I did not think that people thought it was really weird. Like my Hindu friends, the way they questioned me, not like in a maddening tone, but like the Christians came, the missionaries came and forcibly converted Indians and turned us Christian. None of my friends blamed me, but that was the feeling I got. I mean that is when I realized that is what the world thinks, that is what a lot of Indian people think. This is the feeling out there. But I would just go into my history thing and explain that this is not the way it happened. I mean I understand that that is a way a lot of Christianity was spread. But I truly believe that was just, I mean I know my forefathers were Hindu, I mean I know that is where my family comes from, but for as long we know, my family has just been Christian.

As an undergraduate, Binu said "most of my friends were Hindu or Muslim. I attended the Hindu functions, the Diwali and Holis. I did not have any Catholic friends at the time. I was not involved with Catholic things." However, she was involved with the practice of Catholicism.

> I think being religious meant having close communication with God. I felt it was important to pray. Like so many struggles, I would just sit there, not pray and pray, but talk to God. Aside from going to church on Sundays sometimes I would just go and go and sit there and meditate to myself. These are the things that are happening and I need help through them. And so many times He has shown me the light, so many times. It really kept me going back. It has really kept me strong as far as my Catholic faith is concerned. Like my roommate was Muslim, and she always prayed and so I always prayed. They have their religious, which is so much more, I guess, rigorous. It was so much more strict and I liked that. Our religion is, well, there are no set rules, like theirs was. I was really enthralled. I would always ask her about meanings and things. But I never thought about converting. Never! I was just very, very interested.

Binu commented, comparing religion in her life during college and religion in her life during high school. She said the way religion was present in her life "was almost the same. . . . The thing was in high school, I was in a Catholic atmosphere so it was much easier to teach, to practice, it was a lot easier. Everyday we started classes with prayer. I don't want to say I was more religious, because half the time it was kind of done for me, you know what I am saying? I had to pray at times. There was a stronger influence in high school." She described having the same amount of religiosity in college as she did in high school, although it was easier to practice in high school because she was in a Catholic atmosphere.

Toward her junior and senior year of college, Binu said, she grew closer to her Malayali heritage.

> As far as being Indian, in college I really got into my Kerala heritage. I had been into the Indian scene until my junior year and then I got back into my Malayali heritage. I was going to a lot of conferences at that point, like a lot of Keralite conferences and Catholic conventions. And of course there was, you know you heard your parents talking about marrying someone who is Malayali Catholic. I actually never really wanted to marry anyone out of my Catholic religion or out my Malayali heritage. So that was never a problem.

Although Binu was not involved with Catholic campus student organizations, she continued to attend mass every Sunday. For her being religious meant having "close communication with God." The third Sunday of every month she attended Mass at the same Malayali Catholic Church with her parents. She enjoys attending Mass with her parents. "I don't understand everything there, because it is the very high Malayalam they use in the church, but if they don't go too fast, I can get bits and pieces. I would still go. I thought it was very good because the church was done exactly how it is in Kerala."

Adulthood

Binu discussed how during her adult years her regional identity and language, which are interrelated, were somewhat less important to her than during the K–12 or college years. In adulthood, she identifies as Indian, and this identity continues to be situationally contextualized. "When the question is asked of me . . . , if they say, 'what are you?' I'll say I'm Indian. . . . If they say, 'where are you from?' I'll say I was born in Atlanta and then their later question will be, 'Where are you *originally* from?'"

For graduate school Binu left the metropolis she lived in and where she attended college, and spent a year in a "predominantly Caucasian town" attending graduate school. She described this stage of her life as difficult because of the lack of racial and ethnic diversity in the town where her graduate school was located. She felt different most of the time. "I mean, you would walk into a Wal-Mart [and] you could just instantly tell because there was just Caucasian mountain people. . . . Nobody said anything to me, of course, but you could just tell that kind of thing." Although feeling different became part of her life for that one year, she said that she did not experience any discrimination. "I don't know if I was self-conscious about it because I was an Indian person or . . . a colored . . . somebody different than a Caucasian walking into a place. I think I was self-conscious at that point . . . but I don't think anything that awful."

During this year she felt isolated religiously. She described this town as having only two Catholic churches, neither of which she felt comfortable attending. She did associate with other Catholic students on campus. "I joined the Catholic community [on campus]. They are a very small Catholic community and they had Mass in the basement of a house, which I went to religiously, every Sunday."

One of the things she discussed strongly are her reactions to the people she meets who have so many misconceptions about India and the traditions and cultures.

> If anybody says anything about Indians and if they have a misconception or any type of wrong perception of whatever it may be, arranged marriages are a very typical example, or poverty in India, I mean, obviously it's developing country, but I will also say that . . . India is a very intelligent country—I would always stick up [for India], all my life, I'd never say anything bad about it. I've never lied about it, I've just given them another side, regardless of what my opinions may be because I really think there's a lot of ignorance out there.

For Binu today, in adulthood, "Indian culture is being involved in the community, whether it be myself in the Indian community or whether it be the, you know, my north Indian community . . . to be involved in these functions that go on in our community." She feels that her community will play a vital role in the transmission of "Catholic processes and most definitely Malayali traditions and cultures" to her children. She wants to send her children to India and "try to keep the language in the house."

> As far as my kids, when my kids come along, I will definitely instill the Catholic processes and most definitely Malayali traditions and cultures and, you know, do the same thing my parents did . . . take me India as often as I can go, you know, try to keep the language in the house, speak the—just so they understand it. I mean, I don't speak it perfectly, but, you know, as long as they understand it, if that's possible. I—those are the things that I would, I would love to happen, you know, and, and definitely have them have Indian friends. . . . I think that's important, like surrounding yourself with, with your, with your own kind if it's—not just, um, friends—not to sound prejudiced, that may not be, but definitely so you can understand other people's cultures and traditions. I mean my world only opened up as a freshman in college, only because I understand their roots, you know, I was into the, you know, learning about Islam and Hinduism and that kind of thing, so, I definitely think that's important.

Binu continues today to struggle with an issue she first encountered in college with regard to her Catholic identity and being Indian. "I think I felt that Indians perceived Catholicism as a Caucasian religion and so they saw us as a Caucasian type of family or people, and I think I had massive problems with that." She is inviting many "north Indian" friends to her upcoming wedding. "They've never seen anything like it and I am like so thrilled. I've invited people back in college who I don't even talk to, Indian folks, a lot of north Indian kids, I've invited them to the wedding because they've never seen it and only because I want them to see it. . . . I invited them for the church ceremony, you know, I think I'm always trying to prove . . . I'm definitely trying to show that things are possible, like I'm different—I'm not only this Indian, and that's being different, but I'm Catholic, as well."

Discussion

Binu's life illustrates a variety of themes: (1) the ways in which Indian Americans interpret religion and relate it to culture and ethnicity; (2) situational identity and how an identity's being targeted (by both Indians and non-Indians) can lead to defensive reactions; (3) how an ethnic label's definition can change over time; (4) the competing concepts of authenticity in Indian America; (5) the role of transnational experiences in ethnoreligious maintenance; and (6) bicultural conflict.

WHAT "BEING RELIGIOUS" MEANS TO BINU. As a Catholic in a Catholic school, Binu did not have to think very much or work very hard to be Catholic. Everyone her family socialized with was Catholic. It was not until her late high school years and into college that she first socialized with Indian Americans who were not Catholic. It was then that her religion went from being a matter of course to being a matter of contention, attention, and reflection. During her college years, "being religious meant having close communication with God. . . . I did not have any Catholic friends at the time. I was not involved in Catholic things." The discussions that arose with her Hindu and Muslim friends caused her to reflect on the tenets of Catholicism as well as what the religion meant to her. Deep discussions of religion and faith are common during the college years, for reasons related to both the social environment and the cognitive development that occurs in late adolescence. For Binu, these interactions were particularly salient because of her religious minority status among coethnics. Binu was challenged to justify and defend Catholicism to people who, unlike her K–12 classmates, did not know its tenets and in some cases harbored hostility toward it because of their own adolescent experiences. Because she needed to respond to new questions and critiques, her knowledge of Catholicism increased and her sense of adherence and commitment to her faith became stronger as a result.

Binu's struggle with questions of values and principles is a facet of her broader process of identity development.[2] Religion's role in this process is often to offer explanations for existential issues and to provide a sense of connection to society and the religious group through rites and rituals. Religion connects the individual to a group that is imbued with particular importance by its connection to an eternal divine. Yet participation in and practice of worship can decline during the college years, as parental influences and family obligations are replaced with the relative social freedom of the college campus, and late-adolescent cognitive development may lead to doubts and questions regarding matters of faith. Being called to answer for her religion—to explain Catholicism's tenets and its history in India to skeptical coethnics—caused in Binu's religious identity to become more important to her.

The reader will by now have gathered that religion is very important to Binu. In actuality, her *ethnoreligion* is what matters most in her life. Just as Hindu and Muslim communities may form around and through participation in a temple or mosque community, Binu's Malayali Catholic church helps in the expression and maintenance of her ethnic identity. Recall that during college, Binu did not participate in mainstream Catholic organizations on campus; she went to Mass and returned to her home church—an hour's drive away—at least once a month. When she could only attend Mass with white congregants during her graduate-school year in Tennessee, both her tone and choice of words show that church that year was a distasteful obligation rather than the sought-after refuge it was when she worshiped with other Malayalis. Although ritual and the religious obligation of attendance were important enough to outweigh her distaste, her identity and the appeal of her faith was wrapped up in her ethnoreligion. As a Catholic, Binu allows us to isolate this distinction; Indian American Hindus, Sikhs, and Muslims have few houses of worship to choose from, of which most are ethnoreligious communities. Binu could have attend any of several Catholic churches near her college, and today could attend one of a multitude of mainstream Catholic churches in the Atlanta area. But she does not. Her story shows us that it is indeed the ethnic maintenance function of religion that resonates for many second-generation Indian Americans.

The reader might also see Binu as one of the most "religious" members of the research participant cohort: She wears a crucifix, attends Mass, and identifies strongly with Catholicism as a source of personal strength. But we should be careful not to fall into this easy trap of identifying religiosity. Binu attends Mass weekly because weekly attendance is part of Catholic (and, more broadly, Christian) tradition. If we evaluate religiosity on the basis of congregational practice, Christians and other adherents of the Abrahamic faiths—each of which has a weekly sabbath that incorporates, to a greater or lesser extent, and obligation of congregational participation—will probably come out ahead. Hindu traditions, such as the maintenance of a shrine in the home, the performance of private devotions, and mandir attendance performed on specific festival days rather than by a weekly schedule, do not lend themselves to such easy classification. Indeed, a major weakness of many public opinion polls is that they treat attendance as a proxy for religiosity by asking whether the respondent attended church "in the past week" or "in the past month." To accurately measure religiosity of non-Christians—and particularly followers of non-Abrahamic faiths—requires us to reconceptualize practice and participation.

SITUATIONAL ETHNICITY. During most of Binu's K–12 years, she identified as Indian. She was an ethnic and racial minority among coreligionists at her Catholic school. In this context, her Indianness—that is, the difference between her home culture, her parents' national origin, and her racial identity and those of her classmates—was the focal point of her otherness. Binu asserted her Indian identity, and identified as Indian at an all-Catholic school. Later in high school and throughout her college career, When in the company of young Indian Americans who were not Catholic, she came to use the ethnic identifier Malayali Catholic instead of Indian. The change of social surroundings resulted in a change of label, as Binu's religious identity became more salient than it had been before.

The scenarios above show how Binu exhibited situational ethnicity, both during K–12 and in college. Situational ethnicity is the shifting of identity based upon the social context which may include a range of factors such as local environment, the particular population present, individual interactions, and geographic location. For Binu, her social context changed when she encountered other Indians, and the resulting discoveries changed how she identified herself to others. Now it was her Catholicism that set her apart from her peers, who were mostly north Indian Hindus. This change in social context proved to be critical in terms of Binu's socialization process. Although it was now her Catholicism, not her Indianness, that marked her as different from the counter-group, she still remained ethnically self-aware as a result of her K–12 experience of differentness from other Catholic Americans. The Indian American elements of her identity did not disappear or become entirely irrelevant. Rather, in her own mind she went from being a *Malayali* Catholic to being a Malayali *Catholic*. Her religious identity became more salient—moved to the foreground of her self-image, if you will—because it came to represent the major line dividing her from her peers. It is not that her interaction with non-Catholics was unimportant to Binu before these critical incidents; Binu's identity as a pious and practicing Catholic seems always to have been important to her. But it became even more central to her identity when she found herself for the first time a religious minority within her Indian American youth subculture.

Both ethnicity and religion are very important to Binu, and she is clearly comfortable with and conversant in both identities; she can move one or the other to the fore quickly and easily. Under these circumstances, she emphasizes—to herself and others—the identity that becomes salient in a particular set of circumstances. Individuals like Binu who have two or more social identities that are each quite prominent are more likely to exhibit situational ethnicity often.

THE ETHNIC LABEL. As Binu's understanding of herself as an Indian changed, her usage of the term *Indian* changed. Until she encountered what she called "north Indians," the term *Indian* meant Malayali Catholic to her; her understanding that there were non-Malayali Catholic Indians in the world was at best academic. Once she befriended some "north Indian" youth and discovered the ways in which they saw themselves as more Indian than she, her definition of the term *Indian* came to mean north Indian Hindu. By adulthood, she is using the term Indian as shorthand for north Indian Hindu—and a contrast to her "Malayali heritage": "I had been into the Indian scene, until my junior year and then I got back into my Malayali heritage." This evolution of the term in Binu's life shows how situational ethnicity is not merely about moving between social worlds but also about how those worlds change one's identity. It also illustrates both the relative weakness of the ethnic identifier as a research tool, and the value of in-depth qualitative work.

During graduate school, geography prevented Binu from even sporadic access to a Malayali Catholic community. She worshiped with a white American Catholic population. Although she was self-aware as a brown-skinned person in an almost entirely white town, this reference to skin color was all she had to say about being Indian during that year of her life. This illustrates an essential consideration with respect to ethnicity which is foundational: In order to engage with a particularly identity, one must have a space in which to perform it. Religion did not become more important than ethnicity during Binu's graduate school year; it is more accurate to say that because of geographic limitations, she did not have the opportunity to perform the ethnic component of her ethnoreligious identity. Rather, being Malayali Catholic was still very important to her, but her situation was such that she could "only" be Catholic and not Malayali Catholic.

AUTHENTICITY. When Binu began socializing with north Indian youth during her junior year of high school, she hit a brick wall of sorts. She realized that she is not perceived as a "real" Indian because she is Catholic. Her Hindu peers, for whom Hinduism may have been the paradigmatic marker of Indianness, doubted Binu's Indian authenticity because she did not share a religious characteristic they considered essential to Indian identity. In Binu's world view, by contrast, to be Indian was to be a Malayali Catholic; Catholicism, not Hinduism, was an essential element of her ethnic identity. But her Catholicism made her less Indian to the north Indian Americans with whom she associated.

Until these interactions, Binu understood Hinduism and Islam to be part of an undifferentiated category of "other" Indian Americans. Because she'd never had any significant experiences or exposure to these Indian Americans, she had not considered whether there even existed any balance of Indianness—she didn't see herself as more Indian than non-Catholic Indians, nor was she aware that they might see her as less Indian. As a college freshman, she took a great interest in Islam and had many lengthy theological discussions with her Indian American Muslim roommate—"not that I was going to convert or anything." She initially enjoyed the questioning from Hindu and Muslim peers, but she became upset once she realized that the questions reflected not curiosity but doubt and skepticism. When she discovered that her religion raised questions about her ethnicity—the authenticity of her Indianness—in the eyes of other Indians, she experienced cognitive dissonance. She considered herself to be very Indian and therefore was confused as to why others would doubt her Indianness. She was compelled to think through her identity and her own definition of Indianness. Although Binu continued and continues to socialize with north Indians, she also continues to experience anguish over the fact that these friends see Catholicism as a "Caucasian religion."

Despite experiencing so much unfavorable attention directed at her religious identity, Binu continues to wear a visible marker of it: a crucifix pendant. The cross around her neck makes her stand out when in the company of Hindu coethnics. She expressed displeasure with feeling targeted by north Indians as less Indian or less authentic, yet she also chose to continue to wear her religious minority status literally around her neck.

This growth in the importance of Binu's identity as a Malayali Catholic is a result of some of the negative experiences associated with that identity during her college years. To this day, Binu is out to challenge her north Indian peers' belief that Hinduism is the only authentic Indian religion. Hence, she planned to invite "all [her] north Indian friends" to her Malayali Catholic wedding so they could see a thoroughly Indian ceremony—a Catholic ceremony.

Without passing judgment on whether there is a right or wrong answer to the question of whether Hindu, Muslim, or Christian Indian Americans are more or less authentic, it is worth considering the backdrop against which Binu's experiences occurred and which informed the viewpoints of her Hindu peers. To the extent that it has a mainstream, the Indian American community that has exploded in size since 1965 can be described as having an identifiable ethos reflective of India's dominant Hindu milieu. Indian American culture is hegemonically Hindu, in part because most Indian Americans are Hindu and in part because Indian Americans import the culture of the country of origin; India is a legally secular state that is in fact characterized by a pervasive and omnipresent Hindu hegemony. Indian American culture is also hegemonically north Indian; language data indicates that majority of Indian Americans trace their backgrounds to the northern states of India.[3] "Indian food" most often refers to north Indian, specifically Punjabi cuisine. When non-Indians speak of Indian holidays, they are most often referring to Hindu holidays. (Indeed, in all these respects, the relationship between Hinduism and legally secular India is similar to that between Christianity and the legally secular United States.) Hindi, officially a national language of India but fundamentally a north Indian language, is promulgated in the United States through Bollywood films, as is the Hindu ethos and imagery of the traditional Bollywood love story. Other examples abound. A notion of Indian culture heavy with Hinduism has thereby been transmitted to the second generation, and the effects of this conflated Indian American/Hindu-Hindi identity can be seen in Binu's experiences.

IMPACT OF TRANSNATIONAL EXPERIENCES. Binu also engages in some authenticity judgments of her own. For her, India is the place where the most authentic form of Malayali culture is practiced. She described enjoying Mass at her Malayali Catholic Church because she feels that the church was "doing it the right way, because that is what is done in Kerala." The "it" in that sentence is the act of worship. As a Malayali Catholic, Binu looks to how religious practice is done in India—specifically, in the state of Kerala—as an indicator of the authenticity of her religious practice. Like virtually all the research participants, of all religious backgrounds, Binu views religion as static and unchanging; hence, religious practice in India is the barometer of whether her community's religious practice is correct. Worshiping the "way . . . it is done in Kerala" provides Binu with those sensations most connected to religion: association with an historical continuity of faith and practice which in turn is a reflection of what God desires of the faithful. Binu believes that if the way to "get right with God" is to worship correctly, then tradition points the way to proper worship. She believes that as tradition is diluted or changed—that is, as it becomes less authentic—the faithful's relationship with God may become similarly diluted or changed. Binu was the only non-Hindu research participant to express these sentiments.

Understanding authenticity as the key to right worship illuminates why Binu sees her transnational experiences of travel to India as so important. By traveling to India almost every year, Binu connects again with everything she considers the source of her culture, faith, and religious practice. She develops a cumulative and continuing sense of connection to family, is exposed to the dimensions of culture, maintains her own facility with Malayalam, and is reexposed to "authentic" religious practice. Binu goes beyond what might be characterized as nostalgia for India—a yearning for the sights and smells of childhood holidays. Binu's sense of connection to India is magnified and renewed with each visit because she perceives a primordial link between her religious identity and the history and culture of Kerala.

LIVING IN MULTIPLE WORLDS. One of the largest sources of stress for immigrant and second-generation Indian American students is the bicultural conflict, a sensation of not fitting in on either side of the gap between home and school culture, and between "Indian" and "American" culture. Even as a Catholic in an all-Catholic school, Binu experienced bicultural conflict. Like all the research participants, Binu was growing up in the American context and attending American schools while living with Indian immigrant parents who are doing there best to create "little Keralas" in their home and communities and to shelter their children from certain American vices. Binu was not allowed to attend sleep-overs or parties at non-Indian friends' homes or to go to her school's homecoming dance. Because of her parents' rules—which she associated with her ethnic culture—she felt isolated from her non-Indian peers in school. The negative impact of a bicultural gap is often aggravated by the absence of any acknowledgment or understanding on the part of the socially dominant white peers, teachers, and school administrators of the difference between home and school culture. As India and Indian American culture go unacknowledged, the implication is that they are unimportant and that, by extension, the young person and her "issues" are not worthy of attention.

By early adolescence, Binu began building a wall between her home/weekend life and her day-to-day life in school—not an uncommon reaction among research participants. Binu never finished the wall, however, because of a factor that distinguishes Binu's experience from that of many other Indian Americans: She encountered a teacher in high school who asked about Binu's home culture. Binu confided in this teacher about these family disputes arising from the gap between Indian (home) and American culture. Through this "extremely close bond" with the high school teacher, Binu had an in-school outlet for her frustrations and a source for positive feedback from a member of her school's white majority. By taking an interest in Binu's life and providing that kind of outlet, the teacher sent a message that she cared about Binu and her culture and that Binu—ethnicity and all—was welcome at school. One of the most important characteristic students look for in their teachers was caring; having this connection diminished the overall negative impact of the bicultural gap.[4]

The support of her teacher and the opportunity to express her "Indian self" contributed to Binu's belief that her ethnic identity was welcomed at school. She was encouraged at in-school and extracurricular events to talk about her struggles. As she engaged in performances and presentations where she received positive attention for the Indian elements of her identity, her association of positive emotions with her ethnic identity grew exponentially. Validation of ethnic/cultural identity by outsiders (here, her school's non-Indian majority) can lead Indian American to take pride in their culture and heritage. The salience of a Binu's ethnic identity is affected by the opportunity to express it—to affirm and reaffirm it in arenas with social and emotional meaning to the individual (see Royce 1982). The outlet of school performances and summer camp speeches enabled Binu to express dimensions of her culture; this allowed her peers to have a better understanding of who she was, which in turn helped alleviate some of the stress Binu encountered due to the bicultural gap.

Binu has spent most of her life showing people—first non-Indian Catholics and later non-Catholic Indians—that being Catholic and being Indian are not mutually exclusive concepts. The need to constantly defend her ethnoreligious identity not only results in the increasing importance of this identity in her life but it also results in her sense of faith and religiosity growing even stronger. The numerous questions she fielded about being Catholic, along with the questioning of her authenticity (is she really Indian, if she is Catholic?), kept religion in the foreground of her life. To some nonquantifiable extent, this surely affected the degree to which she adheres to the tenets and obligations of her Catholic faith today.

After finishing graduate school, Binu promptly returned to the metropolitan area where she grew up and resumed her regular attendance at the Malayali Catholic church there. Community, although not essential for the practice of her religion as such, is for Binu the impetus to engage in practice and the thing that makes it enjoyable. As an adult and a newlywed (having married another Malayali Catholic), she identified another reason for her ties to her community: She believes community will help her transmit Malayali rituals, traditions, language, and other dimensions of culture to her children. For Binu, returning to her ethnoreligious community after college meant coming back to the core of what makes her Indian.

Questions to Consider

1. What does Binu's experience tell us about contemporary "standards" of Indianess?
2. How do the assumptions made by coethnics affect Binu's feelings about and expressions of her Catholicism?
3. Binu is on a mission to prove to her north Indian friends that Catholicism is as "Indian" as Hinduism. Will she ever succeed? Why or why not?

Neha

Neha is twenty-four years old. She was born in Dearborn, Michigan, to Indian Hindu parents who both emigrated from India. Her father arrived in the United States in 1970; her mother followed in 1973. Her parents were part of the first wave of Indian professionals immigrating after the passage of the 1965 Immigration and Naturalization Act. Her father, a physician, served on the faculty of various American medical schools and later went into private practice. Her mother is a "stay-at-home mom." Neha is the middle of three children, with an older sister and a younger brother. Her family moved several times during her toddler years, settling for a while in Birmingham, Alabama, the first place she remembers living. Neha's family lived in middle-class, semiurban areas; she attended public school until the end of sixth grade. At age thirteen her family moved to New Orleans, where her family lived in an "expensive" neighborhood and she attended a secular private school for grades 7–12. She described both schools as predominantly white with sizeable minority populations.

Neha began her undergraduate studies at a prestigious university in the Northeast, was not happy there, and moved on to another highly prestigious university in the Midwest. An economics major, she relished her studies and threw herself into academics. Three months after graduating from college, Neha returned to the Northeast for law school. She was preparing to graduate from law school at the time of her interview.

Neha's Experiences in K–12

Neha reported that during her K–12 years, she probably would have identified herself as Indian. In each community Neha lived in as a child, she said, her "parents would always join like the Indian American professional association—whatever it is called in your local city. There's always an association of Indian professionals, immigrants who came here." As a result, she said, "I always knew lots of Indian kids who—although they weren't at this specific school or class I was in—were in the same schools and the same neighborhood. That made it not seem like I was the only Indian kid in middle school or the only Indian kid in the city." However, Neha reported having few friends in the ethnoreligious community. Nor did she describe in detail any ethnoreligious function; the impression she gave was of a girl who was always present but rarely involved or interactive at ethnoreligious community events.

Neha did not "feel a connection to being Indian," but said she would have self-identified as Indian because she knew that was how "people would label me." Neha described in detail the numerous reasons why she was "not really Indian." She mentioned having some Indian friends, learning to cook the food, hearing from family in India, "but as far as something deeper, like a religious connection, I've never really had that. And I can barely understand Punjabi." All of her relatives in India "except for a couple of cousins" spoke only Punjabi, so when she traveled to India she couldn't communicate with many people. Neha's last trip to India took place when she was twelve.

Growing up, Neha recalled, she felt ethnically and racially different.

Down South is sort of interesting. Okay, I mean, quite frankly, the right word is people there are less trained in the politically correct phraseology. Like when I would go up North, people would say, 'Where are you from? What ethnicity are you?' People down South would say, 'What are you?' . . . I think I learned really early on that that didn't mean anything. It was just sort of odd, I remember, but some people were sort of interested because they could probably tell you weren't black, and they could tell you weren't white, but they weren't sure what you were.

In school, Neha experienced what she referred to as "the regular stuff." When Neha felt different growing up, it was generally in reaction to questions or statements from peers or teachers; unlike some other research participants, she did not report engaging in spontaneous contemplation of her differentness.

The experiences of feeling different that Neha remembers most distinctly from the K–12 life period relate to religion rather than to her racial or cultural minority status. When pressed for more details about when and how she felt different as a child, Neha described experiences where she felt targeted in school not because of her ethnicity or skin color but because of her religion: "In elementary school, some teachers had a more Christian emphasis. some of them would talk about that in class, but I didn't really pay any attention to it or really understand it much. . . . I just blocked out the teacher for ten minutes and then I'd listen again. . . . I would never complain about it but I was really opinionated. I would just [say to myself] 'I don't think this is appropriate and you shouldn't be talking to us about this, so I'm just going to block you out for ten or fifteen minutes.'" She described Christianity as playing a constant but unspoken role in the classroom. "It's not like we prayed or anything in class but we would talk about things like values in general, or whatever, and the teacher would some-times, in that context, mention Christianity or Christ and I was just like, 'what-ever,' and I just blocked it out because I thought that was just silly."

Even though Neha felt different racially, ethnically, and religiously, she said she never wished that she was not Indian and never tried to deny her Indian-ness. Although she mentioned a few occasions when she was teased for being Indian and briefly thought she wanted to be white, she stated clearly that she "never wished I had blonde hair like a Barbie. There's this white ideal of beauty and you play with white dolls and you want to have paler skin, but I never like felt like any of that. I never even regretted being as tan as I was or wanted to be lighter." However, Neha said she was affected by "Indian beauty ideals"—the im-ages and standards of beauty conveyed in Bollywood films. She felt pressure from the Indian American community to conform to these beauty standards. "When I was little, like there was a lot of pressure to have straight hair, but that was oddly all internal to the Indian community because you know when like you watch the Indian movies, the women all have uniform, stick-straight hair. . . . I remember when I was younger, I felt sort of bad. It was like, 'oh, I wish I had straighter hair like my sister or my mom.' . . . But that was all like internal to the family, not necessarily [from] outside, from the white community."

College

During her college years, Neha said, she identified herself as "Indian American." Neha explained that one of the reasons for the shift in her identity—from Indian to Indian American—was to differentiate herself from the Indian students from India. There were many international students at her university, and "if I said [I was] Indian, people would think I was one of them."

College was "the first time I felt somewhat self-conscious about" being In-dian, Neha remarked. She said she felt a lot of pressure to join the campus In-dian American association and attend the events, but that she resisted that kind of "grouping by skin color or race." Neha expressed the clear, strongly felt and unabashed opinion that some reasons to get together are good and others are not. She felt religion was a good reason to gather as a group, but that culture and race were not. Because of this philosophical objection, she did not attend such functions. Despite her view that religion is an appropriate characteristic around which a group might coalesce, and that culture is not, she also remarked that she probably still wouldn't have gone to the events even if they had been based on the Hindu religion.

> To say you're a part of culture means a fundamental commitment; it means you seriously take the beliefs about culture seriously, and follow the religion and actually live it, not just go to cultural fairs or wear the clothes or cook the food. . . . I wasn't Hindu. . . . I probably still wouldn't have gone, but I think what really made me resist was the idea of there's some sort of pressure or some sort of group identity aspect and I just didn't like the tone of it. . . . I probably wouldn't have gone because I just felt that if I'm not Hindu, I really don't have the connection, so there's no legitimate reason to get together based on group.

In remarking that the she wasn't Hindu, Neha expressed a sentiment that she clarified more in discussing her adult identity: that she was "born Hindu" but does not consider herself at all religious.

Neha said her undergraduate academic coursework had a significant impact on her thinking about culture and religion. Majoring in economics, she came to define herself—and, indeed, to think about concepts of identity—in terms of individual achievements: "It's all about your own accomplishments and your own thoughts; other people don't have that much to do with it." She identifies as an individualist, which she believes separates her from Indian culture, something she sees as more "collectivistic." "I've just always sort of had the idea, which carried over into college and law school, that as an individual you're not defined by background or region, like Southern or Northern, or like Indian or American, or things like that, but the ideas you chose to adopt and the belief system you choose." Starting from this individualistic philosophy, Neha identifies herself as a 'Western' thinker—drawing what seemed to her like another line between her personal identity and the culture of her birth: "As far as a commitment to a mode of thought, I've been much more Western than Eastern, much more American than Indian in that regard." During college and since, Neha says what matters most about any individual is his or her ideas. Other traits are unimportant by comparison: "And you don't evaluate the way it was said, you evaluate the substance. . . . I just thought that was such a wonderful not looking at gender or race or even presentation, but were so looking for the substance of what someone said."

"In college, Neha thought it would be beneficial for her to take classes to learn more about India and "Indian things." She said that taking an Indian philosophy course solidified her self-image as a Western thinker and that she didn't feel a connection to Indian thinking. Rationality outside of religion is "a hallmark of Western civilization," with which Neha identified herself very strongly. She consistently used the pronoun "we" when speaking of Western thought and individualism; she did not always do so when speaking of her Indian tradition.

Adulthood

When asked to identify herself as an adult, Neha says, "My parents emigrated from India but I was born and raised here." Her family is important in her life today, though she rarely discussed them. Interestingly, she reports giving "a lot of thought" to religion. As "a real individualist," her religious choice is "nonpracticing." However, she identifies as Hindu because, she says, she believes in God:

> I believe in God. I don't practice any religion 'cause I wasn't really raised with one. I also don't like the sort of weird pattern of people our age mixing and matching religions to their own convenience, which I'm somewhat guilty of 'cause I'm not following any established religion, which I feel very bad about. But I don't like the idea of [approaching religion with a thought process like], "I find it convenient to believe in reincarnation because I think that's fun so I'm going to take a little bit of that, and I think I don't like to believe in a wrathful God, so I'm not going to believe in that." . . . Religion is not something convenient—it's not like Santa Claus, it's not [just meant] to make you feel good through the day. . . . I believe in God, I do believe in God, but I haven't committed to any religion.

Neha continues to put a premium on the idea that as an individual one should be defined not by background—the "ideas and modes of thought you're raised with"—but instead by "the ideas you adopt and the belief system you chose." "I mean, part of it's probably being raised in America where if you have a more traditional education. . . . The American value system, like what the government is founded on, is a very individualistic conception. I guess when I learned it as a kid, I took it somewhat seriously and I just sort of ran with it."

Neha describes her ethnicity as not "an issue" for her day-to-day life, but takes notice of her ethnicity when people bring it up. On this topic, she discussed several experiences around some of her extracurricular involvements as well as her process of finding a job. She is the president of her law school's chapter of a politically conservative organization of lawyers and law students. She is the only nonwhite in the organization and is surprised by the number of people who comment about her being a women of color present and active in a conservative organization. "I go to all the events, obviously. . . . I actually don't feel self-conscious about it there at all or I don't really notice it, I mean, even though I'll usually be the only minority woman . . . but I sort of feel like conservative students here are pointed out to me sometimes—it sort of takes me by surprise because I really don't think of it that way." She also expressed annoyance at comments she heard from her classmates when she received job offers from prestigious law firms:

> There's been comments. . . . There have been conservatives and liberals who say, "It's different for you to get like law firm job offer because you're a minority woman" or "it's different for you, like you have the advantage of being a minority woman when you applied for your clerkship," or whatever. . . . I oppose affirmative action . . . [and although] we have this bad program out there, that doesn't excuse you being a moron. Like, it's just a very stupid reaction, like even if you feel some people don't deserve to be in X place because of affirmative action doesn't mean everyone [who is nonwhite] is there because of it, and I feel like it's rather an ignorant way to live life to let other people to, to make— you know, like to react to a bad program by becoming even more ignorant and stupid.

Neha believes affirmative action is not needed. As proof, she points out that she believes she "got everything [she] wanted"—getting into the colleges, law school, and the law firm of her choice—without the benefit of affirmative action. She said about her father, a physician on a medical school faculty, reported facing discrimination for being Indian at his workplace; he thought he was discriminated against and denied a promotion because he was Indian. Neha's response was "I was just like, 'You really don't believe that, [do you?]'" She believed her father was exaggerating his situation at work because "if you looked at the staff at [the university hospital], there were so many Asians who were heads of the department that I don't think it was a direct result." Although she vigorously challenged her father's perception that he had been discriminated against, she also stated: "I guess I wouldn't have any way of knowing. I mean, how can you tell? Like, I got into every college I applied [to]. I got into every law school. I got the firm job I wanted, so as far as any sort of indication [of discrimination, there has been] none that I really know of."

Discussion

Neha's perspectives illustrate one response to the experiences of growing up Indian in America. For Neha, these experiences led her away from an identity heavily influenced by ethnic factors and toward more identification with aspects of the dominant (white, American) society. Neha subscribes to white American norms, values, and standards, many of them based on Christian ideals or the philosophies of the European Enlightenment. She identifies Indian culture with modes of thought she sees as archaic and ineffective. Although she acknowledges her status as a minority woman, she denies that this status has had any meaningful effect on her life. According to Neha, language and religion are the two most important components of Indian culture. Her lack of Punjabi language skills, combined with her thoughts on Hinduism and religion in general, allows us to understand the reasons behind her ethnic identity and its orientation toward dominant white society.

ETHNIC IDENTIFICATIONS AND MEANINGS. One of the ways to understand Neha's ethnic identity shift is see the change in her use of ethnic identifiers. Although an ethnic label by itself may not provide much meaning because the same label can have different meanings for different people, the label can provide a window on how the identity development process unfolds when illuminated by more detailed qualitative data from the interview (Hurtado, Gurin, and Peng 1997). Ethnic labels are both imperfect (with the potential to be defined differently by each individual) and superficial (with brevity that limits the depth of their meaning) as analytical tools, but they can at times be useful as indicators of an individual's ethnic orientation. During her K–12 years, Neha believes she would have identified as Indian. Here she identifies herself with a label that shows the major socialization influences of parents and ethnoreligious community (Barth 1969; Stephan and Stephan 2000). The K–12 period is a life stage when individuals are more likely to define and understand themselves by reference to that which is most immediately around them: their parents and family, the food they eat, the people they socialize with, and so forth. Neha also "didn't feel like the only Indian kid in the city" during this period; she was exposed to other Indian Americans young people during her K–12 years, although she made it clear that her participation in ethnoreligious community events was not something she would have chosen to do but for her parents' insistence. In addition to being Indian because of who and what she saw in her immediate surroundings, she compared herself and those surroundings to the white- and Christian-dominated context of her other social world: school, where Neha was often the only Indian American in the classroom and where even schoolwide she saw few other Indian Americans. Even though she reported few specific incidents of racial (as compared to religious) discrimination, being the only student brown skinned in the classroom surely made her aware that others would see her as Indian.

Having grown up around relatively few Indian Americans, Neha became self-conscious with respect to her ethnicity and race when she encountered a more populous and more visible Indian American population in college—one that included different "types of Indians" from those she'd known as a child. Neha's self-ascribed label of Indian American during college shows her efforts to separate herself from the international students from India. She may also have seen it as a way to separate herself from those second-generation Indian Americans around her who immersed themselves in the ethnic student organization. The social context of high school developed in Neha a habit of downplaying in her own mind the fact that she was racially, ethnically, and religiously different from her peers. Her collegiate experiences caused her to maintain this orientation. College students' reports of ethnic identity often match not their report of their parent's background but their own feelings of identity. They "overemphasize" groups with which they identify and "underemphasize" groups with they do not identify. Having an American facet to her identity, even as she realized that she was seen as Indian, was important to her; including the word "American" was, to Neha, a way to combat situations where she was misidentified.

Her movement from a nominally ethnic orientation toward a long-considered and intricately conceived dominant orientation continues into the present day. If pressed to answer the question "What are you?" Neha now responds, "My parents emigrated from India, but I was born and raised here." Neha has come to define "Indian" to mean from India. By extension, being born here gives her ownership in the American ideal as she understands it: individualism, opportunity, and the chance not to be defined by her background. Her wordy ethnic label shows her continuing movement away from an ethnic orientation and attachment to Indian culture and toward an individualistic orientation consistent with her personal philosophy and ambition.

There are a number of factors that may have contributed to this shift, including her lack of connection to the two attributes—language and religion—she sees as the essential elements of her family's Indian culture. We can also see in Neha's thinking the adult echoes of a childhood desire to fit in with mainstream society; her attachment to Enlightenment thinking and scholarship in economics and American law; and her relative disregard of race or ethnicity as a reason for grouping people or as an explanation for who she is or what she has achieved.

INDIAN CULTURE IS . . . . Neha saw two key factors as legitimate sources and expressions of her parents' Indian "culture": the Punjabi language and the Hindu religion. Her identification of these two factors is consistent with responses of other research participants in the study. They are the two factors that reflect communication and common ground among many Indian American coethnics. Respectively, they represent the ability to share ideas and the experience of worshiping together and sharing a commonly understood belief system.

In Neha's case, of course, the identification of these factors is also ironic: The very factors she identifies as the most essential to an ethnic identity separate her from such an identity. Neha never learned to speak Punjabi, although she says she understands it; she spoke English at home with her parents. And although she attended Hindu Sunday school on two brief occasions, she does not subscribe to Hinduism as a belief system (although she does "believe in God"). Invoking language and religion as her key markers of ethnic identity causes—perhaps allows—Neha to conclude that she is *not* "really Indian." Maybe she even chose these factors because they are the two with which she is least able to connect; this would be consistent with her rejectionist stance toward Indian ethnic identity. But whatever her motive, Neha's selection of these two factors is consistent with what we know about ethnic identity development.

Likewise, Neha's most recent transnational experience was a trip to India more than fifteen years ago, when she was forced by her parents to go. At that time, she found herself unable to communicate with most members of her extended family. Speaking the home language and traveling to India are a mutually supporting pair of experiences, each reinforcing and adding value to the other. Having home-language speaking skills is a critical element in creating and fostering relationships with family in India, and thereby of generating positive associations with transnational experiences. In turn, frequency of travel to the home country—by definition an immersion experience of language learning—supported the development of language skills.

Neha's lack of relationships with family in India is both cause and effect of the fact that she has not been to India since the age of twelve. In younger years, children do not have the choice to go to India or not to go—that choice is the parents'. But it is during these trips that second-generation Indian Americans form transnational relationships with cousins and other family members that often become a major reason for voluntary return trips to India in later life. In Neha's case, the lack of language skills, exacerbated by an overall lack of travel to India, are part of a cycle of disconnection that continues to discourage her from returning to India. This causal connection between language loss and transnational ties is consistent with data from other research participants in this study.

Neha also identifies religion as centrally important to her idea of Indianness. Although she also described occasionally feeling connected to Indian culture through dimensions of culture such as eating Indian food and hearing the Punjabi language spoken around her, all but religion are "superficial" to her. She also does not see herself as religious, attributing her lack of attachment to not knowing much about Hinduism—a characteristic that is also both cause and effect of her continuing disconnection from Indian American communities at every life stage. Although she attended functions, she did not understand the prayers and rituals and found it boring when adults attempted to explain them. Celebrating holidays was fun, but she never understood the religious significance of the day. Not understanding the prayers, and not wishing to learn about the rituals—or, in some cases she described, considering her parents' explanations unsatisfactory—contributed to her lack of identity with Hinduism. In identifying religion as a legitimate manifestation of and connection to Indian culture, she shows that she believes there is the possibility of deeper, more meaningful connection—but that a sense of connection to the religion is something she never developed. Having now come to define herself by reference to Western mores of individualism and personal achievement, and expressly rejecting Hinduism and Indian culture as undesirably "collectivistic," religiosity is a characteristic she is not likely to develop in the future.

With reference to other ethnic groups, some have speculated that the second and subsequent generations may become less religious over time.[5] In the case of an Indian American, Neha, these speculations are borne out and the causes of Neha's turn away from Hinduism can be identified. They relate to language loss and a lack of understanding of Hinduism's rituals and traditions themselves. Not understanding Hinduism is one of the reasons that ultimately led her to not identify with Hinduism.

Neha's lack of understanding of the elements of Hinduism despite her childhood exposure to them is coupled with a view of religion as static. This view of religion is consistent both with the manner in which the home religion was often practiced and taught by the research participants' parents and with the simplified and rule-oriented Christianity many were exposed to as part of their upbringing in the United States. Neha's Christian public school teachers probably espoused a view of Christianity as hidebound as Neha's view of Hinduism. For Neha, this view of religion as unchanging and dogmatic results in an absolutist approach to religion; she feels it is better to accept or reject the entire package than to adopt "bits and pieces" to suit one's conveniences, hopes, and fears.

Neha's all-or-nothing approach to religion also becomes a sort of ammunition against her coreligionists. She criticizes Hindus—particularly those in the collegiate Indian American organizations she disdains—for picking and choosing the convenient or comfortable elements of the faith. Perhaps taking a cue from the dogmatic Christians she encountered in childhood, Neha considered those Hindus who choose to follow some but not all tenets of the religion as she understands it to be hypocrites. Her view also reflects another common theme among research participants: All second-generation Indian American Hindus in the study understood the Hinduism of their childhood and the manners of practice they observed in their family members to be the definitive Hinduism; in criticizing her coreligionists, Neha may also have been exhibiting a failure to recognize the diversity of Hindu practice and mores. At the same time, she is manifesting her own version of the critical lens society directs at Hinduism, comparing Hinduism to a Christian/Western norm she considers inherently worthy.

When asked, Neha continues to proclaim a belief in God, a fact that itself demonstrates that religion and the idea of faith continue to play a role in her life even today. However, the disconnection reigns; moreover, this disconnection from her home religion has developed beyond mere uninformed agnosticism. Neha has found an alternative worldview in the American civil religion of individualism. She rejects Hinduism and Indian culture as such because they are too "collectivistic" in their philosophical approach to human affairs. She cannot fit them into a Christian box—the Western, monotheistic norm that defines in her mind that which is worthy. Hinduism is unsophisticated by comparison. Yet it is also the religion of her childhood. Her sense of disconnection from the religion, and her essential association of it with Indian culture, combine to generate her sense of disconnection from the entire image of Indianness as she understands it.

INDIVIDUALISM. As a child, Neha had the opportunity to develop friendship with coethnic peers; she "knew lots of Indian kids" because her "parents would always join" the local ethnoreligious organization. Yet her description of her Indian community is remarkably sterile. She describes being in the company of coethnics when she was growing up, but she never describes these other young Indian Americans as her friends. She mentions that her parents were involved with local Indian American associations, but never described herself as part of a community; indeed, she never described community functions at all. She never even used the word *we* when describing an ethnoreligious function.

Neha's sense of distance from Indian culture—which continued to grow during her college period—became the lens through which she critically assesses the behavior of her coethnics. In college, Neha believed the Indian students' organization on campus to be an artifice built on skin color and a few cultural characteristics. She considers Indian culture and brown skin to be inappropriate reasons for group formation. Indeed, these were the characteristics that Neha had come to downplay in her own relations with non-Indians during K–12 and college. Although this is consistent with her view of religion as the paramount legitimate basis for social group formation, note that in the next breath she adds that she probably would not participate in the Indian American campus organization even if they were based on religion. Giving Neha the benefit of the doubt, one could point out that she felt no particular connection to Hinduism, and that whatever connection she did feel grew more tenuous as her college studies exposed her to Enlightenment thinking. One could also see Neha as simply a rejectionist, someone who avoids association with coethnics for reasons unconnected to her explanations; taking this view, her ascription of cultural rather than religious characteristics to the Indian American students' organization is mere excuse-making. Whichever viewpoint is correct, the level of significance Neha gives religion as part of Indian culture coupled with the fact that she does not identify with Hinduism as a belief system can be one of the components of her distancing mechanism from her Indian ethnicity that develops and takes shape through her life.

The one time Neha felt a desire to look or be different—when she wished she had straighter hair and fairer skin—she blamed not the dominant American culture but Indian culture's fixation on skin tone and straight hair, as expressed in Bollywood movies and by her own family. To be sure, there is an Indian beauty myth which is conveyed unceasingly by Bollywood: the image of the straight-haired, fair-skinned beauty with the aqualine features. As the availability and popularity of Bollywood films in the United States has increased in recent decades, these images have begun to have a profound effect on young women in particular. The films were a large part of the socialization process for those who watched them. They provided insight on the norms, beliefs, and values of what was accepted, rejected, and considered ideal. The notion of beauty was effectively conveyed in the films—but in a way that was positive for some and negative for others. But as critics point out, the Bollywood image of beauty is itself a product of India's contact with the West—that is, with the Euro-American beauty standard. Neha won't engage with such critiques; she denies that her occasional wish to look different bears any relation to "looking like Barbie." Instead, when she feels appearance-related pressure from her family the blame is directed at people and ideas that are Indian. So, her home culture is again identified as the source of her displeasure, and her "Western" worldview is preserved.

As a result of her academic course work, Neha came to the conclusion that she was "more comfortable with Western thought than Eastern thought." This too has had an impact on her sense of connection to her Hindu religion. Although she describes herself as "not atheist," she says she is only "Hindu because [she] was born in it." She won't actively reject the religion—for example, she implied that if her mother wants her to attend and participate in a puja she will—but her coursework helped her confirm the alienation she already felt toward Hinduism. Instead, she is drawn to those philosophies of the European Enlightenment that inform America's civil religion and its creation myths.

She has developed this mindset in part by absorbing the dominant ideology that privileges Western thought and Christianity over Eastern thought and Hinduism. She admires Western economists and philosophers whose teachings strongly reinforce her early ideas of "doing your own thing." Her undergraduate coursework reinforced her most salient identity—an individualist. For Neha, being an individual is associated with being American. Being individualistic separates her from Indian culture. Starting from this individualistic schema, Neha identifies herself as a Western thinker—drawing what seemed to be another line between her personal identity and the culture of her birth: "As far as a commitment to a mode of thought, I've been much more Western than Eastern, much more American than Indian."

RACIAL IDENTITY. One way to understand Neha's experience is through the lens of Hardiman and Jackson's (1997) social identity development model. In the context of this model, Neha exhibits the characteristics of a person at the "acceptance" stage. This stage is characterized by conscious identification with and rationalization of the dominant's logic system; Neha is infatuated with "Western thought." An individual at the acceptance stage often imagines a world that approaches race relations with the core principle that "people are people"; by extension, the individual believes that if people of color would just work hard they would be judged by their merits. Neha's opposition to affirmative action, and her apparent unwillingness to believe even her own father's allegation that he had been discriminated against, illustrate this characteristic. Neha holds in high esteem those individuals who "see people for their ideas" and not for other things such as gender, culture, and race. She believes in pulling oneself up by the bootstraps—after all, she thinks she has. She says she has not experienced any type of discrimination and has gotten everything she has wanted in terms of academics and career; she questions others' experiences of discrimination, even her father's. She does not recognize the systemic nature of oppression, which in turn clearly explains her political position as an opponent of affirmative action.[6] Neha characterizes all her negative race-based experiences as somehow not the product of racism or racial/ethnic animus.

An individual at this stage of ethnic/racial identity development will also accept and conform to white social, cultural, and institutional standards. Neha has not only accepted the dominant ideology of Western thought's superiority to Indian/Hindu thought and theology, she has also become a vocal advocate of the proposition. As the president of her law school's chapter of a politically conservative organization that opposes affirmative action and supports a "strict constructionist" interpretation of the Constitution, she argues white America's case for it. Her overall notion: All things American (read Western, individualist, and nonethnic) are good. Those who coalesce around the false markers of culture and race are intellectually lazy or excuse-makers.

Neha's rejection of and distancing from her ethnic background is another way of accepting the dominant society's ideology. Just as a racial minority will accept and parrot dominant ideologies about race, an ethnic minority will seek to shed the trappings of the home culture because they are seen as an undesired marker in society.[7] Neha has consistently disclaimed interest in being part of ethnic student organizations or an ethnoreligious community; she said she would attend an Indian function only if her parents asked her to attend one with them. She has adopted the dominant group's ideology and accepted the subordinate status of Indian culture and Hinduism as deserved and inevitable. She has come to eschew that which associates her with her ethnicity, not only by declining to participate in an ethnoreligious community but also by holding in disdain those (Indian and non-Indian, but particularly Indian) people who imply that her race or ethnicity is somehow a salient element of her own life.

Taken as a whole, Neha's case study shows the impact on an individual's ethnic identity when she feels disconnected from and rejects contact with other Indian Americans and even family members in India. It also shows that religion can be salient even in the lives of individuals who are not religious. As a belief system she cannot bring herself to ascribe to—yet one she sees as a major component of Indian culture—Hinduism has become a source of distance between herself and other Indian American Hindus. Importantly, she believes that Hinduism is the most legitimate source and reason for a connection to India and

Indian culture. Identifying cause and effect in the complex story of her alienation from Hinduism may be impossible, but Hinduism's role in her ethnic identity development is substantial, even though she does not identify with the religion.

Questions to Consider

1. When asked about "feeling different" during the K–12 life period, what example(s) did Neha give? Knowing Neha's worldview, is this surprising? What does her response indicate with respect to the salience of particular ethnic identity factors?

2. What elements of the lives-to-date of second-generation Indian American Hindus like Neha might have allowed them to feel "religious" even though they do not engage in the traditional worship practices like their immigrant parents? Going forward, what life changes might have such an effect?

3. In the contemporary American social context, how realistic is Neha's philosophical approach to her life—that ethnicity is irrelevant and communities coalescing around commonalities other than religion or political philosophy are unworthy or spurious?

4. Is Neha exhibiting internalized oppression?

5. Is it fair to call religion a salient factor in the life of a person who identifies herself as Hindu only because she was born of Hindu parents? Why or why not?

Salim

Salim, an Isma'ili male, was born in the United States and has lived most of his life in the same Southern metropolitan area. His parents and older sister immigrated to the United States from Uganda in 1972, during the expulsion of Asians from Uganda by Idi Amin. Salim's father is a physician, and his mother held various different jobs while Salim was growing up. Salim grew up in this nuclear family, with many other relatives living nearby. He described growing up in a diverse suburban area until he was twelve, and then moving to another suburban neighborhood that he described as predominantly white. His exposure to Indian Americans in school was a mirror image of his neighborhood experience. In the public school he attended until the sixth grade, he was the only Indian student; at the prestigious private school he attended for grades seven through twelve, there were "many Indians in the school." After graduating, Salim started college at a small liberal-arts institution in Texas that had "no diversity." He left after his first year, returning to his hometown and taking a year off during which he sold various items out of the back of his car. He then completed his undergraduate studies at a large, urban, predominantly commuter university. At the time of the interview he was working as a software consultant in the Atlanta area. He describes the Isma'ili religion as a very young religion in terms of the way its practiced today. I think my grandparents practiced Hindu[ism] or their parents practiced Hindu[ism]. . . . So at some point along the line, we were converted, but it was recently. So, nobody in my family is like fifth- or sixth-generation Isma'ili where they were very comfortable with the religion with the rights and rituals concerned with Muhammad. A lot of our own rights and rituals, even since I was a young kid, have evolved. We had a lot of very Hindu-esque traditions that are sort of being phased out and being much more mainstream Muslim type traditions. Like, we say more prayers in Arabic, or certain traditions that were very Hindu traditions, certain songs that we used to sing and prayers that were from a very Hindu context now we're phasing out.

Salim's Experiences K–12

As a child and as an adolescent, Salim was aware of himself as racially and religiously different from those around him. Salim identified religion as a "challenge" that he struggled with as a child: "I was very aware of the fact that I was Muslim, and back in, you know, 1979, 1980, that was a very unpopular religion to be, because of a lot of what happened with the Iran hostages." Salim's initial awareness of what it meant to be Muslim came from the American mainstream media "when I was six or seven," and it was negative. He said his parents, although observant, never talked to him about religion; religion was simply "something we did"—"sort of do what we tell you because that's the way it is." He added that he did not know what the rituals meant; the only things he knew about Islam he learned from the media. Growing up in a white, Southern milieu, Salim felt the media reported the Iran hostage crisis as a "Muslim thing . . . I just knew that everything I heard about 'Muslim' was bad, so it would have been nice to see others of my color."

Salim thought of himself as an "American kid in terms of the things that I liked, the things that I wanted to do, you know, my tastes in music, my tastes in clothes—everything else [besides his religion and skin color] was very American." He recalled first realizing his skin color was different in second grade. It was sometime in "fourth or fifth" grade when epithets like "sand nigger and camel jockey" were first hurled at him by classmates. At this point, Salim said, he "realized that I wasn't necessarily black, and I wasn't necessarily white."

Schoolyard taunting and fights "made me more aware of the fact that I didn't belong to a group." For Salim, "a group" was something the black kids at his school had. He described fights at school where ethnic slurs were hurled at different groups—and discovering, there on the schoolyard, that he was a group of one. He did not have a community like that of the other students of color: "When we would pick fights, during the fight, that's what somebody, you know, some of the guys would say [ethnic and racial slurs]. So I think it made me more aware of the fact that I didn't belong to a group, you know. At least the black kids, even though there were few of them, they were pretty tight knit and they kind of hung out together. Even though they mixed with everybody else, they, they just had that bond." Salim's lack of a group, in his neighborhood as well as in his school, was what he felt made him different from the kids around him.

> I think I was acutely aware of it all the way through elementary school simply because there weren't any other Indians. I wasn't exposed to a lot of other Indians. The Muslim community that I belonged to was very small, maybe in the two to three hundred range, not a lot of young kids and even then I would see them only every week or every other week. . . . I was conscious of the fact that there were blacks and whites living near us and in school and everywhere else, you know, I didn't realize how many Indians there were living around me.

Salim described being relieved when he switched to a private school that had ethnic and racial diversity. That was the first time he went to school with "another Indian and another person that, who wasn't either black or white. . . . That was actually very comforting—a big relief."

During most of his K–12 life period, Salim reported, his family went to their local Isma'ili mosque every Friday night and "one other night" each week. However, Salim reported not feeling connected to an ethnoreligious community and, as a result, feeling he had no connection to his home culture. Although he was exposed to an Indian culture in his home, which for him meant eating the food and listening to the music his "mom liked," he explicitly drew a distinction between exposure and feeling a connection. Although he had Indian American youth to associate with between seventh and tenth grade, he said this association didn't mean much to him because he felt he had nothing in common with the other Indian kids besides skin color: "The only thing we really had in common was skin color in terms of our Indian culture. You know, all of their families knew each other. They all sort of hung out together. They, they've been friends for years. They went to dinner parties together. My family was not part of that group, so we didn't have all that in common, just the fact that we were brown-skinned." In other words, because his Indian American classmates came from a different community—in this case, a Hindu ethnoreligious community of different socioeconomic means from Salim's family—he saw his connection to these classmates as having no dimensions other than similar skin color.

"The first time that it really became a connection" with other Indian Americans, Salim reported, was "when . . . I met other Indians, and this probably would be like tenth, eleventh grade—I started to forge really good friendships with" other Indian youth. "I started going to the IYA [Indian Youth Association] parties, meeting a lot more Indians, and so, you know, the fact that I was Indian now [felt like it] was okay." Until this point in his life, Salim said, he would have "picked to be white."

In high school, Salim had to deal with his teachers' stereotypes about Muslims as well. He described being very uncomfortable when his ninth grade homeroom teacher frequently "joked" with him. The teacher would say, " 'You don't have a bomb in the backpack, do you?' And he would duck and make a big joke in front of all the other kids. I mean, he was a really popular teacher in school and we all kind of laughed and made a big joke out of it but it made me really uncomfortable. . . . I don't know that I understood enough to go say anything to him about it."

Along with dealing with Muslim stereotypes, Salim was not able to participate in that most famous of American high-school rituals—attending and playing in Friday night football games—because he and his family attended mosque every Friday night for prayers. This too set him apart from his high school classmates. "I could see Christians get to go to church on Sunday mornings so it's very convenient. . . . And I had to go Friday evenings, like the biggest social night of the week, and my God chose that as the [day for prayer]." Salim said missing Friday night games "clearly hurt my, my role on the team. . . . If I was playing well, I should have been starting, but they would never start me because they knew I was going miss every fourth game, or third game, or fifth game. They would rather let the team get into a routine. So I would get to play and other times I did not get to play, sometimes we'd have practices and I'd have to go to mosque and miss practice, which I wasn't a big fan of doing." As a result, Salim said, "I definitely resented my religion. . . . I think that made me resent my religion."

Salim's parents were involved with the Isma'ili community, and he went to events and prayers mostly out of obligation to his parents. During his high-school years, Salim said, he really came to understand the differences between being Isma'ili and being "mainstream Muslim."

> I always knew that I was Isma'ili, which meant, you know, that we go to what's called *Canni*. We don't go to mosque, you know. Most mainstream Muslims speak Pakistani or Urdu or some mainstream Arabic language, and we speak Gujarati or Kuchi. Even a lot of our prayers are Gujarati and Kuchi and Hindi and not in Arabic; whereas Muslim prayers were in Arabic. So I started to learn sort of that way what the differences were.
>
> I'm not sure exactly when I realized that I wasn't part of the mainstream group. But I remember when I realized we were just sort of like one more level that I was different. And that was probably the reason I really drove, or, thrust myself much more into the Indian culture. Part of it was for acceptance; part of it was to be part of a group; and part of it was because I felt much more comfortable with Indians because of the

culture than I did with Muslims because I didn't share any cultural aspects with Muslims. I mean, I don't want to sit around and, you know, talk about prayers or the mosque or anything else. But, you know, with Indians, and my family's culture is very Indian, or, much more Indian than it is Pakistani or Middle Eastern.

Salim said the First Gulf War—which occurred in 1990 and 1991, during his senior year of high school—was the "first time I was really challenged about my religion." He spent a great deal of time in contemplation of whether he identified with the Americans or the Iraqis. Salim called the war "a heavily publicized war about us Americans against—it wasn't so much about us against Iraq, [but rather] it was about us against the Middle East. It was against the Muslims and I think I had to reconcile with myself how I felt about that." Salim wondered "which side of the coin I really belonged to." "At that point, I [had] started to evolve as having a much stronger identity of the Muslim and having confidence in that, and having pride in that, and now all of a sudden, you know, this comes about in early '91. I had to really reconcile in my heart whether, whether I believed that we, that America, was right in what they were doing, you know. Or was Iraq right?" He was angered by how the war was discussed in the media and in his classes with such a "high level of ignorance." For him, the fact that people talked "about 'Muslim' and 'Muslim terrorists' and 'Muslim bombers' instead of Iraqi leaders, Iraqi bombers, Iraqi terrorists" resulted "a stinging every time somebody said that. . . . And, of course, that just exacerbated the whole issue of being Muslim—it just highlighted it." However, he said he sometimes equated being Muslim with having brown skin, which "I would like to shed. If I was a white Muslim, I'm a white Muslim. Who's going to care? Who's going to know, who's going to bother?"

College

In his first year, Salim attended a small liberal-arts college in Texas where there were "very few" people of color. Salim's first collegiate encounter with racism was not through a direct experience of discrimination but through the candor of his roommate, who was white and from "sort of a backwoods family in Texas." Salim and his roommate got a long well, and after some time together his roommate revealed some of the of his family's concerns: "His uncle was a police officer, and was probably one of the most racist people I'd ever met. He used to tell my roommate all the time, 'I don't want you living with that kid. We can get you moved out. You're going to start hanging out with niggers and spics [if you continue living with an Indian].'" Salim said his roommate spoke "very openly" about his family's thinking. "His brother was the same way. His brother would come and stay with us and be very nice to me to my face, but my roommate told me he used to say racist things behind my back." As a result, Salim said, he became "super-consciously aware that the way people treat you to your face is very, very different from what they do behind your back." If one family can act this way, Salim realized, "there must be several families like that, there must be towns, entire towns where maybe the level of discrimination isn't to call you 'nigger' to your face, it's more subtle discrimination." This experience in his freshman year "was the first time I was really exposed to something like that. I think before, if there was racism, if I ever took note of it, it was because it was very blunt and because if they called me a name. Now I started to be more clued in to the fact that racism doesn't always mean they say something to your face."

At the end of his freshman year, Salim left school and took a year off. During this year, he "spent a lot of time learning more about my religion and more about my culture." By getting involved again with "a lot more Indian friends" he found himself able to develop a deeper interest in his ethnicity and home religion. "Freshman year, I had played baseball in college. A lot of rednecks play college baseball, and I don't think that I really grew as an Indian that whole year, and I wanted to sort of get back to my roots, so I really sort of immersed myself more in the culture, into the language, and into the Indian people." Until he took the year off and actually thought about his ethnic, cultural, and religious background, he said "being Indian . . . was very much about the skin color." Thereafter, Salim completed his undergraduate degree at an urban school that served mostly commuter students. During this stage of his education, his circle of friends was "100 percent Indian" and he reported having no white friends. He enjoyed being solely in the company of coethnics: "The fact that I was simply brown skinned was an automatic in to the social circle at the student center. . . . You always have somebody to hang out, have lunch with, you always knew like there was like a spot in the library where everybody sat. . . . You always knew a place where you could just go chill out and, and even though the group would rotate, there was always like five or six people always there, that you just go and just chill with them."

Salim said that he "got more involved in [Indian] culture" at his new university. He enjoyed being in the company of coethnics and felt like he was involved with the culture because he was able to

> sit around and I could understand them. They spoke some Gujarati. . . .
> We could laugh about Indian jokes. . . . We would go to Indian parties. . . .
> I could talk to them about a [Bollywood] movie and they would tell me
> what movie to go see if they were all going to see a movie because they
> were much more involved in the culture than I was at that age. So I defi-
> nitely began to find much more of a cultural connection; whereas in high
> school, there wasn't a cultural connection, it was just [about being]
> brown-skinned. . . . I guess I never really valued being an Indian until
> sophomore year of college because, you know, it was always something

that set me apart from everybody else versus really bonding with a group of people.

Salim preferred to associate with the Indian student organization on campus instead of the Muslim Student Association [MSA] because, he said, he felt he had more in common with the Indian students than the Muslim students. He described how as an Isma'ili he did not fit in with other Muslim students: "So had I ever told other Muslims at MSA or that I was Isma'ili, they would have been like, 'Oh, so you're not *really* Muslim.' That was something else I was aware of as I grew up, which is that I'm not going to find a bond with Muslims, not mainstream Muslims. I'll find a bond with other Isma'ilis, or I'll find a bond with Indians because of the cultural thing."

Salim also said he did not practice religion the way many of them did and therefore was considered an outsider. By contrast, within the Indian cultural group he was considered an insider even though he is not Hindu. "I would always be much more active in [the Indian Student Association] than I was in MSA. . . . A lot of the Muslims were Pakistanis, very conservative. They sort of behaved in a certain way and I didn't like being around them, whereas the Indians were the people who were my friends—the people I hung out at parties with, so it was sort of a natural evolution that was sort of a social type activity, and I didn't really think of it as a religious activity. . . . I wasn't so well accepted by most Muslims."

During college, Salim said, he was not a religious person and not connected to an ethnoreligious community. For Salim, being religious meant "going to [his parents' Isma'ili] mosque on Friday evenings. It meant no drinking, it meant no premarital sex, it meant probably those things more than others." Since he "definitely engaged" in the aforementioned activities, he "didn't consider myself to be a very religious person." As he got older he "reconciled the fact that I could be spiritual and not be super-religious. But you know, there was a conflict there. . . . I didn't enjoy going to the mosque. I mean, I liked being a part of that community because it grew and became a larger community of Isma'ilis, so I [later] had friends my age. That was nice, but I didn't really want to go for the prayers at the mosque."

During college, Salim said, he became more comfortable with his identity because he realized "that Indian doesn't mean 'Indian,' Indian means several different things." The transformation resulted from his discovery, at his larger commuter university, of the diversity within his collegiate community of Indian peers: "[I had] exposure now not just like to Punjabis or Gujaratis, but it is the Punjabis, Gujaratis, Tamils, Telegu people, Bengalis, and whatever else. . . . I was much more comfortable with myself as an Indian [in this] plurality, the diversity." After associating with other Indian American youth, he believed he could be one of them.

He contrasted this new realization with his earlier understanding of Indian identity, the product of his relatively limited childhood exposure to non-Isma'ili communities and of a trip to Africa when he was fifteen years old.

> I associated India with Hinduism. I had gone to Africa; I had gotten back to what I considered to be my roots. So, in my mind, I was sort of asserting myself as an African and then at some point I just realized that I don't have to be African and know everything about the culture when we go back there. . . . That probably happened in college, when I really was accepted by an Indian group. By late high school, early college, all my friends were Indian and I wasn't treated any differently from everybody else. So that was when, you know, my attitude towards India as a place changed a lot.

As a result, he said, he "grew more into the Indian part of my identity. . . . I never really realized that it's okay to consider myself Indian [until] all this other plurality . . . made me much more comfortable with being Indian." Salim described doing

> things which I never would have never considered doing in high school. . . . I was very involved in Indian culture and in the community, dated Indian girls. . . . Yeah, my identity definitely developed much more as an Indian. . . . It's not that we'd just sit around and be ultra-Indian all the time, but when those moments did come, it was like one of those shared connections that I had with somebody that I wouldn't have no matter how close my friend was, you know, my freshman year, my roommate, we never shared that bond. So being Indian it meant, it meant color up until college; after that, it meant something I valued a lot.

Adulthood

Salim identifies culture and religion as two separate and mutually exclusive concepts: "Cultural [traditions] would be like the language or the food or, the Hindi music . . . and the Isma'ili ones would [be] saying a certain prayer or a certain ceremony or going to mosque." Culture, Salim said, is "one hundred times more important to [him] than religion."

Even though his family came to the United States from Uganda, in adulthood Salim traveled to India "because all [his] friends" had done so. "I went to learn more Hindi." Salim visited thirteen cities in three weeks, and found that what he encountered buttressed his collegiate understanding of diversity as a hallmark of the Indian community. He said he found that "India really isn't one country, it's hundreds, and I wanted to experience the culture of all the different regions." He said the trip "really challenged my conscience," and made him "more socially aware than I was before."

The two of us landed in Bombay with, and just started getting around. And even though everyone wanted to speak in English with us, we would always speak Hindi. I would learn Hindi and I would ask people to correct me and tell me how to say it properly. So I feel like I left after three weeks with probably very good conversational Hindi language. At the airport, the customs agent tried to rip me off and I didn't realize how good my Hindi was until then. So, my Hindi's gotten a lot better. Now it's waning, but we still watch Indian movies. I can pick out three times more than I did before I went to India. . . . Gujarati I still speak fine. I mean, I still speak—I make more of an effort with my family.

Religion becomes salient for Salim in adulthood not because he is "more religious than other years," but rather because the "religion is now a tie to my Islamic community, which is very important to me." Although Salim says "I consider myself a practicing Muslim," he considers himself not to be "so religious": "I probably wouldn't win any Muslim of the Year awards. I definitely drank and engaged in other activities that were considered sort of non-Muslim."

Salim described sensations of awkwardness experienced during Ramadan: "I didn't fast during Ramadan because that's not so much emphasized in our sect of Islam. . . . When Ramadan would roll around, other Muslims were fasting, I wouldn't feel very comfortable eating, but I would eat anyways. And, of course, my Hindu friends were, like, 'Aren't you Muslim? Shouldn't you be fasting?' My Muslim friends were also, like, 'Shouldn't you be fasting?'" He said that he felt that he was having to defend why he was eating during Ramadan. He never observed it while growing up and he was "very comfortable answering" such questions and he believed that he "couldn't articulate why" he was eating. Due to not observing the Ramadan fast and not understanding "a lot of the rights and rituals" he said that "Our sect is so different than the rest of the mainstream Muslims. . . . I consider myself a practicing Muslim, but not comfortable as a practicing Muslim." Based upon his collegiate and adulthood experiences, he said, he believes "a lot of the Muslims I met were much more fundamentalist sort of the way that we believe in. [Their attitude is that] 'If it's not this way, then you're wrong.' So I didn't really feel comfortable around Muslims at all. To this day, actually I don't. I don't associate myself with any Muslim groups in general." Yet Salim also says he is "more religious now, probably because I understand why the religion says to do certain things. Before, it was just, 'Don't do this, don't do that.' There was no context behind it, it was like, 'Do it because I said so.' Now, I understand the value of it. . . . [At the same time,] some of the things that maybe I would do before, maybe I wouldn't do them now, now that I understand a lot more of the, the faith aspect of it. I still don't subscribe to all of it, but I understand the big picture."

The main reason he identifies as a practicing Muslim today, Salim says, is that he believes very strongly in the concept of *sewa*, or social service. He believes his most important Muslim acts are when he gives back to his community by spending time with Isma'ili kids at a youth camp in New Jersey. In a way that is intimately bound up with his identity as a Isma'ili, Salim hopes to help today's teens grow up with a positive sense of self. The camps also force him to "learn about Islamic history, passages in the Qur'an, interpretation, debates, that type of stuff. So I definitely spent more time with Muslim scholars now than I used to. . . . I don't necessarily think that I consider myself any more religious than I [was in high school]. I still consider myself very spiritual, but the religion is now a tie to my Islamic community, which is very important to me." So, Salim says, religion is not so much about being "a practicing Isma'ili, but [about] the connection that I have to these kids who are struggling with the same sort of religious issues that I was struggling with as a kid. It bonds me to the kids, the fact that I am Isma'ili, they are Isma'ili. So I learned much more about Islam, I learned much more about Isma'ilism, so that I could help them struggle through certain issues."

It is so important to Salim to participate in these camps every year that he has negotiated with his workplace to take most summer Fridays off in order to participate in the long-weekend camp program; he negotiated this arrangement with his employer as part of his contract, and has now been with the company for three years. "It is the ethic [of service] that I believe very firmly in, and so the way that I view service or giving back to the community. . . . So the role of Islam in my life has certainly influenced that aspect, but it hasn't ever made me put down a drink."

Salim rarely attends the mosque near his adulthood home, which is a panethnic mosque. He says he goes there "once in a while for Friday afternoon prayers, but I don't have any Muslim friends there. I don't go there and just chit chat with people . . . our prayers are fairly different. . . . At night I go to our mosque" (that is, his parents' Isma'ili mosque, farther away but in the same metropolitan area).

Discussion

Salim's life experiences to date illustrate a number of themes common to second-generation Indian Americans and some of particular importance to Muslims in this cohort. Of these, seven will be discussed here: (1) experiences of overt and covert religious and racial discrimination, (2) the development of a connection to other Indian Americans, (3) the paramount importance for Salim of community as the reason and vehicle for cultural discovery and maintenance, (4) the resulting distinction Salim makes between religion and culture, (5) religion's role as a moral compass, (6) the influence of transnational experiences—particularly international travel—on ethnic identity, and (7) how all of this affects Salim's conceptions of his own ethnic and religious authenticity.

DISCRIMINATION AND ALIENATION. Salim's status as an Isma'ili Muslim has been a marker of difference and a source of discomfort in multiple respects over the course of his life. This status as a religious other not only influenced Salim's self-understanding but also shaped how he was treated by classmates, teachers, and American society. From his exposure to the mainstream American media during the Iran hostage crisis when he was six and seven years old, through and including the First Gulf War, when he was a high school senior, Salim came to understand that Islam was associated with enemy status in the American mind. Although religiously observant, his parents rarely discussed with him the meaning and tenets of Islam or why being Muslim was important to them. This is probably because they, like many Indian immigrant parents, did not have enough knowledge to provide the information Salim would require; it may never have occurred to them that religious identity and practice would be something more troubling and less automatic for their son in the United States than it had been for them growing an Isma'ili community. As a result, Salim felt he had no information to counter the the negative mainstream portrayals of Muslims and Islam.

Today, the Isma'ili ethnoreligious community plays a large role in Salim's life. Looking back, he sees childhood experiences of discrimination as ones involving anti-Muslim religious bias. This is the product of a recent process of thought and integration on Salim's part. It is impossible to say with certainty whether as a child Salim understood insults like "camel jockey" and "sandnigger" as religious attacks, racial slurs, or as some undifferentiated type of attack on his differentness as such. As an adult, with the hindsight that has come with cognitive development and his own personal return to a strong identification with Isma'ilism, Salim now sees his childhood victimization as unequivocally religious in nature.

Just as it is hard to say exactly how Salim took these attacks at the time, it also difficult to know the perpetrators' intent. When elementary- and middle-school-aged children use epithets that target the victim's race and religion, what is it that they mean to say? Setting aside the semantic debate over whether these particular epithets refer to religion, race, or national/cultural origin, we can at least say this: The perpetrators were exposed to the same negative ideas about Islam and brown-skinned people as Salim was, and were probably repeating what they had heard from the media and popular culture without a meaningful understanding even of a distinction between race and religion. At a time when popular culture exhibited anti-Muslim characteristics, the fact that they knew to target Salim because he was visibly—that is, racially—different from them shows how religion is racialized in the United States.

Whether racial, religious, or equivocal, experiences of discrimination have been a major factor affecting Salim's ethnic identity. They have had both a momentary and a cumulative effect on Salim—what we might call the cut, the immediate impact of discrimination, and the scar, its lingering toll. For Salim, the lasting effect of his discrimination experiences was aggravated because he had virtually no positive images or knowledge to counterbalance the discrimination and the American popular media's damaging mischaracterizations of Islam. Salim's experiences illustrate how racial and ethnic identity intertwine, and how childhood incidents can build upon each other and reverberate into the adult's identity and behavior. However he interpreted them at the time, the experiences contributed to a sense of alienation that led at first to feeling distant and disconnected from his religion but then later resulted in a strong connection to Isma'ilism in adulthood. His commitment to his religion today is intimately bound to his desire to protect young Isma'ilis from experiences like his own.

In some cases, of course, Salim's religious identity was attacked clearly and unequivocally. The starkest example is surely his homeroom teacher's frequent "joke": "You don't have a bomb in your backpack, do you?" In these and other situations, when his religious identity was attacked in school, Salim would laugh off the statements and often colluded with his peers making jokes about Muslim terrorists. Even when he did not collude, he still remained silent rather than speaking out in contradiction to his peers or the teacher. Some might say Salim was exhibiting internalized oppression. Was he? There are at least two possible answers to this question. One distinguishes between his external responses and his internal reactions. Since Salim's internal response was one of turmoil and disagreement, one could conclude that he was not accepting or adopting the stereotypes implicit in the taunt and therefore was not exhibiting internalized oppression.[8] Although his going along with the joke involves the acquiescence to a negative stereotype of his religious group, this view sees it as more fundamentally a response to the social pressures on a ninth-grader when face-to-face with his white, predominantly Christian peers and a popular teacher. The other possible answer requires us to distinguish his cognitive response of rejection from a deeper emotional impact, whereby a person can intellectually reject negative stereotypes but still buy into them at an almost subconscious level. The rejection is a cognitive process and internalizing the stereotypes is more emotional. One can think he is rejecting them without realizing that at a deeper level he is also absorbing them.

The characterizations made by the media and adopted by his teacher and peers were exacerbated by Salim's own impatience with Islam because of its effects on his social life. He resented his home religion for keeping him off the starting football lineup in high school and otherwise isolating him from the all-important Friday night social scene of adolescent America: "the biggest social night of the week, and my God chose that [as the day of prayer]." Salim's internal turmoil about Islam came to a head during the first Gulf War, which caused him to examine deeply the way his religion, his race, and his nationality interacted. As Salim observed, political and military conflicts between the United

States and Middle Eastern nations with Muslim-majority populations were characterized by the media and political leaders as being "about 'Muslim' and 'Muslim terrorists' and 'Muslim bombers' instead of Iraqi leaders, Iraqi bombers, Iraqi terrorists."

Salim's only account of discrimination during his college years was the verbal abuse he suffered behind his back at the hands of his Texas roommate's family; Salim described this abuse in unequivocally racial terms. His roommate's family may indeed have been concerned only with Salim's race. Salim's perception may also have been affected by the perfect confluence of phenomena that the American popular mind associates with old-fashioned racism: a "backwoods" white family and a "police officer" uncle who spoke of "niggers and spics." It may also have been affected by that unique moment in his life. More even than before, Salim felt disconnected from an ethnoreligious community while also feeling a college freshman's hope of escapaing the poisonous social atmosphere of his high school in 1991. Did these internal factors lead Salim to deemphasize, consciously or unconsciously, his identity as a Muslim and therefore to see his roommates' family as merely racist? When Salim was speaking about his college experiences, both during and after his year in Texas, he never mentioned any incident of religious bias, whether from the media or on a personal level. This is not to say he did not hear anti-Muslim sentiment. Rather, it was probably the product of three interrelated factors: Salim had immersed himself in his collegiate Indian American community, was feeling shunned by the campus Muslim organization, and had begun again to attend the Isma'ili mosque of his childhood. Because his focus was on the Indian elements of his identity and on the social aspects of his mosque experiences, an anti-Muslim encounter during this time might be less memorable to him in the present day.

CONNECTION TO COETHNICS. For one thing, Salim's new-found relationship with Indian Americans later in college permitted "Indian," as opposed to "Muslim," to become a defensive ethnicity for him. Part of the connection to Indians, of course, resulted from rejection and alienation vis-à-vis other Muslims. Many other Muslims do not regard Isma'ilis as Muslim, because the latter often pray in Gujarati rather than Arabic and for other reasons related to theological distinctions between Isma'ilism and other sects of Islam. However, Isma'ilis do generally consider themselves to be Muslims—specifically, Shi'a Muslims of the Isma'ili sect.[9] (Hence Salim uses the words "Muslim" and "Islam" to describe himself and his home religion.)

Salim first became aware of the distinctions among the various Islamic sects late in high school and ultimately came to believe that he had more in common with South Asian Americans who were not Muslim than with Muslims. Pushed away in college by a religious group with which he might otherwise have identified, Salim found a welcoming social group of coethnics who were not Isma'ili or

Muslim. He therefore spent his time with Indian Americans and developed the ethnic, as opposed to religious, elements of his identity. It is not that "ethnic" is the alternative to "religious," but that the presence of an ethnic community and his rejection by the Muslim Student Association led Salim toward an ethnic orientation. As an Indian American, he had insider status with this group even though he is not Hindu. He was more comfortable socializing with a group of Indian peers, and participating in Indian American community cultural events, than participating in Muslim student activities.

Like many research participants, Salim experienced a collegiate sense of disconnection from religion resulting from a combination of factors. First, he was no longer living in the parental home, where parents could "force" the individual to attend religious functions in which he did not have an independent interest. Second, there were no religious institutions on or near many college campuses to serve Hindu, Isma'ili, Sikh, and other Indian American religious communities.[10] Few research participants reported attending religious functions during their college years except when they were home visiting their parents and were motivated by the attendant obligations and pressures. Culture— which until college meant little more than skin color to Salim—then took on a high salience. This turn of events was acceptable to Salim because of the dimensions of culture and community he shared with his Indian American peers, and because of his own relative neglect of religious practice as such, which (in conjunction with their rejection of him) made the Muslim Student Association less appealing.

NEED FOR COMMUNITY. Salim consistently draws a contrast between his Indian community and his Isma'ili community. In college, he'd had the former but not the latter. Salim's postcollegiate return to religion is itself not the product of a religious urge per se but rather has occurred because he found a social community. When in later years of college he began periodically to attend his home mosque, he developed friendships for the first time with coreligionists his own age. As an adult, his social ties to Isma'ilism have increased through his involvement with Isma'ili youth camps, where he is accepted for his religious identity and has the chance to make younger Isma'ilis feel accepted for and strong in theirs. As an adult, Salim identifies as a practicing Isma'ili, because he is finally connected to a community that is both ethnic and religious—an ethnoreligious, Isma'ili community. He is developing new habits of learning and attentiveness to the tenets of his home religion. During K–12 and college, Salim's lack of connection to an Isma'ili community, aggravated by uncontradicted negative portrayals of Islam in the popular media, resulted in a disconnection from religion. Once he found himself among Isma'ilis his own age and younger, he felt connected to a community through which he experiences religion and without which he does not. Community is the conduit for religion; without that community of people to gather with for religious purpose, he would likely engage in religious expression.

Salim's evolving experience with other Indian Americans and other Isma'ilis illustrates the importance of ethnoreligious community to identity development. Although he had Indian American classmates between seventh and twelfth grade, he felt that "the only thing we really had in common was skin color." Likewise, although he attended mosque on Friday nights, he did not feel that he was a part of an ethnoreligious community. To understand why, consider the emotional criteria Salim attached to the idea of community. For him, the mere exposure to dimensions of Indian culture or the presence of other Indian Americans did not result in a feeling of connection to a community. His Hindu schoolmates had a separate social world of their own, of which Salim was not a part. At the mosque, Salim found coreligionists, but they were not his own age and therefore he did not want to socialize with them. Moreover, he was not schooled in Islam by his parents, which might have led to a sense of community at the mosque despite a dearth of peers. Because he could-not develop relationships with peers at the mosque, and because the spiritual aspect of group prayer was unappealing, he felt no community and therefore no desire to attend.

It was not until his year off and matriculation as a sophomore at a large, diverse, commuter university that he felt connected to Indian culture. Ironically, the peers with whom he developed this new-found sense of community were demographically similar to his high-school peers: they were Hindus and probably the children of well-to-do professionals. Yet Salim now found he could "understand them," "laugh about Indian jokes," "talk . . . about Indian movies," and "go to Indian parties." Salim resolves this apparent contradiction by explaining: "I guess I never really valued being an Indian until sophomore year of college because, you know, it was always something that set me apart from everybody else versus really bonding with a group of people." His connection to coethnics went from being about something that made him different to something that enriched his life. Once he found that sense of community, it developed (again, perhaps ironically) an automatic quality he had never experienced before. "You always knew a place where you could just go chill out and, and even though the group would rotate, there was always like five or six people always there, that you just go and just chill with them."

The precedent for this desire for community can be found in his public elementary-school experience. Recall the envy Salim felt when he watched black students and white students support their coethnic peers when fights broke out. His lack of this type of community itself affected Salim's ethnic identity development. As an outsider vis-à-vis his coethnic peers, he did not see them as offering such support or refuge. Lacking coreligionists in school, he felt he had no one to back him up. Salim was looking for friendships that took on the automatic communal quality that he saw other students enjoy as early as elementary school. During his freshman year in Texas, Salim found the very opposite: He was more ethnically and religiously isolated than ever before, and encountered the striking racism of his roommate's family.

Until Salim felt connected to a community of coethnics, he felt disconnected from Indian culture. The disconnection was most profound during the year he spent as a college freshman in Texas, because he had absolutely no opportunity for exposure to Indian culture or community, but even during the K–12 period he felt disconnected from the communities with which he had contact. It is surely no coincidence that, after developing a sense of self as connected to the larger phenomenon of Indian culture, Salim went on in adulthood to seek out community by performing service. Once he developed friendships with other Isma'ilis his own age, he began to attend his parents' mosque on his own. The desire and opportunity to connect with others like him, rather than prayer or other religious practice, is the driving force behind his continued attendance.[11]

DISTINCTION BETWEEN RELIGION AND CULTURE. Salim draws a clear mental line between religion and culture. For him, culture is "one hundred times more important . . . than religion." He draws a clear line between the two: "Cultural [traditions] would be like the language or the food or the Hindi music . . . and the Isma'ili ones would be saying a certain prayer or a certain ceremony or going to mosque." Salim's distinction is not surprising in light of a number of factors, some unique to him and others that may reflect the experiences of non-Hindu Indian Americans more generally. Both Isma'ilis' status as a religious minority within the South Asian American community and the fact that Salim ultimately connected and developed a social community with a predominantly Hindu circle of friends inform Salim's understanding of culture and religion as separate. This distinction between Indian culture and the home religion was more common among non-Hindu research participants, whereas the Hindus were more likely to conflate their own home religion with Indian culture. For Salim, there is the additional factor of his own nonreligiousness. Although he now feels intensely committed to *sewa* and other forms of cultural maintenance, these emotions coexist with his continuing practice of not observing those tenets of Islam that he sees as defining the religion, such as eschewing alcohol and premarital sex and fasting during Ramadan.

Being Indian eclipsed being religious in college, as it often did for research participants. As an adult, Salim has come back to religion because he found a place where he is both embraced because of his religious identity and involved in the lives of younger Isma'ilis. As a counselor at an Isma'ili youth camp in New Jersey, he can engage in what he believes are his most important Muslim acts: giving back to his community.[12] In a way that is intimately bound up with his identity as an Isma'ili Muslim, Salim hopes to help today's teens grow up with a positive sense of self. For Salim, his participation in these youth programs is both an outcome of his identity development trajectory to date and part of a continuing process:

> The thing is, as I worked with identity issues through kids, it helped me resolve a lot of my own issues. I mean, you know, they would say, you know, "How did you ever get through this?" You know, "Kids call me this or kids call me that in school." These are kids from ten to seventeen, so a lot of what they were struggling with today I realized I struggled with then. I had to sort of consciously think about what got me through those times and sharing that with them, and just to be a role model [and say] that "you can get through this. It is not impossible."

During the K–12 period, Salim had reacted to experiences of overt religious discrimination and the subtle oppression that comes from Islam's one-sided depiction in American culture not by developing a defensive identity but by exhibiting a weak ethnic connection and thoughts some might consider internalized oppression. He developed an identity oriented toward white Christian society. He turned away from his home faith, and although he had continuous exposure to Indian culture he was "very American" with respect to "the things that I wanted to do, my tastes in music, my tastes in clothes—everything else." With the help of counterbalancing positive experiences related to his ethnic identity in college and adulthood, Salim changed course and ended up with a stronger sense of ethnic identity and the urge to learn more about Isma'ilism. Having clearly concluded (if not entirely consciously) that this is the better path, he now urges young Isma'ilis to develop the strength of self he lacked as a child. In doing so, he has not only grappled with his own childhood experiences but also developed a habit of participating more frequently in the study and practice of Isma'ilism.

MORAL COMPASS. As described in chapter 3, religion—or even the idea of one's association with a given religion—functions as a reminder of moral obligation in day-to-day life. Salim identifies certain specific obligations for observant Muslims, including avoiding alcohol and premarital sex and observing the daytime fast during Ramadan. He considers himself to be less religious—indeed, to identify with Islam in a "spiritual" more than "religious" sense—because he does not fast during Ramadan and has indulged in the prohibited activities. He remarked that although Islam has influenced his life, "it hasn't ever made me put down a drink." Even after offering the apologia that Isma'ilis do not emphasize the Ramadan fast obligation—"our sect is different from the rest of mainstream Muslims"—he nevertheless identifies it as a religious obligation and sees himself as less religious because he does not keep the fast.

At the same time, Salim draws a specific connection between his life's project of helping younger Isma'ilis cope with the challenges of adolescence and the religious obligation of *sewa*, or social service. This is an obligation that Salim could consider a secular one, arising simply from a sense of social responsibility and the travails of his own childhood. Yet he connects it to *sewa*, with all that term's religious overtones. While still describing himself as "not religious," he studies the Qur'an to the extent necessary to function as a counselor for Isma'ili youth and interacts with "Islamic scholars."

Salim is an important example of how religion's moral-compass function applies even for individuals who do not (and do not even wish to) follow the compass's direction. Salim finds a moral compass in Islam even as he states clearly that it has never made him "put down a drink" of alcohol. At the same time, religion's social importance as a source of morality and righteous conduct is so substantial for Salim that he imbues with religious significance life decisions—his *sewa*—that he could just as easily describe to himself and others in merely secular terms.

TRANSNATIONAL EXPERIENCES. Salim's two trips abroad each affected his identity in dramatically different ways; both are illustrative of how transnational experiences can shape an individual's identity and even change the trajectory of identity development. After traveling to Uganda at age fifteen, Salim invented a new label for himself: "African Indian American." His life experiences up to that point give some indication of where this label came from. He had not yet encountered the diversity of Indian identity that he would come to realize in college, he was an Isma'ili whose parents immigrated from Africa rather than India, and he had never traveled to India (as many of his "Indian" peers had, due to their continuing direct connections to family there). For all these reasons, he had not yet been comfortable describing himself with the labels "Indian" or "Indian American." They meant something, he felt, but they didn't exactly refer to him: "I associated India with Hinduism. I had gone to Africa; I had gotten back to what I considered to be my roots. So, in my mind, I was sort of asserting myself as an African." His admiration of black peers' cohesiveness as a social group may also have influenced his choice of moniker.

Salim knew he could trace his ethnic roots to the Indian subcontinent, and was familiar with Indian culture through his parents' use of the Gujarati language and other dimensions of Indian culture present in his home life, such as Gujarati cuisine and Bollywood films. Yet he still understood the term "Indian" as one that to some substantial degree excluded himself—one that, by extension, only Hindus whose parents came from India could legitimately adopt. In college, Salim realized that Indians are not a monolithic group composed only of Hindus or only people who immigrated directly from India. Discovering the range of people who described themselves as Indian somehow gave Salim permission to do so himself—although he also used the phrase "the Indian part of my identity," implying that the term "Indian" is somehow still incomplete as a descriptor for himself.

As a result, Salim's "attitude towards India as a place changed a lot" and for the first time he felt that he wanted to travel there. Unlike those research participants who traveled to India as children, Salim never described India as dirty or gross, did not describe feeling constrained or alienated by family (since he had none there), and had not learned to look the other way when it came to poverty and disease. Nor were his travels confined to a particular city or region, as were those of the research participants who returned to India on family visits. Rather, Salim traveled widely and said the trip had touched his conscience, and as a result he had become "more socially aware than I was before." These reactions make Salim unusual among the research participants; few who went to India, especially after one trip, saw the poverty and pollution there in terms of social responsibility or awareness. Salim went to India in search of a cultural source and sense of connection to the "original" that he could not find in the United States and had not found in Africa. Inasmuch as he discovered the diversity encompassed by the term "Indian," he was finally able to comfortably apply that word to himself.

One of Salim's other purposes in traveling to India was to learn Hindi. (He already spoke conversational Gujarati as a result of growing up with parents who spoke Gujarati in the home.) Knowing Hindi is seen as an marker of ethnic authenticity by many in the second generation. Speaking and understanding Hindi carries a cultural cachet among second-generation Indian Americans that far outstrips the language's usage in their childhood homes. It is the language that most people associate with India. This phenomenon may be traced to a combination of factors: the popularity of Hindi-language Bollywood films, which Salim reported viewing with his friends in college; the likelihood that if a college offers courses in any Indian language it will be Hindi; and the language's legal status as the national language of India. Salim expresses pride at being able to hold his own in a Hindi-language argument with a corrupt customs official. For Salim, long reticent about calling himself Indian, his facility with the language has become another indication that he is indeed entitled to that ethnic label.

AUTHENTICITY. The need for authenticity is a recurring theme in Salim's life. For the reasons described amply above, Salim had grown up seeing himself as somewhat less than authentically Indian. Like other many Indian Americans in the cohort, he looked to India as a source or guide of what was authentic. He was not Hindu, and his parents had come to the United States from Africa rather than India. Only when he forged a connection to ethnic and ethnoreligious communities and thereby developed a sense of himself as Indian was his interest in India—or any aspiration toward authenticity as an Indian—even piqued. He then opened himself up to the possibility that he could self-identify as Indian. When he finally traveled to India several years later, his experiences confirmed that he could be Indian, for two oft-expressed but contrasting reasons: first, because he came to realize that the term encompassed far more than the predominantly north Indian and Hindu subgroup to which he had been exposed in the United States, and second, because he developed his ability to speak Hindi.

At the same time, Salim faced crises of authenticity related to his religious identity as well. Non-Isma'ilis viewed him as insufficiently Muslim, and even non-Muslims questioned him when they observed him engaging in conduct considered inconsistent with "observant" Islam. Salim took these questions to imply doubt as to his identity as a Muslim. The evaluation of non-Christians against the known (or presumed) ideals of their home religion is common in the United States. It springs from a combination of a small amount of knowledge about non-Christian religions and the presumption that followers of "foreign" religions will necessarily be doctrinaire. No one would assume that every last American Catholic observes the obligation to attend Mass on all the Holy Days of Obligation, yet there is no similar consideration given to the range of beliefs, practices, and levels of observance present among Muslims (or, for that matter, Hindus or Sikhs). Rather, the assumption is made that any Muslim will observe all of Islam's "five pillars." It is not only Christian Americans or white Americans who engage in these unwarranted assumptions; indeed, Salim implied that many of the friends who asked why he was not keeping the Ramadan fast were in fact fellow Indian Americans. The result for Salim was that, because he and his family observed different (some would say incomplete) Islamic traditions, his authenticity as a Muslim was called into question by both Muslims and non-Muslims.

Salim has responded by increasing his participation in the Isma'ili community and his knowledge of Islam. Although he is still reticent about characterizing himself as a practicing Isma'ili, he described learning "about Islamic history, passages in the Qur'an, interpretation, debates, that type of stuff," and spending "more time with Muslim scholars now than I used to." He has armed himself with knowledge, so although he doesn't practice Islam in a manner other might consider fully observant or orthodox, he has the knowledge to respond. By attending worship services at his masjid and engaging in *sewa*, he also has a sense of his own personal connection to an active Muslim community; this enables him to feel Muslim in all the ways that matter to him.

Questions to Consider

1. Does religion function as a moral compass for Salim?
2. How was Salim's ethnic identity affected by his feeling that he was neither "Indian" enough for coethnics nor "Muslim" enough for his coreligionists?
3. When he was rejected by other Muslim students in college, was it a foregone conclusion that Salim would then gravitate toward an Indian American

ethnic community? What other directions might his identity have taken in response to his experiences with the MSA?

4. How should educational institutions (both K–12 and higher education) adapt their calendars and policies to respond to religious diversity?

5. What should families and ethnoreligious communities do to bridge the bicultural gap?

Epilogue

This work, like any in a nascent field of scholarship, is more a beginning than a resolution of the questions, opportunities, and challenges of the subject matter. It can and should nevertheless be the basis for rethinking both how we do our scholarship on religion and how America's K–12 school system responds to and protects Indian American students.

The years-long process of developing this book has convinced me that we must consider religion at the level of the individual. Approaching religion only by reference to congregational function is inadequate to consider what religion means and how it acts in the individual life. Even theology is at best a tiny corner of how Indian Americans live religion. There are avenues of research I did not follow, gender being the best example. Providing gendered approaches to lived religion would advance our studies in this field. Women are traditionally seen as the bearers and perpetuators of religious tradition. Yet with the exception of Avya, most of the research participants in this study who had thought deeply about and grappled with their own relationship with religion were men: Nikhil, Salim, Aziz, and others. The women were, by and large, comparatively unreflective on matters of faith. How, then, is lived religion gendered in this population?

This study also showed how lived religion changes by life period. In the next half-decade, most of these research participants will marry and many will have children. Will the preparation for and fulfillment of these life transitions change how the research participants live religion? If so, how? I plan to undertake a follow-up study with this cohort about six years hence in order to answer this question.

Indian American Religions in America

In the coming years, we should begin to explore what might be called American Sikhism, American Hinduism, and American Islam. India's image as a touchpoint

for authenticity notwithstanding, religions are inevitably reinvented and rein-
terpreted in new social arenas. How will the second generation interact and coexist in religious communities with the constant influx of new immigrants from
India? Will language loss result in the development of English-language prayer
liturgies? Will the cultural influence of Christian dogmatism result in the development of the "Ten Commandments of Hinduism" one research participant
wished for, or in other reinterpretations of scripture that focus on rules over stories? In the public sphere, how will Indian American religious organizations respond to the growing influence of fundamentalist Christianity on everything
from biology textbooks to U.S. foreign policy? The next time a town like Palos
Heights tries to pay Muslims to go away quietly, will they?

In undertaking this exploration, we must be particularly careful not to assume that members of any given religious group will agree on its tenets or practices. There is a tendency, even among many scholars, to treat Indian religions
as monolithic. There is no more "one Hinduism" than there is "one Christianity." Indeed, perhaps we will see the further development and diversification of
sects within the American recreations of Indian religions. Even if we do not end
up with sects per se, we will see the development of divergent philosophies and
approaches to theology and practice. Some may look like the Hindutva movements now ascendant, but others may constitute the development of a "religious left."

Inasmuch as the U.S. government does not collect data on religious affiliation and few of the major public polls do so, social scientists need to work on
our models both to track religious affiliation in new populations and to explain
why and how the turn to religion has become meaningful for these transnational minorities. The researchers who undertake the study must ensure that its
design fully and appropriately includes South Asian Americans. This means not
only ensuring that South Asian Americans are adequately represented in the research cohort but also that the program is designed to elicit useful information
on lived religion among Hindus, Sikhs, Muslims, and other Indian American re-
ligionists. It should avoid undue attention to the congregation and inquire not
only into ritual practices but also about how religion functions as a moral compass, a source of identity, and an impetus for study among respondents.

September 11, 2001

September 11, 2001, was a critical incident for many Indian Americans—in particular, those living in the New York and Washington, D.C. areas. The post-9/11
backlash galvanized the Sikh community. As Jaideep Singh has noted on numerous occasions, the sometimes violent backlash was a wake-up call for Sikhs; it
showed them that they needed to build bridges beyond their ethnoreligious communities, increasing their mainstream civic involvement in order to challenge

misconceptions and acquire allies. For non-Muslim Indian Americans, the back-lash was a reminder that social distinctions that are second nature to them may be invisible to mainstream Americans—hence the large number of Hindus, Sikhs, and Christians who fell prey to violence and harassment.

One recurring theme in the mainstream dialogue after September 11 has been interfaith communication. We need to develop a better understanding of the relationships among Hindus, Sikhs, and Muslims in the United States, and in particular to examine the attitudes of these second generations toward each other. Have they inherited the biases of their parents? As more seem to be fol-lowing the trend of British Asians to identify primarily by their religious affilia-tion, should specific efforts to maintain a dialogue be undertaken?

At the same time, we should not overemphasize the impact of September 11 and the backlash. The image of the Muslim terrorist predated September 11 by decades, and the popular association of Islam with brown-skinned people like Indian Americans is of similar vintage. The attacks' impact on Indian American communities may be profound in New York, Washington, and backlash killing sites like Dallas and Phoenix, whereas its effects on ethnic and religious identity of Indian Americans elsewhere was negligible. Although there is a dearth of pre-9/11 data on which to base a comparative analysis, a well-designed qualitative study could still reveal much.

As we begin to review and interpret the lives of Second Generation B, new avenues of inquiry open. For example, what effect is exposure to Bollywood films having on how these second-generation Indian Americans form an under-standing of their religions? One female research participant in this study de-scribed learning most of what she knows about Hindu wedding rituals from Bollywood movies; viewing them sparked conversations with her mother about Hindu tradition and even about her parents' own arranged marriage. How will experiences like these be repeated and built upon as Bollywood films' appeal grows? What negative effects might be found? For example, Sikhs often play the role of buffoon or comic relief in Bollywood films. How may this affect how the second generation—both Sikhs and non-Sikhs—understand Sikhism and Sikhs' place in Indian and Indian American culture?

Implications for Educational Policy

We have seen the role religion plays in the lives of second-generation Indian Americans, and that its place goes beyond ethnic maintenance or nostalgia. For decades, public schools have shied away from religion, mostly because they fear the consequences of violating students' constitutional rights under the Estab-lishment Clause. They have gone so far beyond what the Constitution requires that they are allowing harm to befall religious minority students and failing to prepare all students for a multicultural world where religious identities are growing ever more salient. Indeed, as the National Council for the Social Studies writes in its position paper on religion:

> Knowledge about religions is not only a characteristic of an educated person but is absolutely necessary for understanding and living in a world of diversity. Knowledge of religious differences and the role of religion in the contemporary world can help promote understanding and alleviate prejudice. Since the purpose of the social studies is to provide students with a knowledge of the world that has been, the world that is, and the world of the future, studying about religions should be an essential part of the social studies curriculum.[1]

We have seen in this text how the unpreparedness of teachers to understand and deal with religious differences has harmed students, from Salim's homeroom teacher ("You don't have a bomb in that backpack, do you?") to Nikhil's soccer coach who benched him for refusing to say the Lord's Prayer.

Curricular reforms are essential, and the study of contemporary America should include a thorough consideration of religion's role as an organizing place and principle for immigrant communities. But if we stop at curricular reform we will still have failed Indian American students. The typical American classroom now contains at least one religious-minority student, and all teachers must be trained to respond to their needs on issues from assignments to discipline. As teachers, they must be trained to treat religious-minority students with sensitivity, such as by adapting testing schedules and assignments when they conflict with holidays and other obligations. This does nothing more than put Hindu, Muslim, Sikh, and other students on a level playing field with their Christian classmates, who receive the same benefits structurally through everything from school holiday schedules to "fish-stick Fridays" during Lent. As disciplinarians, all teachers must be aware of and conversant with religious oppression; they must be taught to recognize and respond to religious hazing as forcefully as they would to racial violence and epithets. The importance of the latter reform cannot be overemphasized, because religious oppression has a negative impact on both identity development and academic achievement. Recall that Asian Americans are most likely to face harassment from peers. As a group leader for a program serving Asian American students in the Northampton, Mass., public schools, I encountered an Indian American Hindu seventh-grader who had recently been held down in the cafeteria and force-fed a beef hot dog by his classmates. The experience had affected the boy's attitude toward school; he began acting out in class and even starting bringing a pocketknife to school "to defend myself next time." Had teachers present in the cafeteria intervened, and had the students' curricula been designed to promote recognition and respect for religious difference, a discipline problem and a dangerous situation could have been avoided.

More broadly, the field of multicultural education must begin addressing religion as a social identity of equal importance to race, gender, and sexual orientation. A few leading scholars (Nieto 2003; Banks and Banks 2004) have made tentative first steps toward incorporating religion into multicultural education texts, but much more needs to be done. Religion's treatment must be commensurate with its demonstrated importance in the lives of students. Faculty in schools of education nationwide must overcome their unease with religion, fill the gaps in their own training through professional development, and begin truly preparing teachers for the twenty-first-century classroom.

Finally, more Indian Americans should consider pursuing careers in teaching. Even if the reforms recommended above miraculously occur in the coming years, the next generation needs allies and role models in their K–12 social world. This "next generation" will be a mix of third-generation students, second-generation children of recent adult immigrants, and new young immigrants as well. They will be socioeconomically diverse and found in every corner of America. The opportunity to work with them may be more personally rewarding than any other career choice.

A Singular Experience

All these speculations and endeavors have one thing in common: they bear upon each of us as individuals. The capacity of individuals to interact and to understand and appreciate what religion means to each other is essential in the twenty-first-century classroom, workplace, and world. Studying the tenets of Islam or Hinduism or Sikhism, while fascinating, is only a small step in the right direction. We must develop understandings of how the followers of those faiths see religion, how they embrace it and act it out—in short, how they live religion every day. To do so we must avoid the glib assumption, the "profile," and the easy traps of lists and categories. To succeed is to more deeply appreciate, to be more deeply appreciated, and perhaps even to gain a clearer view of our own path to God.

APPENDIX

Interview Protocol

Introduction

I will provide an overview of research project and my rationale for study.

I will have the participants sign consent forms and explain confidentiality and my reasons for recording the interview.

I am interested in researching how people construct their identities. I will be asking you some questions concerning your identity at three specific stages of your life: adolescence, college years, and today.

Self-Identification and Related Components

Explain to interviewee: I am going to use a cardboard pie as a visual cue. I will ask the interviewee: Here is a pie that has many pieces. If the pieces represent different components of your identity, what do the pieces represent? What is your identity and what has gone into the making of your identity? How were these contents expressed behaviorally or attitudinally?

Would your answer been different in college? If so, how? What pieces of the pie would contribute to your identity?

What about as an adolescent? How would you describe yourself? What pieces of the pie would contribute to your identity?

Adolescence

Now let's go back to your adolescence; tell me the story of how your identity has evolved.

Who were the significant people in your life at the time?

Did you ever consider yourself different from other kids? (neighborhood and/or school). How?

What was the racial and ethnic composition of your school/neighborhood?

If so, when did you first realize you were different from other people?

How did you feel? What did you think? What effect did this event have in your life, your feelings about yourself, your family? Your friends?

Who were the key people in your life (with regard to race and ethnicity)?

What were key events (with regard to race and ethnicity), positive and negative—How did you deal with the situation(s)?

Upon reflection, are there one or more significant events or individuals that you feel played a crucial role in your achievement of an ___ identity?

What was the ethnic/racial/religious background of your friends?

Who were your role models? Any significant people in your life?

In what ways did these people impact on your attitude and behavior about yourself?

Was there ever a time(s) that you wished you were not of Indian ancestry? Why?

Were there times you denied your Indianess? Why?

How did you feel about being Indian American at this time?

In what ways did these feelings translate into behaviors?

College

Now let's go back to your college years; tell me the story of how your identity has evolved (developed).

Where did you attend college?

Did you ever consider yourself different from other students? How?

Who were the key people in your life (with regard to race and ethnicity)?

What were key events (with regard to race and ethnicity), positive and negative—How did you deal with the situation(s)?

As a college student what does it mean to you to have an identity as an ___?

Upon reflection, are there one or more significant events or individuals that you feel played a crucial role in your achievement of an ___ identity?

What was the ethnic/racial/religious background of the majority of your friends?

Who were your role models?

In what ways did these people impact on your attitude and behavior about yourself?

How does your ethnic heritage have a place in undergraduate life in the United States?

Was your ethnic identity in conflict with being an "American" college student? If so, how?

Did you experience isolation as an Indian American student from the Indian community on campus?

What was it like in class?

What is it like to be in school with other Indian American students? Without other Indian/Indian American students?

Was there ever a time(s) that you wished you were not of Indian ancestry? Why?

Were there times you denied your Indianess? Why?

Did you belong to any ethnic student groups?

Did you take any courses related to Indian religion/literature/languages/politics, etc.?

Tell me about the difference in your experience as an Indian American college student between your first year and last year of college.

Adult

Now consider your life today. Tell me how your identity has evolved since college.

Do you ever consider yourself different from other people today? How?

Who are the key people in your life (with regard to race and ethnicity)?

What are key events (with regard to race and ethnicity), positive and negative—How do you deal with the situation(s)?

What do you view to be significantly different about your background and experience which allowed you to develop an identity as an ___?

How do you identify today?

What does it mean to you to have an identity as an ___?

Upon reflection, are there one or more significant events or individuals that you feel played a crucial role in your achievement of an ___ identity?

What are the ethnic/racial/religious background of your friends?

Who are your role models? An significant people in your life?

What type of impact have these people had on your life?

Have there been moments in recent times you wished you were not of Indian ancestry?

Have there been times you have denied your Indian ancestry?

Religion of Your Family: Role in Your Life

ADOLESCENCE

Religiously, how do you identify?

Where did you (your family) worship?

Was religion your primary reason for participating in group worship? Was it to preserve tradition? Was it for social reasons? Was it to celebrate home culture? Was it to strengthen local community? Was it for fun? Was it to speak the language?

How often did you attend religious events?

Did you attend "Sunday school" classes? If so, for how long? Frequency?

How well did you understand the rituals and traditions of the religion?

Were you aware of your caste, jati or nat (for Hindus)?

COLLEGE

How religious were you? Did you perform individual acts of worship in college (did you attend a temple, mosque, church, gurdwara)?

How often did you attend religious events? Did you attend "Sunday school" classes?

Were you more or less religious as a college student compared to as an adolescent?

What kind of knowledge did have about your religion? How well did you understand the rituals and traditions of the religion?

How did you practice your faith?

What was your main reason for participating in group worship? Was it to preserve tradition? Was it for social reasons? Was it to celebrate home culture? Was it to strengthen local community? Was it for fun? Was it to speak the language?

How important was it for you to go to a temple, mosque, church, gurdwara?

ADULTHOOD

Are you still religious? How religious are you?

Are you more or less religious when you were in college?

Do you have a shrine at home/dorm room (for Hindus)?

How much knowledge do you have about your religion?

How well do you understand the rituals and traditions of the religion?

How do you practice your faith? Where do you worship?

Do you perform individual acts? Or do you participate more in group worship?

Is religion your primary reason for participating in group worship? Is it to preserve tradition? Is it for social reasons? Is it to celebrate home culture? Is it to strengthen local community? Is it for fun? Is it to speak the language?

How often do you attend religious events?

What do you need to retain the religious traditions and rituals?

How important is it for you to go to a temple or mosque?

How does belonging to _____ faith make you feel about your Indian identity?

Discrimination

Over the years did any of your family members experience racial or religious discrimination? How did they deal with it?

Did you experience any racial or religious discrimination?

When did you first begin to see yourself as a racial minority? Religious minority?

How did this happen? How did these experiences influence your life at the time?

How have they affected your ethnic, racial, or religious way of identifying?

Interactions with Dominant Society

Do you feel that you have had to reject any of your family's values in order to "make it" in this society? What were they?

Do you believe that you have had to adopt any white values in order to make it in this society?

In what ways would you say these events, behaviors, attitudes of yours represent identity conflict over being an Indian American? How were you able to resolve these identity conflicts? What did you do?

How would you characterize your behavior towards white people? Please give two or three illustrative examples (members of other racial minorities, members of the Indian American community).

Other

Is there anything that we did not touch on or discuss fully in the interview? Anything you want to clarify?

NOTES

INTRODUCTION

1. The population of foreign-born residents and their children in the United States—that is, the first and second generations combined—is now larger than it has ever been, rising to 56 million from 34 million in just three decades (Scott 2002).
2. For the first time, individuals had the option of checking more than one box on the 2000 census (United States Bureau of the Census 2001).
3. Indian American Center for Political Awareness 2003. These distributions are relatively unchanged since 1990, when the Northeast had 35 percent, the Southeast 24 percent, the West 23 percent, and the Midwest 18 percent (Lee 1998).
4. Because not all research participants continue to identify with the religion in which they were raised, I use the phrase "home religion" to describe that religion and connote its role in their upbringing. As the reader will discover, the home religion remains relevant to the identities of even those research participants who no longer identify with it.
5. For their histories, see Takaki 1989; Jensen 1988; Chandresekhar 1982; Prashad 2000. For their communities and culture, see Khandelwal 2002; Rangaswamy 2000; Seth 1995; Helweg and Helweg 1990; Bacon 1996; Lessinger 1995; Leonard 1997; Saran 1985.
6. See Hawley and Mann 1993; Tinker 1977; Eck 1996; Fenton 1992; George 1998; Gonzales 1986; Kurien 1998; Leonard 1997; Williams 1992a, 1992b, 1996, 1998.
7. See R. H. Kim 2004a; Portes and Rumbaut 2001; Portes, Fernandez-Kelly, and Haller 2003; Portes and Zhou 1993; Min 2002; Gibson 1988; Levitt and Waters 2002; Kibria 2002; Bankston and Zhou 1995; Chong 1998; Zhou 1997; Lee 1994.
8. See Gupta 2000; Asher 2001, 2002; Vyas 2001; Mukhi 2000, 2002; Dasgupta 1997; Dhingra 2003; Purkayashtha 2005.
9. See Bankston and Zhou 1995; Chong 1998; Kim and Pyle 2004; R. H. Kim 2004a, 2004b.
10. See Jacobson 1998; Brodkin 1998; Roediger 1991.
11. The interview questions that formed the basis of my semistructured interview protocol can be found in the Appendix.
12. Throughout this text, "the South" refers to Alabama, Arkansas, Delaware, the District of Columbia, Florida, Georgia, Kentucky, Louisiana, Maryland, Mississippi, North Carolina, Oklahoma, South Carolina, Tennessee, Texas, Virginia, and West Virginia. This is consistent with the terms used by the United States Census Bureau. http://www.census.gov/population/www/cps/cpsdef.html.
13. One research participant, the son of one Sikh parent and one Hindu parent, identifies himself religiously as "Sikh and Hindu"; and although there was one Jain research participant, Girish, no material in his interview spoke to a Jain experience as opposed to his experience of being an Indian American, and therefore a racial and religious

minority in America. His experiences are discussed in that context without specific reference in the text to Jain religious identity or practice.

14. I was more interested in participants' perception of the racial/ethnic composition of the neighborhood and school than in the actual figures; accordingly, I did not ask them to complete a demographic sheet.

15. These research participants had been married for between one and five years.

16. This was a result of the 1965 law and the specific visa preferences—what Prashad (2000) discusses as "state selection," because the decision about who may immigrate is in the hands of the American government rather than in the hands of the would-be immigrants themselves.

17. See Wang and Wu 1996; Prashad 2000. Between 1965 and 1980, thousands of highly educated, professional-class Indian immigrants arrived in the United States (Jensen 1988; Steinberg 1989). This high educational and occupational level of the first wave of Indian immigrants permitted to enter the United States under the Immigration and Naturalization Act of 1965 was the result of several factors. First, a large number of Indian physicians, pharmacists, nurses, and other medical professionals were allowed to immigrate because of the shortage of domestic medical personnel during the Vietnam War and the increased need for such personnel with the creation of the Medicare and Medicaid programs (Prashad 2000). Second, the space race started by the Soviet Union in the late 1950s created a sense of demand for skilled scientists and engineers; many of the Asian countries were considered to be intellectually ahead of the United States on scientific matters, hence the preference for PhDs and engineers. Third, there was a political motivation: to end the prevailing image of the United States abroad as a racist nation. Fourth, many Indians who came as foreign students and completed their master's and PhD programs in the United States changed their status to permanent residents (Chandrasekhar 1982; Seth 1995). In addition, approximately 70,000 Indian refugees from the business and professional classes, expelled by the Idi Amin regime in Uganda in the early 1970s, were admitted to the United States under a special provision. Thousands more people of Indian descent immigrated from the Caribbean Islands and the British Commonwealth countries (Seth 1995).

18. South Asia includes Bangladesh, Bhutan, India, Nepal, Maldives, Pakistan, and Sri Lanka.

19. Idinopolus 1998.

20. Many research participants do see religion as a rigid set of rules or requirements. Measuring their own lives and conduct by reference to what they understand (usually from their parents) to be religion's rules, most therefore see themselves as not religious. By contrast, others may develop a sense of themselves as religious by merely following such rules.

21. See Graves 2001, who shows that scientific, not political, correctness underlies the critique of the race concept, and Gould 1996, who discusses the racism of science and attempts to debunk scientific racism.

22. In addition to the conflation of these terms in American speech, both ethnicity and religion, among other factors, are frequently racialized (Pierce 2000).

23. Cross and Fhagen-Smith 2001; Cross 1991; Adams 2001; Helms 1995.

CHAPTER 1   RELIGION IN AMERICA

1. Leonard 1997; Fenton 1988; Williams 1988; Khaldi 1991; George 1998; Kurien 1998; Mazumdar and Mazumdar 2003.

2. See Williams 1988; Narayanan 1992; Eck 2001; Haddad 2002.

3. 26 U.S.C. section 102 reads in full: "The Secretary may collect decennially statistics relating to religious bodies." The Census Bureau says "Public Law 94–521 prohibits us from asking a question on religious affiliation on a mandatory basis; therefore, the Bureau of the Census is not the source for information on religion." http://www.census.gov/prod/www/religion.htm. In fact, the referenced public law, passed in 1976, doesn't bar questions about religion but rather prohibits the punishment of respondents who decline to state their religion because doing so would violate its tenets. The relevant law is found at 26 U.S.C. section 225(d): "Where the doctrine, teaching, or discipline of any religious denomination or church prohibits the disclosure of information relative to membership," a respondent may not be punished for "a refusal, in such circumstances, to furnish such information." Because of its unique effectiveness in the collection of populationwide data, the Census should include in future decennial and other surveys *optional* questions on religious affiliation. (It would remain free to include in its presentations of data a caveat regarding the number of respondents who declined to answer.)

4. The Pluralism Project (www.pluralism.org) lists population statistics from many different sources, including governmental and community-based organizations. See also T. W. Smith 2002.

5. As the reader will see later in this chapter, many research participants differentiate between religion and spirituality. They consider religion to be the ritual practice of their parents. Many of the research participants self-identify as "not religious, but spiritual." I think if more people understood religion the way we are considering it here—as lived religion, the dynamic relationship between individuals and their beliefs and how that relationship affects their outlook and actions—they might be less inclined to make the distinction between "religious" (read doctrinaire or orthodox) and "spiritual" (connoting belief or faith outside the ritual sphere).

6. Given the focus of lived religion scholarship on case studies and other qualitative approaches, it will be exciting to see how the work of ethnographers and social scientists—once they incorporate religion into their work—will enrich religious studies, and vice versa. Even more exciting is the potential of lived religion and other approaches that focus on the experiences of religious minorities in the classroom, the workplace, and the commercial sphere to make a substantial contribution to shaping social policy in America.

7. There is a growing body of literature on the intersections of Asian Americans and Christianity, discussing the intersections of race and religion. See Alumkal 2003, Busto 1999, R. H. Kim 2004b.

8. For reasons relating to the interaction of culture and religion for non-Western Christians, the same could be said of the Christian children, but to a substantially lesser extent.

9. I am not out to blame the United States for having been founded by Christians or for having a Christian-majority population. In chapter 5, I do begin to point fingers at individual habits and structural phenomena that result in religious oppression of non-Christians in the United States. In the present chapter, America's overweening Christianity is merely a fact of the research participants' lives, like climate or topography.

10. White Christian American youth have a similar development and negotiate religion in similar ways (T. W. Smith 2002; Regnerus, Smith, and Fritsch 2003).

11. Gibson 1988; Maira 2002; Asher 2002.

12. Gibson 1988; Suárez-Orozco 2003; Pang and Cheng 1998.

13. If anything can be said about Leela's remark, it is that, remarkably, she didn't say that Hinduism and the *Gita* were never discussed in class. Because she went to a parochial school, she had a mandatory Bible class; one day in that class the teacher said to her, "Leela, why don't you tell us a little bit about Hinduism?" That, Leela reported, was the full extent of Hinduism's visibility in school.

14. One can speculate that Leela's parents had one of three motives. Perhaps they genuinely held the philosophical belief that Christian worship, including Communion, is one appropriate way to perform Hindu devotions—or at least an adequate substitute for the latter. Perhaps they were not particularly religious, or had a social agenda focused on assimilation rather than ethnic maintenance. Or maybe Leela's questions raised concerns about whether and how Leela might feel different from her Christian classmates and neighbors; by telling her to take Communion, her parents were avoiding a situation where she could be targeted as different. (Whether Communion bread and wine is *prasad* (food offering to deities), and whether it is better to hide one's Hinduism when in another religious context, could of course be debated.)

15. I am sad to report that, according to the in-service teachers I work with today, this type of directed and illegal religious practice is still occurring in public schools today.

16. Kelly Chong (1998) described a similar experience among young Korean Americans.

CHAPTER 2   ETHNICITY AND RELIGION

1. Religiosity and religious participation did have a gender component which, although it is not my focus, should be acknowledged. The process of childhood and adolescent development involves the internalization of gender roles; we can therefore expect the influences of both the family and ethnoreligious community and the (sometimes conflicting) influences of the dominant society to be incorporated into the gender identities of second-generation Indian Americans. Gender identity develops through a process of processing and internalizing diverse influences (as does ethnic identity, described in more detail below). Religion historically has been considered an institution that promotes gender role "traditionalism," including the role of motherhood for women, and research shows that across religions girls and women are more likely than boys and men to participate in regular worship and to report that religion is "very important" to them (Regnerus, Smith, and Fritsch 2003). A study that examines influences on the gender identity of Muslim high-school girls in the United States seems to bear this out, finding that greater religiosity and ethnic group identity predicts greater "femininity." The researchers locate their findings at the crossroads of cultural and religious influences on gender, concluding that the religiosity/femininity connection reflects "the role of institutionalized Islam and traditional ethnic cultural norms at work in an immigrant population" (Abu Ali and Reisen 1999). To the extent that any cohort of just forty-one people can be spoken of in terms of averages or trends, the findings of Abu Ali and Reisen and of Regnerus et al. are largely borne out by the research participants in the present study.

2. I draw upon the works of several scholars: Stephan and Stephan 2000; Spickard and Burroughs 2000; Saeed, Blain, and Forbes 1999; Zhou 1999; J. Kim 1981; Phinney 1990; Hoare 1991.

3. The phrase *situational ethnicity* refers to the person's assuming different ethnic roles based on the situation he or she is in or the person with whom he or she is interacting. See, for example, Root 2000.

4. In the course of the interview two research participants also identified with a caste/*jati*.

5. "Indian American" was the second most often chosen label. See also Morning 2001, 165.

6. Maira 1998, 2002; Kibria 1999, 2002; Min and Kim 2002; Min and Park 1999; Hurtado et al. 1993; Hurtado, Gurin, and Peng 1997.

7. All of these factors are dimensions of culture, ways in which the research participants expressed and engaged with their culture. Culture—defined primarily by traditional cultural markers associated with the homeland, India—provided a pathway for building relationships based on commonalties.

8. See Helms 1995 and Omi and Winant 1997.

9. See Rosenthal and Feldman 1992.

10. Tajfel 1978, 1981; Hardiman and Jackson 1997; Tatum 1997.

11. Ethnic awareness for some of these second-generation Indian Americans developed and led to a racial awareness even without critical incidents of discrimination. For others, discrimination was the catalyst that led to a racial awakening and consciousness.

12. See Thai 1999.

13. Discussing "Nigrescence," the process of becoming black, William Cross describes encounter experiences. An encounter is an experience that catches the subject off guard. "The encounter must work around, slip through, or even shatter the relevance of the person's current identity and world view" (Cross 1991, 199). September 11, 2001, and the resulting 9/11 backlash against people who looked Arab or Middle Eastern may prove to be a critical incident for South Asian Americans. The data in this study were collected prior to the September 11 attacks.

14. Whereas transnationalism is often discussed by reference to remittances (what one might call Western Union transnationalism), no research participants reported remittances, see Levitt and Waters 2002; Portes, Fernandez-Kelly, and Haller 2003.

15. Many U.S.-born Asian Americans consider themselves American when they are children, but increasingly adopt the ethnic identity of their parents as they grow older (Kim 1996; Kim and Yu 1996; Thai 1999).

16. Espiritu 2002, 38.

17. Basch, Schiller, and Szanton Blanc 1994; Foner 2001; Schiller and Fouron 1999.

18. See Durkehim 1995/1915; Warner and Srole 1945; Weber 1961; Smith 1978; Stout 1975.

19. Language was the runner-up to religion among the most important components of ethnic identity, which echoes the scholarship from the time of Kallen [1915] to as recently as the work of Lopez and Espiritu, 1997, which identifies religion and language to be the building blocks of ethnicity.

20. For Hindus, see Jackson and Nesbit 1993; Vertovec 2000. For Muslims, see Saeed, Blain, and Forbes 1999; Jacobson 1997.

21. This allowance, about one hundred people per year, was not extended to most other Asian nations as part of the 1952 law.

22. Most of the existing academic typologies relating ethnicity to religion are therefore unhelpful (Yang and Ebaugh 2001). They are not flawed; they are simply not suited to the purpose here, which is to understand what religion looks like and how it functions in the individual lives of the second-generation Indian American research participants.

23. Chong 1998; Kurien 1998, 2004; Yang and Ebaugh 2001; Yang 1999; Min 1992, 2000a, 2000b; Haddad 2000.

24. A third important distinction between pre-1965 and post-1965 immigrant groups relates to theological differences. Distinctions between the belief systems of the Western

faiths (Judaism and Christianity) and Hinduism, Sikhism, and Islam are both obvious and difficult to summarize. Even differences in the manner of religious practice between South Asian and other Muslims make the Indian Muslim experience unique. This subject, however, is beyond the scope of this book.

25. That is to say, scholars cannot expect to get the same quality and thoroughness of exposure to religious practices from going to a gurdwara as they can from observing and attending church services.

26. On hybrid identity, see Hutnyk 1999; Maira 1999; Bhabha 1994; Anthias 2001.

27. Ramesh 1998; Williams 1988; Helweg and Helweg 1990.

28. See Bloul 2003 for a survey of the different definitions of the term *ethnorelgious*.

29. The importance of an ethnoreligious community to the religious identity development of second-generation Indian Americans may be best illustrated by Aziz's experience without one. In college, he recounted, "there was no Muslim community where I lived. [The] nearest one was forty-two miles away. That was difficult. I would try to do things on my own, but without a community you're dead." For Aziz, the individual experience of religion and worship was impossible without a group of people—a community—with which it could be experienced. Disconnection from a religious community meant disconnection from religion itself. For him, praying had always been something you did in the company of others. Binu, a female Malayali Catholic, expressed a similar sentiment. As a graduate student living in an area without a Malayali Catholic congregation, she rarely went to church, and whenever she could she drove home from school and to attend Malyali services with her family. Binu's and Aziz's feelings and actions show how religious practice, the vehicle through which faith is acted out (if not also experienced), may be dependent upon access to a community of coreligionists.

30. Although cross-attendance by Muslims at Hindu events or Hindus at Muslim events was rare, several Sikh research participants talked about attending Hindu celebrations. Research participants' ethnoreligious communities typically celebrated appropriate religious holidays and Republic Day, or Indian independence day, each August 15.

31. For reasons relating to the interaction of culture and religion for non-Western Christians, the same could be said for the Catholic and Christian children, albeit to a lesser extent.

32. Yoo 1999; Williams 1988, 1996; Fenton 1988.

33. See also Jacob and Thakur 2001; Williams 1988; Fenton 1988.

34. Portes and Rumbaut (2001) show that immigrants with a high level of education and income are better able to provide a grounding in their own culture.

35. Seema's case is both illustrative and unusual. Although they were Christians, Seema and her family participated actively in the Indian American Hindu community in Nashville.

36. Perhaps ironically, this was particularly true of Hindu parents. These Indian Hindu parents grew up in a country where one can be Hindu as effortlessly as one can be Christian in the United States. They also grew up in a country where the academic study of religion is virtually unheard of.

37. Jacob and Thakur 2001; Eck 2001; Kurien 1998; Miller 1995.

38. Ironically, Sunday school was often the one cultural event that Indian Christian young people could not attend; several Catholic research participants who went to the "white" Catholic Sunday school faced a schedule conflict. They wanted to go to the Hindu Sunday school because all their friends were going; but their parents decided their religious obligations dictated otherwise.

39. On the basis of the tone and context in which the research participants characterized these feelings, they appear to have been influenced by one or both of two factors: the normal adolescent and preadolescent rejection of parents' ideas and activities as boring, and a particular rejection of these events because they represented the uncomfortable ways in which research participants felt different from their non-Indian peers.

40. Note that Ahalya is engaging in the conflation of religion and ethnicity described above. In all likelihood, Ahalya would also say she feels less Hindu, but her word choice during our discussion of religion was "less Indian."

41. It should be borne in mind that access to an ethnoreligious community was a product of parents' decision as well. Because children are dependent upon their parents for transportation and the social access that comes with it, geographic isolation can be experienced even when an ethnoreligious community is present. Among this cohort of research participants, however, parents with geographic access and the economic wherewithal did participate, at least passively, in an ethnoreligious community.

42. Rosenthal and Feldman (1992) have shown parents' involvement in the ethnic community is directly related to an adolescent's positive sense of ethnic identity.

43. In an illustration of the changeability of ethnic priorities, at least one research participant who said it was important to her to marry a coethnic has since married a white American.

CHAPTER 3   FACETS OF LIVED RELIGION

1. On "what matters," see Roof 1999, 204; Hall 1997; Orsi 1985.

2. Salim's approach to *sewa* is discussed at length in his case study in chapter 6.

3. *Sewa* is not uniquely a Muslim concept. *Sewa*, or *seva*, is a Sanskrit word literally meaning "service."

4. This shorthand expression refers to the five religious obligations of a Sikh male: *kesh* (uncut hair), which is kept covered by a distinctive turban; *kirpan* (religious sword); *kara* (metal bracelet); *kanga* (comb); and *kaccha* (undershorts).

5. As discussed at greater length later in this chapter and in chapter 4, Western religious concepts and practices, such as weekly communal attendance at a house of worship and what research participants perceived as a clear structure of hard-and-fast rules (the "Ten Commandments"), are strikingly different from home-based prayer and other forms of domestic ritual, nonweekly worship schedules, and holidays that lack legal recognition. Comparing the family's religious ways with the concept of religion represented by the American Christian norm seems to have led some research participants to distinguish between their own belief system, however deeply held, and religiosity. In addition, many research participants reported negative encounters with Christians; as noted in chapter 4, such encounters often had a profound effect on the research participant's religious and ethnic identity.

6. Attending worship gatherings also had a language-maintenance function. When their parents gathered with other adults, research participants got to hear the native language spoken. Particularly for those whose parents conversed with them in English at home, this was important.

7. This, of course, relates back to the issue of parents as imperfect conveyors of religious knowledge. When children ask their parents during a puja, "What does this mean?" or "Why do we do that?" parents are rarely able to translate and only sometimes able to explain. See Neha and Salim's case study in chapter 6 for a more detailed analysis of the issue.

8. I borrow from Schiller's (1992) definition of *transnationalism*: "the frequent and wide-spread movement back and forth between communities of origin and destination and the resulting cultural and economic transformation." My usage notwithstanding, one can have transnational experiences without leaving the United States because of the constant flow of people and cultural commodities, such as viewing Bollywood films, having relatives from India visit for extended periods of time, and the like. These experiences can also be seen as transnational experiences, to the extent that they expose people directly to images, ideas, and people from the country of origin. There is no agreement on the exact nature of transnationalism. However, most of the research and theoretical discussion are based on the lives of immigrants. There is a similar situation when theorizing about the second generation and transnationalism. For a review of the term *transnationalism,* and the various definitions, see the Introduction in *The Changing Face of Home* (Levitt and Waters 2002b).

9. Although scholars have identified several kinds of second-generation transnationalism—social and financial remittances, engagement in political activity, and retention of language are examples of transnationalism examined in other second-generation groups; see Levitt and Waters 2002a—religion has scarcely been considered. I think Jones-Correa (2003, 223) is correct when he says: "It is less than certain what the real significance of these behaviors is and whether these markers of transnationalism make a person truly 'transnational.'"

10. In this respect, transnationalism is an illustration of the meaningful distinctions between Indian Americans and the immigrant waves of the nineteenth and early twentieth centuries. Technology—from transatlantic flights to cheap phone cards—has made it possible for immigrants and the second generation to maintain regular contact with family and friends in the "old country" and even to return periodically to the ancestral home. This is a counterpoint to the merely emotional transnationalism experienced by immigrants of previous centuries when a trip "home" would have involved a prohibitively expensive six-week boat trip.

11. One of the reasons that many who traveled to India during the K–12 period did so during summer vacation was to make the most of the significant financial outlay involved.

12. Many Sikh emigrants still support the fight for Khalistan, an independent Sikh state in the Punjab region; many activities at gurdwaras across the country have been organized around such a movement. As to where the religious authority lies, there are two schools of thought. The first believes that all spiritual authority lies with Akal *Takhat* (Throne of the Timeless) which is located on the grounds of the Golden Temple. The second school of thought believes in being involved with this particular religious authority but does not see it as the ultimate religious authority. This too may be a window on how the development of a religiously identified diaspora will affect the religion's development in India and globally.

13. Although the concept of diaspora is more frequently associated with a national or ethnic affiliation, religious diasporas do exist. For a discussion on religious diasporas, see Cohen 1997 and Vertovec 2000.

14. As Vertovec (2000, 3) observes with respect to Hindus, "the tie to India goes beyond ethnic . . . origins. . . . [For Hindus,] India is a sacred space abounding with sacred places, from local shrines venerated by castes and clans to sites described in central religious texts like the *Mahabharata,* where the most widely recognized gods and legendary humans are believed to have undertaken some of their most significant deeds."

15. Amazingly, Wolf's otherwise excellent work (2002) presents neither data nor any substantive discussion of religion's role in transnational experiences or of the relationship of transnational experiences to religious identity or practice.

16. The research participants in my study had some emotional ties with relatives or friends, and for the most part their transnational life is lived primarily at the emotional level. As they manage and inhabit multiple cultural and ideological zones, the resulting emotional transnationalism constantly juxtaposes what they do at home with what is done at Home. Although this may offer the security of a source of identity, it also creates tensions, confusion, and contradictory messages that, as has been demonstrated, can lead to intense alienation and despair among some.

17. Research participants who traveled to India frequently over their lifespan were more likely to have developed relationships with their extended family there—not only grandparents but also cousins and neighbors close to their own age. These research participants now return to India, among other reasons, to see family. For those with gaps between trips of a decade or more, the quality of the connection is different; it is characterized more by familial obligation than by an emotional bond. These research participants are less likely to have close relationships with family, less likely to have facility with the home language (which has a debilitating effect on relationships with extended family in India), and are more likely to feel and act like tourists when they visit India.

18. Some research participants never enjoyed traveling to India, and nearly 25 percent have not been there since graduating from high school.

19. This is precisely what their immigrant parents hoped they would achieve by immersing their children in the Indian culture they had left behind and to exposing them to the culture of the extended family.

20. Harjit, a Sikh, attended Sikh Sunday school at the gurdwara in his home town: "Every Sunday at the gurdwara, I learned a lot about my religion, as well as a lot of the culture."

21. Some argue that the prevalence of Hindi language betrays a north Indian bias on the part of many Indian American communities. It seems more likely that the real reasons for the prevalence of Hindi are, first and most important, the majority of Indian Americans trace their lineage to the northern parts of India where Hindi and the other Indo-Aryan languages predominate, and second, to the extent the immigrant parents are trying to impart an "Indian" (as opposed to religious or regional) identity in the second generation, Hindi—as one of just two official languages of India (along with English)—is an obvious choice. On the other hand, in Burlington, Mass., today, a single Sunday school teaches Hindi, Tamil, Telegu, Gujarati, and Marati, because it serves such a large and diverse Indian population.

22. The Vishva Hindu Parishad, founded in 1964 by leaders of the Hindu nationalist organization Rashtriya Swayamsevak Sangh (RSS) and the Hindu guru Swami Chinmayanand, is a movement that simultaneously tries to reach out globally to all Hindus in the world and mobilize Hindus in India for anti-Muslim politics. Between 1984 to 1992 the VHP mobilized Hindus for the destruction of the Babri Masjid in Ayodhya, a mosque allegedly built on a Hindu site. Not only did this action achieve its target of destroying the sixteenth-century mosque but it also has made the Bharatiya Janata Party (BJP), a political party allied to both VHP and RSS, one of the largest political parties in India.

23. Fenton acknowledged as much in his commentary. His death in 1994 prevented him from returning to examine the second generation in its adulthood.

24. As noted at the beginning of this chapter, the hegemonic nature of Christianity in American culture exacerbated this situation.

25. Developing a questioning attitude about Hinduism had also led Avya, earlier in life, to discover more about her own background and why her parents had taught her only a limited version of Hinduism.

26. Aziz claims never to have used drugs, advising his interviewer: "Don't get high off your own supply."

27. About half the research participants described themselves as "spiritual," an appellation related more to religion's function as a moral compass than to its performance as ritual. Only a few said they were "religious."

28. Though Smita discussed "not knowing why she was doing the ritual," which could be labeled "symbolic religion" (Gans 1979), that might be an oversimplification of the issue.

29. Here, we acknowledge the virtual truism that religious practice is situational. It may mean one thing during high school and something very different in adulthood—and it may do so without being inconsistent or diminishing the depth of meaning respondents feel toward their religious practices and identities.

30. See Prashad 2000; Kurien 1998, 2001; Maira 2002.

31. Along with the fact that the literature on ethnic identity has overlooked religion, the nascent research on second-generation transnationalism has also for the most part overlooked religion.

CHAPTER 4   WHAT DOES RACE HAVE TO DO WITH RELIGION?

1. I would argue that religion is on at least equal footing with race as an American social organizing principle, as is surely obvious to anyone who has made it this far into the text.

2. There is even a word for such a test: *shibboleth.* See Judges 12:6 (KJV).

3. This is a topic being wrestled with by scholars examining the intersections of race and religion among East Asian American college students and evangelical student organizations (Alumkal 2004; R. H. Kim 2004a and 2004b; Busto 1996).

4. Whiteness emerged in the seventeenth century in the British colonies as a common identity across class lines among Europeans in opposition to African slaves and Native Americans. Eventually, white, Christian, and free were metonyms.

5. The scholarly preoccupation with the black and the Jew is arguably changing in the years since September 11, 2001.

6. Pierce (2000) discusses how race is also a cultural identity for blacks.

7. For a recent review of this controversial issue, see Koshy 2001.

8. In this particular context, the term *Indian* has a different meaning. It refers to a group that in today's parlance we would refer to as *South Asian*—incorporating the entire subcontinent that was in the first half of the twentieth century the British colony of India.

9. *United States v. Bhagat Singh Thind*, 261 U.S. 204 (1923).

10. For more regarding the racial ambiguity of Indians in the United States, see Visweswaran 1997; Kibria 1998; Koshy 1998; Takaki 1989.

11. The other fundamental dynamic of U.S. racial thinking is characterized by an understanding of race as "pure" and thus easily divided into a limited series of mutually exclusive categories (Omi and Winant 1997; Kibria 1998).

12. Among Asian Americans, they are "A Part Yet Apart," the pithy title of Shankar and Srikant's (1998) anthology.

13. Ricky Martin, *Livin' la Vida Loca* (1998).

14. In *Indiana Jones and the Temple of Doom*, the villain is a priest of the Hindu goddess Kali. Early in the film, the protagonist and his cohorts are served "chilled monkey brains" in an Indian palace.

15. Singh (2003) argues that contemporary events have caused religion to join race as one of the most powerful and prominent channels through which to identify the other, or "enemy," in America's national life. As amply discussed by Singh and in the present work, this disturbing tendency affects primarily non-Christian people of color. As a result, Singh argues, the intersection of white supremacy with Christian supremacy—the intermingling of racial and religious bigotry—has become an increasingly prevalent and influential trend in the United States, both in the media and among the general population.

16. Here it is important to acknowledge a gender component to the phenomenon of religious oppression; for example, black or white Muslim women who wear *purdah* or *hijab* (head scarf) may be targets because of this nonracial marker. I would posit that even this is less likely, however, because it is really the brown skin that sticks out in the American mind as a representation of religious difference.

17. The term *redlining* refers to once-legal and written (now illegal and unwritten) policies that functioned to maintain racial separation and white economic advantage, such as by denying mortgage loans to blacks and residents of "black" neighborhoods, real estate rental and sales policies that discourage racial integration, and racially restrictive covenants.

18. Much of the contemporary scholarship on discrimination distinguishes between agents—those engaging in or benefiting from the racist act or structure—and those targets who are victimized by the racist act or fact. See Freire 1996, and Hardiman and Jackson 1997. With respect to Indian Americans and other groups that are neither black nor white, we can identify a new phenomenon of "American privilege." Similar to McIntosh's (1998) discussion of "white privilege"—the advantages one enjoys merely by being seen as white—American privilege is enjoyed by a person presumed to be American (black or white) as compared to one who, for racial reasons, is assumed to be a foreigner or a foreign-born person. A number of research participants described experiences (many chronicled below and in chapter 5) that are manifestations of this American privilege.

19. Race as a black-white divide does not exist in India, but a social hierarchy does exist that links privilege to skin color through the intermediary concepts of caste and social class. As Mazumdar (1989a, 47) points out, "South Asians, regardless of national origin on the subcontinent, cling to a mythography which holds that the elite (upper caste/class) are 'Aryan' and by extension 'Caucasian.' They are themselves acutely color conscious."

20. Min and R. Kim (1999) acknowledge as much, writing: "The fact that highly successful Asian American professionals identify with African Americans and Latinos and adopt a moderate level of racial identification as a person of color goes against our expectations. Asian immigrants are generally prejudiced against African Americans and have a tendency to align with whites in a white-black biracial dichotomy."

21. Some research participants tried to get involved with collegiate pan-Asian student organizations, but found that these organizations were made up predominantly of East Asian Americans. As a result, the research participants reported feeling physically that they did not belong, and further that their concerns were not the group's concerns. None remained active in Asian student organizations, nor are any currently active in anything that might be described as a pan-Asian movement.

22. Covert racism, of course, is much harder to identify or to prove. To put it another way, the "white man's burden" has become a burden upon other racial minorities; the stark and familiar examples of Civil Rights era–like lynchings, beatings, and hosings—have meant that nonblack minorities who point out that they have been denied an opportunity for academic or professional advancement for racial reasons are accused of "crying racism." The same burden affects much scholarship in the field. The work of Batts (1989), McConahay (1986), and other scholars who examine overt and covert racism, while offering a helpful theoretical foundation for the present effort, is so oriented toward and based upon the experiences of African Americans that it is self-limiting in ways that will become clear in this section and in the analysis to follow.

23. The model minority myth is the American belief that Asians work hard and are smart, particularly in math and science. The public first became aware of the idea of a model minority in December 1966, when *U.S. News and World Report* published an article lauding the success of Chinese Americans. The term *model minority* was coined in the mid-1960s by William Petersen, a social demographer, who believed that the success and achievement of Asian Americans paralleled those of the Jewish Americans (Lee 1996, 6).

24. See Tuan 2001; Lee 1994, 1996; Osajima 1988.

25. See Palmer 2001; Lei 2003; Tatum 1997.

26. Tuan 2001; Ancheta 1998; Takaki 1989; C. J. Kim 2001.

27. Lowe (1996) uses the phrase "foreigner within" and Tuan (2001) uses "forever foreigners" to discuss the same concept.

28. If the reader feels inclined to defend the sorority, that is precisely the power of covert racism; it can be difficult, even impossible, to prove. Questions about one's culture or ethnic identity are not out of line per se, but it is easy to see how such questions—or even the display of certain attitudes, or using a certain tone of voice—could make an individual feel unwelcome. They are manifestations of the fraternity/sorority member's unease about bringing someone different into the group. The issue here is not the sorority's intentions but how Binita understood the experience. Because they focus on a conspicuous difference between the group and the individual, questions about a person's background in this context become a proxy for the message, "You are different by virtue of your race and ethnicity, and we're not sure you'll fit in with us." This is, of course, the flip side of McIntosh's (1998) white privilege. White privilege is an "elusive and fugitive subject," but it surely includes the assumption of belonging and immunity from the kind of "where are you from" questioning that Binita endured.

29. In fairness, some of the experiences described, although occurring in the school environment, were at times and places that were beyond the ears of the teachers and other school personnel.

30. Fisher et al. (2000) reported on the distress associated with instances of perceived racial prejudice encountered in educational contexts by African American, Asian American, and Hispanic adolescents.

31. A similar movement in Great Britain emphasizes the primacy of second-generation Indian Britons' religious identity. As Raj (2000) notes, this movement reveals the attractiveness of religious identity (Hindu) over over an Asian one. (The term *Asian* in the United Kingdom, in contrast to the American, refers primarily to people of South Asian extraction.) The promotion of an explicitly religious (Hindu) identity provides British Asian young people a way to distinguish themselves from South Asian Muslims. By way of comparison, it is interesting to note that the movement toward a primarily

religious identity in the United States is immigrant-initiated, while in Britain the provenance of the religious emphasis is the second generation.

32. Notwithstanding the fact that some religious markers—such as the *hijab* (Muslim headscarf), *dastaar* (Sikh turban), or religious jewelry such as a crucifix—are indeed visible.

CHAPTER 5   RELIGIOUS OPPRESSION

1. As one of the three Abrahamic faiths, some might argue, Islam is a Western religion. Here, however, I refer to the Western canon as traditionally understood, with its European theology, art, culture, and intellectual moorings. In this schema, Islam is indeed an outsider.

2. Virginia banned Catholics from public offices in the 1640s, Massachusetts expelled Catholic priests in 1647, and after 1689 New York, Pennsylvania, Virginia, and Maryland refused to grant citizenship to immigrant Catholics (Spring 2003).

3. The adoption of the First Amendment did not put an end to government-sponsored religion. The First Amendment imposed restrictions only on the federal government, and barred it from interfering with or being involved in religious communities, including those supported by the states. Only after *Cantwell v. Connecticut* (1940) and *Everson v. Board of Education* (1947) were the First Amendment's free-exercise guarantee and establishment prohibition also made applicable to the states through Fourteenth Amendment incorporation.

4. See also Roediger and Barret 2004; Jacobson 1998; Sanchez 1997.

5. In reality, religious oppression affects all non-Christian faiths. One well-known form of religious oppression is antisemitism; even anti-Catholicism has not disappeared entirely from American culture. Inasmuch as the present work deals with my cohort of forty-one Indian Americans, however, the focus is on the oppression of Hindu, Muslim, and Sikh Americans.

6. Christian denominations that pray in tongues as well as African American and Asian American Christianity are also seen as others. As Lincoln (1999) has noted, religion is structured in such a way that "religion in America" has usually meant the religion of white Americans, unless words like Negro, folk, or black were specifically mentioned.

7. When the Muslim community in Palos Heights, Illinois, attempted to buy the old Reformed Church of Palos Heights and turn it into a mosque, they were met with strong resistance from the community and the city council. There were rumblings among residents that a mosque would hurt property values in the mostly white, middle-class suburb (a concern not raised with respect to the approximately twenty Christian churches there). A member of the city council was heard to remark on National Public Radio that she would prefer that the church be occupied by a "normal" religion "like the Catholics." In the end, the city council offered the Al Salam Mosque Foundation $200,000 to abandon their plans for building a mosque in Palos Heights. The foundation accepted the offer because the group would rather remove itself from the politically charged debate. At a special city council meeting a member of the group stated, "Our people want to be able to worship in peace . . . and without fear of stigma"(Edwards 2000).

8. Hindus themselves have mistakenly used the word *idol* to describe *murtis*. See Fenton 1992.

9. It is important to note that an established norm does not necessarily represent a majority, but those who have the ability to exert control over other. (See Pharr, 1995).

10. On June 26, 1991, a Muslim imam, Siraj Wahhaj of Brooklyn, opened a session of the U.S. House of Representatives for the first time. In February of 1992, Imam W. Deen Mohammed of the Chicago-based American Muslim Mission opened a session of the U.S. Senate with prayer, again the first Muslim ever to do so (Eck 2001).

11. Despite their religious origin, the U.S. Supreme Court has upheld blue laws, concluding that although the laws had roots in the Christian religion, it is within the powers and rights of a state to set aside a day of rest for the well-being of its citizens. See, for example, *McGowan v. Maryland,* 366 U.S. 420 (1961). Again, the question is begged: Why Sunday?

12. Most presidential inaugural speeches contain references to God other than the traditional closing, "God bless America." Likewise, President Bill Clinton quoted Matthew 5:9, a verse from the Christian Bible, during the signing of the peace treaty between Israel and Jordan in 1994, and President George W. Bush quoted the Hebrew Bible's book of Deuteronomy in a 2002 speech on Palestinian statehood. See http://www.thenation.com/doc/20031222/stam and http://www.pbs.org/newshour/bb/middle_east/jan-june 02/bush_speech_6-24.html.

    To his credit, Bill Clinton in 1996 became the first U.S. president to sign a proclamation commemorating the celebration of Eid ul Fitr and to invite Muslims to the White House to celebrate the holiday. Several states' governors now regularly issue proclamations concerning Ramadan. President Clinton also issued a proclamation on the birthday of the Sikh Guru, Guru Nanak, in 1998. The proclamation read in part: "Religious pluralism in our nation is bringing us together in new and powerful way." *San Diego Union Tribune,* November 13, 1998.

13. The phrase "In God We Trust" was introduced by eleven Protestant denominations. In 1886 Congress passed legislation sanctioning the printing of the phrase on American currency. The U.S. Department of Treasury started printing the phrase on penny starting in 1909. President Theodore Roosevelt did not approve of the phrase and the penny was taken out of circulation. Later, during the upheaval of the Cold War, in further wanting to distance itself from the communist USSR, the United States asserted itself as a Christian nation and the phrase was again used on money, including paper money, by a resolution of the eighty-fourth Congress signed into law by President Eisenhower. See http://www.religioustolerance.org/nat_mott.htm.

14. The Great Hall of the Supreme Court was used for Christmas celebrations hosted by Chief Justice William Rehnquist despite opposition voiced by some of his colleagues and non-Christian law clerks (Klain 2005).

15. I use the term *stories* rather than *myths* because the latter word seems to assume that the tale in question is not actually true.

16. This term refers to a person born into Christianity.

17. Olsen 1997; Edwards 2000; see also Aronowitz 1999.

18. I would like to thank John Bartlett for this phrase and the Joshi Five for their enthusiasm when learning of the term and description.

19. Also see Mazur and McCarthy 2001 and Moore 1994 for excellent discussions on the economics of commodification.

20. Scholars acknowledge the harmful impact of racism on students of color in the educational context, particularly the negative impact that teacher bias can have on students. Cochran-Smith 1997; Darder 1991; Delpit 1995; Pang 2004.

21. The impact on South Asian religious communities of these misperceptions can be real and difficult. The distortion and constant association of Islam with terrorism creates and perpetuates a fear of Muslims, and particular wariness of groups or communities

of Muslims. Muslim communities have encountered hostility when attempting to erect masjids in towns across America, even when they were going to be built in areas designated by special zoning ordinances as space for churches and worshipers (see note 8 above). Hindu and Sikh communities have also encountered problems when trying to build their respective houses of worship.

22. The participation requirement, without an option to engage in a nonreligious alternative project, means that the program would in fact have been illegal even if it promoted multiple religions because the establishment clause also prohibits the promotion of religion *as against irrelgion*. Two federal Circuit Courts have concluded that coach- or teacher-led group prayer outside the classroom is a violation of the First Amendment's Establishment Clause. See *Doe v. Duncanville Independent School District*, 994 F.2d 160 (5th Circuit, 1993) (preliminary injunction), 70 F. 3d 402 (5th Circuit, 1995) (final decision) (holding that a basketball coach may not lead team in prayer at practice or prior to a game) and *Steele v. Van Buren Public School District*, 845 F.2d 1492 (8th Circuit, 1988) (holding that a band teacher's practice of leading the band in prayer at rehearsals and performances violated the Establishment Clause).

23. Parental response has been shown to have a substantial impact on whether young people choose to confront prejudice or accept it. See the works of Ponterotto and Pedersen 1993; Tatum 1997.

24. The misconception that Hindus worship idols is among the most persistent and frustrating inaccuracies in common understanding of the religion. Unfortunately, it is perpetuated by Hindus and non-Hindus alike.

25. Again, I don't wish to present a theological argument about proselytzation, but rather discuss it in terms of harassment and discrimination as it was described by several research participants.

26. The term "South Asian" here appears to refer to people with national or ethnic origins in Bangladesh, India, Maldives, Nepal, Pakistan, and Sri Lanka.

27. Several Asian American organizations have published hate crime audits.

28. See http://www.rediff.com/us/2001/sep/17ny2.htm.

29. The possible exception being a nonbrown person who was in some other respect visibly and identifiably Muslim, such as a *hijab*-wearing woman.

30. The Sikh Coalition was founded a few days after September 11, 2001.

31. Islam is seen as evil not only in the Christian-influenced American popular mind, but also by many Hindus, Jews, and others. Ironically, this has enabled a certain degree of coalition-building between Hindus and Jews, applying the "enemy of my enemy" theory of political positioning.

32. Harjit's experience also offers another example of Christian privilege: A Roman Catholic wearing a crucifix would never encounter a coworker asking glibly, "Hey, what's with the dead guy around your neck?" Christian imagery is familiar and understood, and there is a known obligation to act and speak respectfully about it. By contrast, the elements of Indian religious are "foreign" and therefore remain subject to ridicule, misunderstanding, and marginalization.

33. The man who was killed, Navroze Mody, was Zorastrian (a Parsi), and the other man, whose severe injuries resulting in brain trauma, is Hindu.

34. The statement is based on the research participants' own descriptions of their contemporaneous reactions.

35. During their interviews, it was clear that some research participants began applying this new depth of feeling to their K–12 experiences; in recollecting them, the experiences took on an emotional power that in some cases they had not earlier had.

However, this should not be understood to mean that experiences during K–12 are without both immediate and long-term religious impact. Overall, this research shows that the opposite is true.

36. One might also surmise that experiences in college and adulthood are seen as more part of the "real world," whereas childhood teasing can be written off by adults as a temporary artifact of childhood itself.

CHAPTER 6   CASE STUDIES

1. Kerala is one of the southern states in India.

2. Erikson's (e.g., 1968) theory of psychosocial development could be interpreted as a model of religious faith development.

3. According to the 2000 U.S Census, Hindi and Gujarati speakers—a combined 600,000 people—outnumber all the other Indian languages combined (United States Bureau of the Census 2003).

4. See Nieto 1999.

5. See Fenton 1988 and Kurien 1998.

6. Prashad (2001) would describe her one of the "fervent proponents of racism as the colorblind."

7. The social identity development model is based on theories of race rather than of ethnicity, and therefore does not consider the effects of the acceptance stage on nonracial aspects of ethnicity.

8. Of course, while he was questioning them, he still lacked the knowledge or resources that might have counterbalanced the discrimination and perhaps led him to challenge the teacher.

9. As this is not a theological text, I decline to discuss in detail the purported distinctions among the various sects of Islam. For purposes of the present analysis, the key point is that most Isma'ilis, like Salim, consider themselves to be Muslim, but that many mainstream Sunni and Shi'ite Muslims do not consider Isma'ilis to be Muslim.

10. Another factor is the decline in religious attendance and practice observed across American college students, as students use the freedom of college to explore other social identities and activities (Pascarella and Terenzini 1991).

11. This too is typical of those research participants who reported attending religious functions in adulthood; most said they were seeking community rather than religion as such.

12. Consistent with Salim's story, research shows that youth who hold religion to be an important part of their life were more likely to have participated in community service. See Regnerus and Elder 2003.

EPILOGUE

1. http://www.socialstudies.org/positions/religion.

REFERENCES

Abu Ali, Azhar, and Carol A. Reisen. 1999. Gender role identity among adolescent Muslim girls living in the U.S. *Current Psychology: Developmental, Learning, Personality, Social* 18:185–192.

Adams, Maurianne. 2001. Core process of racial identity development. In *New perspectives on racial identity development: A theoretical and practical anthology*, edited by C. L. Wijeyesinghe and B. W. Jackson. New York: New York University Press.

Ahlstrom, Sydney E. 1972. *A religious history of the American people.* New Haven: Yale University Press.

Akram, Susan M. 2002. The aftermath of September 11, 2001: The targeting of Arabs and Muslims in America. *Arab Studies Quarterly* 24 (2/3):61.

Alumkal, Anthony William. 2003. *Asian American evangelical churches: Race, ethnicity, and assimilation in the second generation.* New York: LFB Scholarly Publishing.

———. 2004. American evangelicalism in the post-civil rights era: A racial formation analysis. *Sociology of Religion* 65 (3):195–213.

Ammerman, Nancy T. 1997. Golden rule Christianity. In *Lived religion in America: Toward a history of practice*, edited by D. D. Hall. Princeton: Princeton University Press.

Ancheta, Angelo N. 1998. *Race, rights, and the Asian American experience.* New Brunswick: Rutgers University Press.

Anthias, Floya. 2001. New hybridities, old concepts: The limits of "culture." *Ethnic and Racial Studies* 24 (4):619–641.

Anthias, Floya, and Nira Yuval-Davis. 1992. *Racialized boundaries: Race, nation, gender, color and class and the anti-racist struggle.* London: Routledge.

Aronowitz, Stanley. 1999. Between nationality and class. In *Critical ethnicity: Countering the waves of identity politics*, edited by R. H. Tai and M. L. Kenyatta. Lanham, Md.: Rowman and Littlefield.

Asher, Nina. 2001. Rethinking multiculturalism: Attending to Indian American high school students' stories of negotiating self-representations. In *Research on the education of Asian and Pacific Americans*, edited by C. Park, S. Lee, and A. L. Goodwin. Greenwich, Conn.: Information Age Publishers.

———. 2002. Class acts: Indian American high school students negotiate professional and ethnic identities. *Urban Education* 37 (2):267–295.

Association of Statisticians of American Religious Bodies. 2002. *Churches and church membership in the United States 1990 and religious congregations and membership in the United States 2000.* www.glenmary.org/grc, and http://www.uga.edu/bahai/2002/020929 .html.

Atkinson, Donald R., George Morten, and Derald Wing Sue. 1993. *Counseling American minorities: A cross-cultural perspective.* 4th ed. Madison, Wis.: W. C. Brown and Benchmark.

Bacon, J. 1996. *Life lines: Community, family, and assimilation among Asian Indian immigrants.* Oxford: Oxford University Press.

Ballard, Roger. 1994. *Desh pardesh: The South Asian presence in Britain.* London: C. Hurst.

Banks, James A., and Cherry A. McGee Banks. 2004. *Multicultural education: Issues and perspectives.* 5th ed. New York: John Wiley.

Bankston, Carl L., and Min Zhou. 1995. Religious participation, ethnic identification and adaptation of Vietnamese adolescents in an immigrant community. *Sociological Quarterly* 36:523–534.

Barot, Rohit, and John Bird. 2001. Racialization: The genealogy and critique of a concept. *Ethnic and Racial Studies* 24 (4):601–618.

Barth, Fredrik. 1969. *Ethnic groups and boundaries: The social organization of culture difference.* London: Allen and Unwin.

Basch, Linda G., Nina Glick Schiller, and Cristina Szanton Blanc. 1994. *Nations unbound: Transnational projects, postcolonial predicaments, and deterritorialized nation-states.* Langhorne, Pa.: Gordon and Breach.

Batts, Valerie. 1989. Modern racism: New melody for the same old tunes. Rocky Mount, N.C.: Visions Publication.

Beaman, Lori G. 2003. The myth of pluralism, diversity, and vigor: The constitutional privilege of Protestantism in the United States and Canada. *Journal for the Scientific Study of Religion* 42 (3):311–325.

Beaudoin, Thomas. 1998. *Virtual faith: The irreverent spiritual quest of Generation X.* San Francisco: Jossey-Bass.

Bell, Lee Ann. 1997. Theoretical foundations for social justice education. In *Teaching for diversity and social justice: A sourcebook*, edited by M. Adams, L. A. Bell, and P. Griffin. New York: Routledge.

Bergen Record. 1993. Retrial begins in racial beating. Hackensack, N.J.: Bergen Record Corp., May 18, B05.

Berger, P. L. 1969. *A rumor of angels.* Garden City, N.Y.: Doubleday.

Bhabha, Homi K. 1994. *The location of culture.* London: Routledge.

Bloul, Rachel A. D. 2003. Islamphobia and anti-discrimination laws: Ethno-religion as a legal categroy in the UK and Australia. Paper read at the Challenges of Immigration and Integration in the European Union and Australia, at Sydney, Australia.

Blumenfeld, W. J. Forthcoming. Christian Privilege, the Public Schools, and the Promotion of "Secular" and Not-So "Secular" Mainline Christianity. *Equity and Excellence in Education* 39 (3).

Brodkin, K. 1998. *How Jews became white folks and what that says about race in America.* New Brunswick: Rutgers University Press.

Busto, Rudy V. 1999. The Gospel according to the model minority: Hazarding an interpretation of Asian American evangelical college students. In *New spiritual homes: Religion and Asian Americans*, edited by D. Yoo. Honolulu: University of Hawaii Press.

Chan, Sucheng. 1991. Chronology. In *Asian Americans: An interpretative history.* Boston: Twayne.

Chandrasekhar, S. 1982. A history of United States legislation with respect to immigration from India: Some statistics on Asian Indian immigration to the United States of America. In *From India to America: A brief history of immigration, problems, of discrimination, admission and assimilation*, edited by S. Chandrasekhar. La Jolla: Population Review.

Cheng, Victor. 2004. *Inauthentic: The anxiety over culture and identity.* New Brunswick: Rutgers University Press.

Chong, K. H. 1998. What it means to be Christian: The role of religion in the construction of ethnic identity and boundary among second generation Korean Americans. *Sociology of Religion: A Quarterly Review* 59 (3):259–286.

Cochran-Smith, Marilyn. 1997. Knowledge, skills, and experiences for teaching culturally diverse learners: A perspective for practicing teachers. In *Critical knowledge for diverse teachers and learners*, edited by J. Irvine. Washington, D.C.: AACTE.

Cohen, Robin. 1997. *Global diasporas : an introduction*. Seattle: University of Washington Press.

Cromwell, J. B. 1997. Cultural discrimination: The reasonable accommodation of religion in the workplace. *Employee Responsibilities and Rights Journal* 10 (2):155.

Cross, W. E., Jr. 1991. *Shades of black: Diversity in African American identity*. Philadelphia: Temple University Press.

Cross, W. E., Jr., and Peony Fhagen-Smith. 2001. Patterns of African American identity development: A life span perspective. In *New perspectives on racial identity development: A theoretical and practical anthology*, edited by C. L. Wijeyesinghe and B. W. Jackson. New York: New York University Press.

Darder, Antonia. 1991. *Culture and power in the classroom: A critical foundation for bicultural education*. New York: Bergin and Garvey.

Dasgupta, Monisha. 1997. "What Is Indian about You?": A gendered, transnational approach to ethnicity. *Gender and Society* 11 (5):572–596.

Delpit, Lisa D. 1995. *Other people's children: Cultural conflict in the classroom*. New York: New Press.

Derman-Sparks, L., and Carol Brunson Phillips. 1997. *Teaching/learning anti-racism: A developmental approach*. New York: Teachers College Press.

Desai, Jigna. 2004. *Beyond Bollywood: The cultural politics of South Asian diasporic film*. New York: Routledge.

Dhingra, Pawan H. 2003. Being American between black and white: Second generation Asian American professionals' racial identities. *Journal of Asian American Studies* 6 (2):117–147.

Dickie, Lance. 2001. When symbols of faith become targets of bigots. *Seattle Times*, September 28. http://seattletimes.nwsource.com/html/editorialsopinion/134346907_lanceed28.html.

Durkheim, E. 1995/1915. *The elementary forms of the religious life*. Translated by K. E. Fields. New York: Free Press.

Ebaugh, Helen Rose, and Janet Saltzman Chafetz, eds. 2000. *Religion and the new immigrants: Continuities and adaptations in immigrant congregations*. Walnut Creek, Cal.: Altamira.

———, eds. 2002. *Religion across borders: Transnational immigrant networks*. Walnut Creek, Cal.: Altamira.

Eck, Diana L. 1996. *Neighboring faiths: How will Americans cope with increasing religious diversity? Harvard Magazine*. www.harvard-magazine.com/so96/faith.html.

———. 2001. *A new religious America: How a Christian country has now become the world's most religiously diverse nation*. San Francisco: Harper Collins.

Edles, Laura Desfor. 2004. Rethinking "race," "ethnicity" and "culture": Is Hawai'i the "model minority" state? *Ethnic and Racial Studies* 27 (1):37–68.

Edwards, Steve. 2000. *Palos heights mosque controversy*. Chicago: Chicago Public Radio.

Erikson, Erik H. 1963. *Childhood and society*. 2d rev. and enl. ed. New York: W. W. Norton.

———. 1968. *Identity, youth, and crisis*. New York: W. W. Norton.

Espiritu, Yen Le. 2002. The intersection of race, ethnicity, and class: The multiple identities of second-generation Filipinos. In *second generation: Ethnic identity among Asian Americans*, edited by P. G. Min. Walnut Creek, Cal.: Altamira.

Feagin, J. R. 1997. Old poison in new bottles: The deep roots of modern nativism. In *Immigrants out: The new nativism and the anti-immigrant impulse in the United States*, edited by J. F. Perea. New York: New York University Press.

Fenton, John Y. 1988. *Transplanting religious traditions: Asian Indians in America*. New York: Praeger.

———. 1992. Academic study of religions and Asian Indian-American college students. In *A sacred thread: Modern transmissions of Hindu traditions in India and abroad*, edited by R. B. Williams. Chambersburg, Pa.: Anima Publications.

Fisher, Celia, Scyatta A. Wallace, and Rose A. Fenton. 2000. Discrimination distress during adolescence. *Journal of Youth and Adolescence* 28 (6):679–695.

Foner, Nancy. 2001. Transnationalism then and now: New York immigrants today and at the turn of the twentieth century. In *Migration, transnationalization, and race*, edited by H. Cordero-Guzman, R. C. Smith, and R. Grossfoguel. Philadelphia: Temple University Press.

Form, W. 2000. Italian Protestants: Religion, ethnicity, and assimilation. *Journal for the Scientific Study of Religion* 39 (3):307–320.

Fredrickson, George M. 2002. *Racism: A short history*. Princeton: Princeton University Press.

Freire, Paulo. 1996. *Pedagogy of the oppressed*. 3rd ed. New York: Continuum.

Gans, Herbert J. 1979. Symbolic ethnicity: The future of ethnic groups and culture in America. *Ethnic and Racial Studies* 2 (1):1–19.

———. 1994. Symbolic ethnicity and symbolic religiosity: Towards a comparison of ethnic and religious acculturation. *Ethnic and Racial Studies* 17 (4):577–592.

Gaustad, Edwin S., and Leigh E. Schmidt. 2002. *The religious history of America: The heart of the American story from colonial times to today*. Revised ed. San Francisco: Harper Collins.

George, S. 1998. Caroling with the Keralites: The negotiation of gendered space in an Indian immigrant church. In *Gatherings in diaspora: Religious communities and the new immigration*, edited by R. S. Warner and J. G. Wittner. Philadelphia: Temple University Press.

Gibson, Margaret A. 1988. *Accommodation without assimilation: Sikh immigrants in an American high school*. Ithaca: Cornell University Press.

Goldenberg, I. 1978. *Oppression and social intervention: Essays on the human condition and the problems of change*. Chicago: Nelson-Hall.

Gonzales, J. L. 1986. Asian Indian immigration pattern: The origins of the Sikh community in California. *International Migration Review* 20 (1):40–54.

Gould, Stephen Jay. 1996. *The mismeasure of man*. Rev. ed. New York: Norton.

Gramsci, Antonio. 1971. *Selection from the prison notebooks of Antonio Gramsci*. New York: International Publishers.

Graves, Joseph L. 2001. *The emperor's new clothes: Biological theories of race at the millennium*. New Brunswick: Rutgers University Press.

Gupta, Himanee. 2003. Staking a claim on American-ness: Hindu temples in the United States. In *Revealing the sacred in Asian America*, edited by J. N. Iwamura and P. Spickard. New York: Routledge.

Gupta, Sangeeta R., ed. 2000. *Emerging voices: South Asian American women redefine self, family and community*. Walnut Creek, Cal.: Altamira.

Haddad, Yvonne Yazbeck. 2000. At home in the Hijra: South Asian Muslims in the United States. In *The South Asian religious diaspora in Britain, Canada, and the United States*, edited by H. Coward, J. Hinnells, and R. B. Williams. Albany: State University of New York Press.

———. 2002. *Muslims in the West: From sojourners to citizens*. Oxford: Oxford University Press.

Hall, David D. 1997. Introduction. In *Lived religion in America: Toward a history of practice*, edited by D. D. Hall. Princeton: Princeton University Press.

Hall, Kathleen. 2002. *Lives in translation: Sikh youth as British citizens*. Philadelphia: University of Pennsylvania Press.

Hall, Stuart. 1994. Cultural identity and diaspora. In *Colonial Discourse and postcolonial theory: A reader*, edited by P. Williams and L. Chrisman. New York: Columbia University Press.

Haney-López, Ian. 1996. *White by law: The legal construction of race*. New York: New York University Press.

———. 2003. *Racism on trial: The Chicano fight for justice*. Cambridge: Belknap Press of Harvard University Press.

Hardiman, Rita, and Bailey Jackson. 1997. Conceptual foundations for social justice courses. In *Teaching for diversity and social justice: A sourcebook*, edited by M. Adams, L. A. Bell, and P. Griffin. New York: Routledge.

Hawley, John S., and Gurinder Singh Mann. 1993. *Studying the Sikhs: Issues for North America*. Albany: State University of New York Press.

Helms, Janet. E. 1994. The conceptualization of racial identity and other "racial" constructs. In *Human diversity*, edited by E. Trickett, R. Watts, and D. Burman. San Francisco: Jossey-Bass.

Helweg, Arthur W., and Usha M. Helweg. 1990. *An immigrant success story: East Indians in America*. Philadelphia: University of Pennsylvania Press.

Herberg, Will. 1983. *Protestant, Catholic, Jew: An essay in American religious sociology*. Chicago: University of Chicago Press.

Higginbotham, Evelyn Brooks. 1992. African-American women's history and the metalanguage of race. *Signs* 17 (2):251–274.

Hoare, C. H. 1991. Psychosocial identity development and cultural others. *Journal of Counseling and Development* 70 (1):25–53.

Hurtado, A., P. Gurin, and T. Peng. 1997. Social identities: A framework for studying the adaptations of immigrants and ethnics. In *New American destinies: A reader in contemporary Asian and Latino immigration*, edited by D. Y. Hamamoto and R. D. Torres. New York: Routledge.

Hurtado, A., J. Rodriguez, P. Gurin, and J. Beals. 1993. The impact of Mexican descendants' social identity of the ethnic socialization of children. In *Ethnic identity: Formation and transmission among Hispanics and other minorities*, edited by M. E. Bernal and G. P. Knight. Albany: State University of New York Press.

Hutnyk, J. 1999. Hybridity saves?: Authenticity and/or critique of appropriation. *Amerasia Journal* 25 (3):39–58.

Idinopulos, Thomas A. 1998. What Is religion? *Cross Currents*. Fall. http://www.crosscurrents .org/whatisreligion.htm

Ignatiev, Noel. 1995. *How the Irish became white*. New York: Routledge.

Igoa, Christine. 2000. *The inner world of the immigrant child*. Mahwah, N.J.: Lawrence Earlbaum Associates.

Indian American Center for Political Awareness. 2003. *Indian American Population*. Washington, D.C.

International Mission Board. 1999. Divali: Festival of lights prayer for Hindus. Richmond, Va.: Southern Baptist Convention.

Iwamura, Jane Naomi. 2002. Envisioning Asian and Pacific America. In *Revealing the sacred in Asian and Pacific America*, edited by J. N. Iwamura and P. Spickard. New York: Routledge.

Iwamura, Jane Naomi, and Paul Spickard. 2003. *Revealing the sacred in Asian America*. New York: Routledge.

Jackson, Robert, and Eleanor Nesbitt. 1993. *Hindu children in Britain.* Stoke on Trent, UK: Trentham Books.

Jacob, Simon, and Pallavi Thakur. 2001. Jyothi Hindu temple: One religion, many practices. In *Religion and the new immigrants: Continuities and adaptations in immigrant communities,* edited by H. R. Ebaugh and J. S. Chafetz. Walnut Creek, Cal.: Altamira.

Jacobson, Jessica. 1997. Religion and ethnicity: Dual and alternative sources of identity among young British Pakistanis. *Ethnic and Racial Studies* 20 (2):238–256.

Jacobson, Matthew Frye. 1998. *Whiteness of a different color: European immigrants and the alchemy of race.* Cambridge: Harvard University Press.

Jensen, Joan M. 1988. *Passage from India: Asian Indian immigrants in North America.* New Haven: Yale University Press.

Jones-Correa, Michael. 2003. The study of transnationalism among the children of immigrants: Where we are and where we should be headed. In *The changing face of home: The transnational lives of the second generation,* edited by P. Levitt and M. C. Waters. New York: Russell Sage Foundation.

Kailin, Julie. 2002. *Antiracist education: From theory to practice.* Lanham, Md.: Rowman Littlefield.

Kallen, Horace. [1915] 1996. Democracy versus the melting-pot: A study of American nationality. In *Theories of ethnicity: A classical reader,* edited by W. Sollors. New York: New York University.

Khaldi, Omar. 1991. *Indian Muslims in North America.* Watertown, Mass.: South Asia Press.

Khandelwal, Madhulika S. 2002. *Becoming American, being Indian: An immigrant community in New York City.* The anthropology of contemporary issues. Ithaca: Cornell University Press.

Kiang, Peter. 2002. K–12 education and Asian American youth development. *Asian American Policy Review* 10:31–47.

Kibria, Nazli. 1998. The racial gap: South Asian American racial identity and the Asian American movement. In *A part, yet apart: South Asians in Asian America,* edited by L. D. Shankar and R. Srikanth. Philadelphia: Temple University Press.

———. 1999. College and notions of "Asian American": Second generation Chinese and Korean Americans negotiate race and identity. *Amerasia Journal* 25 (1):29–52.

———. 2002. *Becoming Asian American: Second-generation Chinese and Korean American identities.* Baltimore: Johns Hopkins University Press.

Kim, Claire Jean. 2001. The racial triangulation of Asian Americans. In *Asian Americans and politics: Perspectives, experiences, prospects,* edited by G. H. Chang. Washington, D.C. and Stanford: Woodrow Wilson Center Press and Stanford University Press.

Kim, Henry H., and Ralph E. Pyle. 2004. An exception to the exception: Second-generation Korean American church participation. *Social Compass* 51 (3):321.

Kim, Elaine, and Eui-Young Yu. 1996. *East to America: Korean American life stories.* New York: New Press.

Kim, J. 1981. Processes of Asian American identity development: A study of Japanese American women's perceptions of their struggles to achieve positive identities as Americans of Asian ancestry. Ph.D. dissertation, University of Massachusetts-Amherst.

Kim, Rebecca H. 2004a. Made in the U.S.A.: Second-generation Korean American campus evangelicals. In *Asian American Youth Culture,* edited by J. Lee and M. Zhou. New York: Routledge.

———. 2004b. Second-generation Korean American evangelicals: Ethnic, multiethnic, or white campus ministries. *Sociology of Religion* 65 (1):19–34.

Kim, Sang-Hoon. 1996. Discovering my ethnic roots. In *Becoming American, becoming ethnic: College students explore their roots*, edited by T. Dublin. Philadelphia: Temple University Press.

King, Valarie, Glen H. Elder Jr, and Les B. Whitbeck. 1997. Religious involvement among rural youth: An ecological and life course perspective. *Journal of Research on Adolescence* 7 (4):431–456.

Klain, Ron. 2005. Carols in the court. *New York Times.* http://www.nytimes.com/2005/09/12/opinion/12klain.html.

Kooistra, W. P., and K. I. Pargament. 1999. Religious doubting in parochial school addolescents. *Journal of Psychology and Theology* 27:33–42.

Koshy, Susan. 1998. Category crisis: South Asian Americans and questions of race and ethnicity. *Diaspora* 7 (3):285–320.

———. 2001. Morphing race into ethnicity: Asian Americans and critical transformations of whiteness. *boundary 2* 28 (1):153–194.

Kosmin, Barry A., Egon Mayer, and Keysar Ariela. 2001. *American religious identification survey.* New York: Graduate Center of the City of New York.

Kurien, Prema. 1998. Becoming American by becoming Hindu: Indian Americans take their place at the multicultural table. In *Gatherings in diaspora: Religious communities and the new immigration*, edited by R. S. Warner and J. G. Wittner. Philadelphia: Temple University Press.

———. 2001. Religion, ethnicity and politics: Hindu and Muslim Indian immigrants in the United States. *Ethnic and Racial Studies* 24 (2):263–293.

———. 2004. Multiculturalism, immigrant religion, and diasporic nationalism: The development of an American Hinduism. *Social Problems* 51 (3):362.

Lal, Vinay. 1999. The politics of history on the Internet: Cyber-diasporic Hinduism and the North American Hindu diaspora. *Diaspora* 8 (2):137–172.

Lampman, Jane. 1998. World faiths put down roots in US. *Christian Science Monitor*, June 18, B1.

Lee, Stacy. 1994. Behind the model minority stereotype: Voices of high- and low-achieving Asian American students. *Anthropology and Education Quarterly* 25 (4):413–429.

———. 1996. *Unraveling the "model minority" stereotype.* New York: Teachers College Press.

———. 1998. Asian Americans: Diverse and growing. *Population Bulletin* 53 (2):1–40.

Lei, Joy. 2003. (Un)necessary Toughness?: Those ?Loud Black Girls? and Those ?Quiet Asian Boys? *Anthropology and Education Quarterly* 34 (2):158–181.

Leonard, Karen. 1997. *The South Asian Americans.* Westport, Conn.: Greenwood Press.

———. 2000. Punjabi Mexican American experiences of multiethnicity. In *We are a people: Narrative and multiplicity in constructing ethnic identity*, edited by P. Spickard and W. J. Burroughs. Philadelphia: Temple University Press.

Lessinger, J. 1995. *From the Ganges to the Hudson.* Boston: Allyn and Bacon.

Levitt, Peggy. 2002. The ties that change: Relations to the ancestral home over the life cycle. In *The changing face of home: The transnational lives of the second generation*, edited by P. Levitt and M. C. Waters. New York: Russell Sage Foundation.

Levitt, Peggy, and Mary C. Waters, eds. 2002a. *The changing face of home: The transnational lives of the second generation.* New York: Russell Sage Foundation.

———. 2002b. Introduction. In *The changing face of home: The transnational lives of the second generation*, edited by P. Levitt and M. C. Waters. New York: Russell Sage Foundation.

Lincoln, C. Eric. 1999. *Race, religion, and the continuing American dilemma.* New York: Hill and Wang.

Lopez, D., and Espiritu, Y. 1997. Panethnicity in the United States: A theoretical framework. In *New American destinies: A reader in contemporary Asian and Latino immigration*, edited by D. Y. Hamamoto and R. D. Torres. New York: Routledge.

Maira, Sunaina. 1998. Desis reprezent: Bhangra remix and hip hop in New York City. *Postcolonial Studies* 1 (3):357–370.

———. 1999. Identity dub: The paradoxes of an Indian American youth subculture (New York mix). *Cultural Anthropology* 14 (1):29–60.

———. 2000. Henna and hip hop: The politics of cultural protection and the work of cultural studies. *Journal of Asian American Studies* 3 (3):329–369.

———. 2002. *Desi's in the house: Indian American youth culture in New York City*. Philadelphia: Temple University Press.

Mann, Gurinder Singh. 2000. Sikhism in the United States. In *The South Asian religious diaspora in Britain, Canada, and the United States*, edited by H. Coward, J. Hinnells, and R. B. Williams. Albany: State University of New York Press.

Marler, Penny Long, and C. Kirk Hadaway. 2002. "Being religious" or "being spiritual" in America: A zero-sum proposition? *Journal for the Scientific Study of Religion* 41 (2):289–300.

Mazumdar, Shampa, and Sanjoy Mazumdar. 2003. Creating the sacred: Altars in the Hindu American home. In *Revealing the Sacred in Asian and Pacific America:*, edited by J. N. Iwamura and P. Spickard. New York: Routledge.

Mazumdar, Sucheta. 1989a. Race and racism: South Asians in the United States. In *Frontiers of Asian American Studies*, edited by G. Nomura. Pullman: Washington State University Press.

———. 1989b. Racist responses to racism: The aryan myth and South Asians in the United States. *South Asia Bulletin* 9 (1):47–55.

Mazur, Eric Michael, and Kate McCarthy. 2001. *God in the details: American religion in popular culture*. New York: Routledge.

McConahay, J. B. 1986. Modern racism, ambivalence, and the modern racism scale. In *Prejudice, discrimination, and racism*, edited by J. F. Dovidio and S. L. Gaertner. New York: Academic Press.

McIntosh, Peggy. 1998. White privilege: Unpacking the invisible knapsack. In *Beyond heroes and holidays: A practical guide to K–12 anti-racist, multicultural education and staff development*. Wellesley, Mass.: Network of Educators on the Americas.

Melendy, H. B. 1977. *Asians in America: Filipinos, Koreans, and East Indians*. Boston: Twyane.

Miles, Robert. 1989. *Racism: Key ideas*. New York: Routledge.

Miller, Barbara. 1995. Precepts and practices: Researching identity formation among Indian Hindu adolescents in the United States. In *Cultural practices as contexts for development*, edited by J. J. Goodnow and P. J. Miller. San Francisco: Jossey-Bass.

Min, Pyong Gap. 1992. The structure and social functions of Korean immigrant churches in the United States. *International Migration Review* 26 (4):1,370–1,394.

———. 2000a. Immigrants' religion and ethnicity: A comparison of Korean Christian and Indian Hindu Immigrants. *Bulletin of the Royal Institute for Inter-Faith Studies* 2:1,201–1,240.

———. 2000b. Religion and ethnicity: A comparison of Korean Christian and Indian Hindu immigrants in the U.S. Paper read at conference on Revealing the Sacred in Asian America: Theories and Methods, Santa Barbara, Cal.

———. 2002. *The second generation: ethnic identity among Asian Americans*. Walnut Creek, Cal.: Altamira.

Min, Pyong Gap, and Jung Ha Kim. 2002. *Religions in Asian America: Building faith communities*. Walnut Creek, Cal.: Altamira.

Min, Pyong Gap, and Rose Kim. 1999. *Struggle for ethnic identity: Narratives by Asian American professionals.* Walnut Creek, Cal.: Altamira.

———. 2000. Formation of ethnic and racial identities: Narratives by young Asian-American professionals. *Ethnic and Racial Studies* 23 (4):735–760.

Min, Pyong Gap, and K. Park. 1999. Second generation Asian Americans' ethnic identity. *Amerasia Journal* 25 (1):ix–xiii.

Mittelberg, D., and M. C. Waters. 1992. The process of ethnogenesis among Haitian and Israeli immigrants in the United States. *Ethnic and Racial Studies* 15 (3):412–435.

Moore, Kathleen M. 2002. "United we stand": American attitudes toward (Muslim) immigration post-September 11th. *Muslim World* 92 (1/2):39.

Moore, R. Laurence. 1986. *Religious outsiders and the making of Americans.* New York: Oxford University Press.

———. 1994. *Selling God : American religion in the marketplace of culture.* New York: Oxford University Press.

Morning, A. 2001. The racial self-identification of South Asians in the United States. *Journal of Ethnic and Migration Studies* 27 (1):61–79.

Mukhi, Sunita. 2000. *Doing the desi thing: Performing Indianness in New York City.* New York: Garland.

Narayanan, Vasudha. 1992. Creating the South Indian "Hindu" experience in the United States. In *A sacred thread: Modern transmissions of Hindu traditions in India and abroad,* edited by R. B. Williams. Chambersburg, Pa.: Anima Publications.

Nieto, Sonia. 1999. *The light in their eyes: Creating multicultural learning communities,* New York: Teachers College Press.

———. 2003. *Affirming diversity: The sociopolitical context for multicultural education.* 4th ed. White Plains, N.Y.: Longman.

Nimer, Mohammed. 2001. The status of Muslim civil rights in the United States. Washington, D.C.: Council on American Islamic Relations.

Olsen, Laurie. 1997. *Made in America: Immigrant students in our public schools.* New York: New Press.

Omi, Michael. 1994. Racial formation. In *Racial formation in the United States from the 1960s to the 1990s,* edited by M. Omi and H. Winant. New York: Routledge.

Omi, Michael, and Howard Winant. 1986. *Racial formation in the United States: From the 1960s to the 1980s.* New York: Routledge and Kegan Paul.

———. 1994. *Racial formation in the United States: From the 1960s to the 1990s.* 2nd ed. New York: Routledge.

Orsi, Robert A. 1985. *The madonna of 115th Street: Faith and community in Italian Harlem, 1880–1950.* New Haven: Yale University Press.

———. 1992. The religious boundaries of an inbetween people: Street feste and the problem of the dark-skinned "other" in Italian Harlem, 1920–1990. *American Quarterly* 44 (3):313–347.

Osajima, K. 1988. Asian Americans and the model minority: An analysis of the popular press image of the 1960s and 1980s. In *Reflections on shattered windows: Promises and prospects for Asian American Studies,* edited by G. Y. Okhiro, S. Hune, A. A. Hansen, and J. M. Liu. Pullman: Washington University Press.

Palmer, John. 2001. Korean adopted young women: Gender bias, racial issues and educational implications. In *Research on the education of Asian and Pacific Americans,* edited by C. Park, S. Lee, and A. L. Goodwin. Greenwich, Conn.: Information Age Publishing.

Pang, Valerie Ooka. 2004. *Multicultural education: A caring-centered, reflective approach.* New York: McGraw-Hill.

Pang, Valerie Ooka, and L. L. Cheng. 1998. *Struggling to be heard: The unmet needs of Asian Pacific American children*. Albany: State University of New York Press.

Pascarella, Ernest, and Patrick T. Terenzini. 1991. *How college affects students: Findings and insights from twenty years of research*. San Franscisco: Jossey-Bass.

Peeradina, Saleem. 1996. Erasing god. *Amerasia Journal* 22 (1):217–232.

Pharr, S. 1988. *Homophobia: A weapon of sexism*. Iverness, Cal.: Chardon.

Phinney, Jean. 1990. Ethnic identity in adolescence and adults: Review of research. *Psychological Bulletin* 108 (3):499–515.

Pierce, Lori. 2000. The continuing significance of race. In *We are a people: Narrative and multiplicity in constructing ethnic identity*, edited by P. Spickard and W. J. Burroughs. Philadelphia: Temple University Press.

Pluralism Project. 2004. *Statistics*. The Pluralism Project and Harvard University. http://www.pluralism.org/resources/statistics/index.php.

Ponterotto, J. G., and P. B. Pedersen. 1993. *Preventing prejudice: A guide for counselors and educators*, edited by P. B. Pedersen. Newbury Park, Cal.: Sage.

Portes, Alejandro, Patricia Fernandez-Kelly, and William J. Haller. 2003. Segmented assimilation on the ground: The new second generation in early adulthood. Princeton: Center for Migration and Development, Princeton University.

Portes, Alejandro, and Ruben G. Rumbaut, eds. 1996. *The new second generation*. New York: Russell Sage Foundation.

——. 2001. *Legacies: The story of the immigrant second generation*. Berkeley: University of California Press.

Portes, Alejandro, and Min Zhou. 1993. The new second generation: Segmented assimilation and its variants. *Annals of the American Academy of Political and Social Science* 530:74–96.

Prashad, Vijay. 2000. *The karma of brown folk*. Minneapolis: University of Minnesota Press.

Prewitt, Kenneth. 2004. The census counts, the census classifies. In *Not just black and white: Historical and contemporary perspectives on immigration, race, and ethnicity in the United States*, edited by N. Foner and G. M. Fredrickson. New York: Russell Sage Foundation.

Purkayashtha, Bandana. 2005. *Negotiating ethnicity: South Asian Americans traverse a transnational world*. New Brunswick: Rutgers University Press.

Radhakrishnan, R. 1994. Is the ethnic "authentic" in the diaspora? In *The State of Asian America*, edited by K. Aguilar-San Juan. Boston: South End Press.

Raj, Dhooleka Sarhadi. 2000. Who the hell do you think you are? Promoting religious identity among young Hindus in Britain. *Ethnic and racial studies* 23 (3):535–558.

Rajagopal, Arvind. 1995. Better Hindu than black? Narratives of Asian Indian identity. Paper read at Society for the Scientific Study of Religion at St. Louis, Missouri.

Rajan, Valli. 1995. Using TV, Christian Pat Robertson denouces Hinduism as "Demonic." *Hinduism Today*, July.

Ramesh, Clospet N. 1998. Asian Indian Americans' attempts at dealing with disjunctured selves. Fullerton, Cal: Conference on Interdisciplinary Theory and Research on Intercultural Relations at California State University, Fullerton.

Rangaswamy, Padma. 2000. *Namasté America: Indian immigrants in an American metropolis*. University Park: Pennsylvania State University Press.

Redman, George I. 2003. *A casebook for exploring diversity*. Upper Saddle River, N. J.: Merrill Prentice Hall.

Regnerus, Mark D., and Glen H. Elder, Jr. 2003. Staying on track in school: Religious influences in high- and low-risk settings. *Journal for the Scientific Study of Religion* 42 (4):633.

Regnerus, Mark, Christian Smith, and Melissa Fritsch. 2003. Religion in the lives of American adolescents: A review of the literature. Chapell Hill, N.C.: National Study of Youth and Religion.

Roediger, David R. 1991. *The wages of whiteness: Race and the making of the American working class.* New York: Verso.

———. 2002. *Colored white: Transcending the racial past.* Berkeley: University of California Press.

Roediger, David R., and James Barret. 2004. Making new imimgrants "inbetween": Irish hosts and white panethnicity, 1890 to 1930. In *Not just black and white: Historical and contemporary perspectives on immigration, race, and ethnicity in the United States,* edited by N. Foner and G. M. Fredrickson. New York: Russell Sage Foundation.

Roof, Wade Clark. 1999. *Spiritual marketplace: Baby boomers and the remaking of American religion.* Princeton: Princeton University Press.

Root, Maria P. P., ed. 1996. *The multiracial experience: Racial borders as the new frontier.* Thousand Oaks, Cal.: Sage.

———. 2000. Rethinking racial identity development. In *We are a people: Narrative and multiplicity in constructing ethnic identity,* edited by P. Spickard and W. J. Burroughs. Philadelphia: Temple University Press.

Rosenthal, D., and S. Feldman. 1992. The nature and stability of ethnic identity in Chinese youth. *Journal for Cross-Cultural Psychology* 23 (2):214–227.

Royce, Anya P. 1982. *Ethnic identity: Strategies of diversity.* Bloomington: Indiana University Press.

Rudrappa, Sharmila. 2004. *Ethnic routes to becoming American: Indian immigrants and the cultures of citizenship.* New Brunswick: Rutgers University Press.

Saeed, Amir, Neil Blain, and Douglass Forbes. 1999. New ethnic and national questions in Scotland: Post-British identities among Glasgow Pakistani teenagers. *Ethnic and Racial Studies* 22 (5):821–844.

Said, Edward. 1978. *Orientalism.* New York: Vintage Books.

———. 1996. A devil theory of Islam. *The Nation,* August 12.

Sanchez, George J. 1997. Face the nation: Race, immigration, and the rise of nativism in late twentieth-century America. *International Migration Review* 31 (4):1,009–1030.

Sandhu, Sabeen. 2004. Instant karma: The commercialization of Asian Indian culture. In *Asian American youth: Culture, identity, and ethnicity,* edited by J. Lee and M. Zhou. New York: Routledge.

Saran, Parmatma. 1985. *The Asian Indian experience in the United States.* New Delhi: Vikas.

Schiller, Nina Glick, Linda G. Basch, and Cristina Szanton Blanc. 1992. *Towards a transnational perspective on migration: Race, class, ethnicity, and nationalism reconsidered.* Annals of the New York Academy of Sciences 645. New York: New York Academy of Sciences.

Schiller, Nina Glick, and Fouron, Georges E. 1999. Terrains of blood and nation: Haitian transnational social fields. *Ethnic and Racial Studies* 22 (2):340–366.

Scott, Janny. 2002. Foreign born in U.S. at record high. *New York Times,* February 7.

Sengupta, Somini. 1998a. An attack he cannot remember, a memory problem he cannot forget. *The New York Times,* June 14, 1998, 8.

———. 1998b. Officials see racial motive in attack on Indian-American. *New York Times,* September 22, 1998.

Seth, Manju. 1995. Asian Indian Americans. In *Asian Americans: Contemporary trends and issues,* edited by P. G. Min. Thousand Oaks, Cal.: Sage.

Shaheen, Jack G. 1984. *The TV Arab.* Bowling Green, Ohio: Bowling Green State University Popular Press.

———. 2001. *Reel bad Arabs: How Hollywood vilifies a people.* New York: Olive Branch Press.

Shankar, L. D., and R. Srikanth, eds. 1998. *A part, yet apart: South Asians in Asian America.* Philadelphia: Temple University Press.

Sikh Mediawatch and Resource Task Force (SMART). 2001. Sikh Americans condemn hate crimes and urge nation to unite; Demand protection from police and public officials. Baltimore, Md.: SMART.

Singh, Amrijit. 1996. African Americans and the new immigrants. In *Between the lines: South Asians and postcolonially*, edited by D. Bahri and M. Vasudeva. Philadelphia: Temple University Press.

Singh, Jaideep. 2002. Decoding race, religion and difference: Deconstructing and interpreting racialized media representations of Sikh, Muslim, and Arab Americans. Invited presentation at Princeton University, March 26.

———. 2003. The racialization of minoritized religious identity: Constructing sacred sites at the intersection of white and Christian supremacy. In *Revealing the sacred in Asian and Pacific America*, edited by J. N. Iwamura and P. Spickard. New York: Routledge.

Smith, Christian. 2003a. Mapping American adolescent subjective religiosity and attitudes of alienation toward religion: A research report. *Sociology of Religion* 61 (1):111–123.

———. 2003b. Theorizing religious effects among American adolescents. *Journal for the Scientific Study of Religion* 42 (1):17–30.

Smith, Christian, and Faris, Robert. 2002. Religion and the life attitudes and self-images of American adolescents. *National Study of Youth and Religion* 2:1–42.

Smith, Timothy. 1978. Religion and ethnicity in America. *American Historical Review* 83: 1,155–1,185.

Smith, Tom W. 2002. Religious diversity in America: The emergence of Muslims, Buddhist, Hindus and others. *Journal for the Scientific Study of Religion* 41 (3):577–585.

Spickard, Paul, and W. Jeffrey Burroughs, eds. 2000. *We are a people: Narrative and multiplicity in constructing ethnic identity.* Philadelphia: Temple University Press.

Spring, Joel. 2003. *Deculturalization and the struggle for equality: A brief history of the education of dominated cultures in the United States.* Fourth ed. Boston: McGraw Hill.

Steinberg, Stephen. 1989. *The ethnic myth: Race, ethnicity, and class in America.* Boston: Beacon.

Stephan, Cookie White, and Walter G. Stephan. 2000. What are the functions of ethnic identity? In *We are a people: Narrative and multiplicity in constructing ethnic identity*, edited by P. Spickard and W. J. Burroughs. Philadelphia: Temple University Press.

Stout, Harry. 1975. Ethnicity: The vital center of religion in America. *Ethncity* 2:204–224.

Suárez-Orozco, Carola. 2003. *Understanding the social worlds of immigrant youth.* San Francisco: Jossey-Bass.

Suarez-Orozco, M. M. 1997. "Becoming somebody": Central American immigrants in US inner city schools. In *Beyond Black and White: New Faces and Voices in US Schools*, edited by M. Seller and L. Weis. Albany: State University of New York Press.

Suleiman, Mahmoud F. 1997. Empowering Arab American students: Implications for multicultural teachers. Paper read at National Association of Multicultural Educators.

Suzuki, B. H. 1979. Multicultural education: What's it all about? *Integrated Education* 17: 97–98.

Tajfel, H. 1978. *The social psychology of minorities.* New York: Minority Rights Group.

———. 1981. *Human groups and social categories.* Cambridge: Cambridge University Press.

Takaki, Ronald. 1989. *Strangers from a different shore: A history of Asians in America.* Boston: Little Brown.

Tamminen, K. 1994. Religious development in childhood and adolescence: A viewpoint of religious development between the ages of 7 and 20. *International Journal for the Psychology of Religion* 4 (2):61–85.

Tatum, Beverly D. 1997. *"Why are all the black kids sitting together in the cafeteria?" and other conversations about race.* New York: Basic Books.

Thai, H. C. 1999. "Splitting things in half is so white!": Conceptions of family life and friendship and the formation of ethnic identity among second generation Vietnamese Americans. *Amerasia Journal* 25 (1):53–88.

Thompson, Kenneth. 2002. Border crossings and diasporic identities: Media use and leisure practices of an ethnic minority. *Qualitative Sociology* 25 (3):409–418.

Tinker, H. 1977. *The banyan tree.* New York: Oxford University Press.

Tong, R. 1989. *Feminist thought: A comprehensive introduction.* Boulder, Col.: Westview.

Tuan, Mia. 2001. *Forever foreigners or honorary whites?: The Asian ethnic experience today.* New Brunswick: Rutgers University Press.

Twine, France Winddance. 1997. Brown-skinned white girls: Class, culture, and the construction of white identity in suburban communities. In *Displacing whiteness: Essays in social and cultural criticism*, edited by R. Frankenburg. Durham: Duke University Press.

United States Bureau of the Census. 2001. Profiles of general demographic characteristics: 2000 census of population and housing. Washington, D.C.: U.S. Department of Commerce.

United States Bureau of the Census. 2003. Census 2000, Summary File 3, Table PCT 10. Washington, D.C.: U.S. Government Printing Office.

Vextouec, Steven. 2000. *The Hindu diaspora: Comparative patterns, global diasporas.* London: Routledge.

Vickerman, Milton. 2002. Second-generation West Indian transnationalism. In *The changing face of home: The transnational lives of the second generation*, edited by P. Levitt and M. C. Waters. New York: Russell Sage Foundation.

Visweswaran, K. 1997. Diaspora by design: Flexible citizenship and South Asians in U.S. racial formation. *Diaspora* 6 (1):5–29.

Vyas, Sapna. 2001. Am I Indian, American, or Indian American? In *Research on the Education of Asian and Pacific Americans*, edited by C. Park, S. Lee and A. L. Goodwin. Greenwich, CT.: Information Age Publishing.

Wang, Theodore H., and Frank H. Wu. 1996. Beyond the Model Minority Myth. In *The Affirmative Action Debate*, edited by G. E. Curry. Reading, MA: Addison-Wesley.

Warner, R. Stephen. 1993. Work in progress toward a new paradigm for the sociological study of religion. *American Journal of Sociology* 98:1,044–1,093.

———. 1998. Immigration and Religious Communities in the United States. In *Gatherings in the Diaspora: Religious Communities and the New Immigration*, edited by R. S. Warner and J. Wittner. Philadelphia: Temple University Press.

Warner, W. L., and S. Srole. 1945. *The social systems of American ethnic groups.* New Haven: Yale University Press.

Waters, Mary C. 1994. Ethnic and racial identities of second generation black immigrants in New York City. *International Migration Review* 28 (Winter):759–820.

———. 1999. *Black identities: West Indian immigrant dreams and American realities.* Cambridge: Russell Sage Foundation and Harvard University Press.

Weber, Max. 1961. Ethnic groups. In *Theories of Society, I*, edited by T. Parson. New York: Free Press of Glencoe.

Wendel, Richard. 2003. Lived Religion and Family Therapy: What does spirituality have to do with it? *Family Practice* 42 (1):165–179.

Williams, Raymond Bradbury. 1988. *Religions of immigrants from India and Pakistan.* New York: Cambridge University Press.

Williams, Raymond Brudy, 1992a. A sacred thread: Introduction. In *A sacred thread: Modern transmission of Hindu traditions in India and abroad*, edited by R. B. Williams. Chambersburg, Pa.: Anima.

———. 1992b. Sacred threads of several textures. In *Sacred thread: Modern transmission of Hindu traditions in India and abroad*, edited by R. B. Williams. Chambersburg, Pa.: Anima.

———. 1996. *Christian pluralism in the United States: The Indian immigrant experience*. New York: Cambridge University Press.

———. 1998. Asian Indian and Pakistani religions in the United States. *Annals of the American Academy of Political and Social Science* 558 (July 1998): 178–195.

Wolf, Diane L. 2002. There's no place like "home": Emotional transnationalism and the struggles of second-generation filipinos. In *The changing face of home: The transnational lives of the second generation*, edited by P. Levitt and M. C. Waters. New York: Russell Sage Foundation.

Yang, F. 1999. ABC and xyz: Religious, ethnic and racial identities of the new second generation Chinese in Christian churches. *Amerasia Journal* 25 (1):89–115.

Yang, F., and H. R. Ebaugh. 2001. Religion and ethnicity among new immigrants: The impact of majority/minority status in home and host countries. *Journal for the Scientific Study of Religion* 40 (3):367–378.

Yang, T. 1997. Race, religion, and cultural identity: Reconciling the jurisprudence of race and religion. *Indiana Law Journal* 73 (1):119–185.

Yoo, David. 1999. *New spiritual homes: Religion and Asian Americans*. Honolulu: University of Hawaii and UCLA Asian American Studies Center.

Young, I. 1990. *Justice and the politics of difference*. Princeton: Princeton University Press.

Zaidman, N. 1997. When the deities are asleep: Processes of change in an American Hare Krishna temple. *Journal of Contemporary Religion* 12 (3):335–352.

Zhou, M. 1997. Growing up American: The challenge of confronting immigrant children and children of immigrants. *Annual Review of Sociology* 23:63–96.

———. 1999. Coming of age: The current situation of Asian American children. *Amerasia Journal* 25 (1):1–28.

INDEX

adulthood: ethnic identity development in, 41, 152; ethnoreligious community, 58–61; negotiating religion through, 33; ritual practices, 85; transnational experiences in, 70–71

African Americans, 91, 100–102, 105, 106, 116

alienation, 74, 183–185

alignment, 100–103

American Religious Identification Survey (ARIS), 19

Aryan Nation, 115, 138–139

Asiatic Exclusion League, 93

atheists, 50, 96, 137–138

authenticity: emotional transnationalism, 74; home religion, 50–52, 156–157, 192; language, 191; moral-compass religiosity, 69; religious study, 77–78; transnationalism, 69–70, 157–158, 191–192

Barred Zone Act. *See* Immigration Act of 1917

Bhagavad Gita, 17, 28

Bharatiya Janata Party (BJP), 83

bicultural conflict, 22–27, 31, 37, 38, 158–160. *See also* negotiating religion

bicultural identity, 43, 50, 154–155. *See also* ethnic identity development

black/white paradigm, 94–95, 111

Bollywood, 43, 162, 170–171, 196

case studies: authenticity, 156–157, 191–192; bicultural conflict, 158–160; coethnics, 185–186; collectivism, 167–170; discrimination and alienation, 183–185; ethnic labels, 166–167; ethnoreligious community, 186–188; Hindu female (Neha), 160–173; individualism, 170–171; Isma'ili male (Salim), 173–193; Malayali Catholic female (Binu), 145–160; moral compass, 189–190; overview of, 12–13; participant demographics, 5–7; racial identity, 171–173; religion and culture, 188–189; religiosity, 153–154; situational ethnicity, 154–155; transnational experiences, 157–158, 190–191

categorization. *See* ethnic labels

Catholics, Indian, 77, 79–80. *See also* Malayali Catholics

Chafetz, Janet Saltzman, 20–21

Christian hegemony: and American society, 27–30, 121–122, 125–126; and the bicultural conflict, 22, 24, 71; delegitimization of South Asian religions, 126–128; education system, 23–27, 32, 131–136; institutional level, 124; and religious oppression, 121, 123–124, 136–138

Christian privilege, 125–126, 144

Christian proselytization, 136–138

Christianity: bicultural conflict, 23, 28–30; early immigrants, 46–47; effect on the home faith, 66, 80, 88, 195; lived religion, 20; racialization of religion, 90–91; as societal norm, 27–30, 121–124; white supremacy, 90–91, 117. *See also* Indian American Christians

Civilization Act of 1819, 119

coethnics: discrimination by, 72–73, 156–157; dissatisfaction with, 47, 162, 170, 172; as extended family, 52; knowledge acquisition, 82, 153; religious oppression, 137; sense of belonging, 178–179, 185–188; Sunday School, 56–57; transnational experiences, 71, 73–74

college: ethnic identity development in, 185–186; ethnoreligious community, 31–33, 39–40, 55, 59; and home religion, 79–84, 149–150, 163, 178; moral compass and, 63–64; religious oppression in, 112–113, 143; ritual practices, 85; transnational experiences during, 75

compartmentalization, 31, 38

coreligionists: dissatisfaction with, 63, 169; as extended family, 52; and knowledge acquisition, 55, 82; transnational experiences, 71, 72

critical incidents, 38–39, 41–42, 44, 60

cultural dimensions: as collectivistic, 167–169, 171; as discrimination buffer, 58, 89, 101–102; Diwali festival, 49–50, 53; ethnic identity development, 35, 180; importance of, 188–189; Indo-chic, 43, 127–128; as inseparable from Hinduism, 48–50; as lived religion, 43–44, 47–50; and religious oppression, 141–142; Sunday school, 56

cultural identity. *See* ethnic identity development

cultural mores, 31, 43, 51, 62
cultural transmission, 43, 48–50, 55, 58, 81
culture, 11

Darbar Sahib (Golden Temple), 72
demographics: of research participants, 5–7;
Indian American religious groups, 19–20
discrimination: of coethnics, 71–72; ethnoreligious community as buffer to, 58, 89,
101–102; gray area between
religious/racial, 141–144; parental support
and, 135–136; racialization of religion, 116,
118–119; religious, 26–27, 121, 132–135,
183–184, 197. *See also* racial discrimination;
racism; religious discrimination; religious
oppression; skin color; "whiteness"
Diwali (festival), 49–50, 53
"dot-buster" attacks, 141–142
double minority, 4, 91, 95, 120, 139. *See also*
racialization of religion

Ebaugh, Helen, 20–21
education system: Christian hegemony and
the, 23–27, 32, 131–136, 144; integration, 42,
115; multicultural education, 42, 144, 198;
need for reforms in, 196–197; protecting
Indian American students, 194, 197; and
religious oppression, 121, 134–135
educators: as bicultural connection, 159;
marginalization by, 25–26, 132; model
minority myth, 106–107; need for Indian-
American, 198; non-Indians teaching
Indian subjects, 81; and racism, 101–102,
113, 128
emotional transnationalism, 73–74
ethnic identifications. *See* ethnic labels
ethnic identity development: adolescence,
40–44; adulthood, 41–42; authenticity,
50–52; bicultural, 43, 50, 154–155; college
years, 39–40, 153, 179–180, 185–188; conflation of Indian and Hindu, 43–45, 47–50,
157, 167; critical incidents, 38–39, 41–42,
44, 60; and dominant white society,
163–166, 171–173; and educators, 197; ethnic self-conception, 11, 35–37; ethnoreligious community, 35–36, 38, 44, 53–54,
60–61; group/individual religion, 10–11,
46, 164; home religion's impact on, 24, 34,
47, 60; influences on, 2–3, 13, 35–37; internalized racism, 109–110; K-12 period,
24–30; labels and, 35–37, 155–156, 166–167;
language and, 3, 35, 41, 42, 165–169; and
the life span, 38–43, 159–160; lived religion, 8, 44–45, 52; marginalization, 36–38,
114–115; and mischaracterization of religion, 127–128; mutable nature of, 10,
34–35, 37, 44; race/racial identity, 8–10,
92–95; racialization, 37–38, 103–105, 116,
183–185; religious oppression, 120, 135,
136, 138, 143; religious study, 79–81; ritual
practices, 86; and skin color, 108–109; as a
social construct, 92–94; and social exclusion, 110–111; sociocultural climate and,
42–43, 50; and the third space, 30–33;

transnational experiences, 35–37, 40, 88,
180–181, 190–191. *See also* lived religion
ethnic labels: and ethnic identity development, 35–37, 155–156, 166–167; racism,
113–114, 174–175, 183
ethnicity, 10
ethnoreligious community: adult participation in, 58–61, 186–188; alternatives to,
59–60; college life, 39–40; compulsory
participation, 22–23, 29, 56; and early immigrants, 45, 54–55; ethnic identity development, 35–36, 38, 44, 53–54, 60–61;
geographic isolation and, 37, 56–58;
houses of worship, 18–19; individual faith,
22, 46, 170; limitations of, 79; as monoracial, 89–90; necessary elements of, 56–57;
religious oppression, 143; religious study,
29–30, 77–78; role of, 52–54, 58; and socioeconomics, 36–37, 42, 54–55, 57; Sunday School, 30–31, 55–56, 77–79, 82; term,
53; as a third space, 30–31

family(ies): compulsory religious participation, 22–23, 29, 176, 186; ethnic identity
development, 35, 36; ethnoreligious
community, 52; Immigration Reform Act
of 1965 and, 16–17; lived religion, 44;
ritual practices, 85; transnational
experiences, 70
Fenton, John, 3, 21
First Amendment rights, 135
foreignness and marginalization, 110–112, 115
formalized worship. *See* ritual practices
freedom of religion, 135
future outlook: education system, 196–198;
Hindutva, 87–88, 195; Indian American
religious experience, 66, 67, 144, 194–195

Gandhi, Mohandas, 56, 77, 114
gender, 208n1
"Golden Rule Christians," 66–67
Golden Temple. *See* Darbar Sahib
government, 121, 124, 126, 129–130, 195–197

Hall, Stuart, 34–35
harassment, 137–138
Hare Krishnas, 17, 18, 45. *See also* ISKCON
(International Society of Krishna
Consciousness)
hegemony, 123. *See also* Christian hegemony
Hindi, 56, 77, 191, 213n21
Hindu/Indian conflation: ethnic identity,
43–45, 48–50, 157, 167; ethnoreligious
community education, 56, 77; parents'
cultural transmission, 43, 48–50, 55;
racialization of religion, 96; transnational
experiences, 72–73
Hindus/Hinduism: American Hinduism, 194;
Bharatiya Janata Party (BJP), 83; case
study, 160–173; Christian proselytization
and, 136–138; Christian school participation, 24–25; as "collectivistic," 168, 169;
delegitimization/misrepresentation of,
126–128, 130; discrimination/righ-

teousness by, 69, 72–73, 83; early immigrants, 17, 46–47; ethnic authenticity, 48, 51; ethnic identity, 44, 89–90, 157; ethnoreligious community, 30, 46, 53–54; as foreigners, 91; Hindutva, 87–88, 195; and the Immigration Reform Act of 1965, 16, 18; independent religious study, 79, 81–83; in India versus America, 45; intellectualization of religion, 27–28, 30; lived religion, 47–50, 64–66, 86–87; population statistics on, 19; post-9/11 backlash, 97, 140; prayer languages, 60, 67; racialization of religions, 96, 116, 130, 142; religious oppression, 118–119, 121–123, 126, 135, 136; sociopolitical climate, 21, 87, 196; Sunday school, 77–79; and transnational experiences, 71, 72. *See also* Hindu/Indian conflation

Hindutva, 87–88, 195

historical overview: of ethnoreligious community, 54–55; Immigration Reform Act of 1965, 1, 16–17, 100–101; Indian American immigration, 16–19, 45–46; post-9/11 backlash, 103–104, 111; Puritan migration/ethics, 15–16, 90–91, 118–119; religious oppression, 118–119; racial status of Indian Americans, 92–94

home faith: authenticity, 50–52, 156–157, 192; doubt of the, 24–25, 28–29, 31; effects of Christian norm on, 27–30, 138; ethnic identity, 46, 60, 188–189; evolution of the, 195; houses of worship, 18–19, 122–123, 125, 126; independent religious study, 79–84; language, 61; moral compass religiosity, 68; spirituality and the, 65–66, 76–77; transnational experiences, 72, 76

home/school conflict, 22–27, 30–33, 38, 110

houses of worship, 18–19, 122–123, 125, 126

hybrid identities, 43, 50, 154–155

identity, 34–36. *See also* ethnic identity development

immigrant parents. *See* parents

Immigration Act: of 1917, 16, 17; of 1924, 16; of 1965, 1, 16–17, 100–101, 145

Immigration Reform Act. *See* Immigration Act, of 1965

immigration statistics, 2

independent religious study. *See* religious study

India: emotional transnationalism, 73–74; religious discrimination in, 72–73. *See also* Hindu/Indian conflation; transnationalism/transnational experiences

Indian American, 7

Indian American Christians: challenges of, 45–46; and Hinduism, 48–51; independent religious studies by, 79–80; Indian Catholics, 77, 79–80; lived religion, 48, 64–65; population statistics, 19; and racialization of religion, 96, 97, 196. *See also* Malayali Catholics

Indian culture. *See* cultural dimensions

Indian Muslims. *See* Muslims/Islam

Indiana Jones and the Temple of Doom (film), 96, 130

individual religious practice, 65–66, 76–77, 143–144, 182. *See also* moral compass; moral-compass religiosity

individualism, 163–167, 169, 170–172

Indo-chic, 43, 127–128

institutional-level oppression, 121, 124, 131–136

intellectualization of religion, 27–30, 66. *See also* moral-compass religiosity; religious study

internalized racism, 109–110

International Society for Krishna Consciousness (ISKCON), 17, 18

interview protocol, 199–204

Islam. *See* Muslims/Islam

Isma'ili Muslim: authenticity, 192; case study, 173–193; description of, 173–174; ethnoreligious community, 186–188; individual religious study, 82, 83; and Muslims, 83, 176–177, 179, 185–186

isolation. *See* marginalization

Jews/Judaism, 46–47, 91, 94, 96, 118–119

Johnson-Reed Immigration Act of 1924, 16, 18, 119

K-12 life stage: adolescence, 37, 38, 40–41, 52, 53; effects of religious oppression in, 143; ethnic identity development, 24–30; ethnoreligious community, 30–31, 57–58; home/school conflict, 22–27, 38; mischaracterization of home faith during, 127; racism in, 104–105, 113–115; and ritual practices, 84; and transnational experiences, 40, 70, 71

knowledge acquisition. *See* religious study

Ku Klux Klan, 94, 114–115, 119, 134

language: and ethnic identity development, 3, 35, 41, 42, 165–169; and evolution of the home faith, 195; Hindi, 56, 77, 191; and lived religion, 44; and Sunday school, 56

language barriers, 66–68

life stages: ethnic identity development, 38–40, 44, 159–160; lived religion, 88; moral-compass religiosity, 69; race and racism, 103; transnational experiences, 74. *See also* adulthood; K-12 life stage

lived religion: and Christian norms, 30; congregational worship, 20–21; defined, 8; ethnic identity development, 8, 44–45, 52; Hinduism, 47–50, 64–66, 86–87; Indian cultural practices as, 36, 43–44; individual experience of, 23, 46; Islam and, 47–48, 63, 64, 66; manifestations of, 62; marginalization, 25–26, 189–190; moral compass, 62–65; moral-compass religiosity, 66–69, 73; as new scholarship, 20–21, 194; over the life span, 88; and politics, 87–88; religious oppression, 119–120, 144;

lived religion (*continued*)
  religious study as, 79–84; ritual practices
  as, 84–87; Sikhism and, 64, 65, 78; sociohistorical context, 21; Sunday school,
  77–79; transnationalism, 44, 70–76. *See
  also* ethnic identity development; negotiating religion
Luce-Cellar Act of 1946, 16, 17

Madonna of 115th Street (Orsi), 20
Mahabharata, 17, 28, 56, 77
Malayali Catholics: case study, 145–152;
  coethnics, 156–157; ethnoreligious community, 45–46, 52, 54, 153–154; identifiers
  and, 154–156; transnational experiences,
  72, 157–158
marginalization: and the Christian norm, 131;
  effect of religious, 143–144; ethnic identity
  development, 36–38, 114–116; foreignness,
  110–112, 115; and lived religion, 25–26;
  and skin color, 108–109, 114–115, 117;
  socioeconomic class, 122–123
McCarran Walter Act of 1952, 16, 17
media: Bollywood, 42, 162, 170–171, 196; mischaracterization of South Asian religions
  by, 96, 127; racialization of religion,
  129–131; religious oppression, 121
"meltable" ethnics, 4, 47, 90
misrepresentation, 130–131
model minority myth, 105–107, 116
monoethnic experience, 89–90
moral compass, 62–67, 69, 189–190
moral-compass religiosity, 66–69, 73
Muhammad, 83, 212
Muslims/Islam: American Islam, 194; delegitimization of, 126–130; ethnic identity, 44,
  46, 185–186; ethnoreligious community,
  53, 87; as foreigners, 91; and Hinduism,
  48–51; immigration history of, 17–18, 45,
  47; and the Immigration Reform Act of
  1965, 16; independent religious study, 82,
  83; intellectualization of religion, 28; lived
  religion, 47–48, 63, 64, 66; media perception of, 29, 130–131; population statistics
  on, 19; post-9/11 backlash, 97, 139–140, 196;
  prayer languages, 67; racialization of religion, 96–97, 116, 128, 130, 142; religious oppression, 118–119, 121–124, 126, 135, 140;
  righteousness, 69; *sewa* (service), 63, 182,
  188–189, 192; Shi'a Islam, 83; sociopolitical
  climate, 174, 177, 183, 196; Sunday school,
  77; transnational experiences, 72. *See also*
  Isma'ili Muslim

National Asian Pacific American Legal Consortium (NAPALAC), 139
National Honor Society (NHS), 134, 135
National Origins Act of 1924, 16, 18, 119
negotiating religion: in adulthood, 33; Christian norms and, 27–30; compulsory religious participation, 21–22; home/school
  conflicts, 22–27; religious oppression, 120;
  third space, 30–33

Omi, Michael, 8, 9
"1.5 generation," 7
oppression. *See* religious oppression
Orsi, Robert, 20

parents: alignment and, 100–101, 105; and
  the bicultural conflict, 24–25, 31, 37; compulsory religious participation and, 22–23,
  29, 176, 186; as cultural transmitters, 55,
  62, 65, 81, 144; discriminatory acts toward,
  102, 148, 165; ethnoreligious community,
  52–53, 55, 56; Hindu/Indian conflation
  and, 48–50; and mainstream society, 37;
  and the model minority myth, 105; religious instruction and, 25, 29–30, 183; ritual practices, 85; social boundaries
  created by, 31, 43, 147; views on
  race/racism, 112, 116, 133, 135–136
participant demographics, 5–7
perpetual foreigner. *See* foreignness and
  marginalization
policymakers, 121, 124, 126, 129–130,
  195–197
politics. *See* policymakers; sociopolitical
  climate
post-9/11 backlash, 97, 103–104, 130–131,
  139–140, 195–196
proselytization, 136–138
Protestant American. *See* Christianity
public school. *See* education system; educators; home/school conflict
Punjab region, 17, 72, 212n12
Puranas, 56, 77
Puritans, 15–16, 90–91, 118–119
puja (ceremony), 35, 48, 59, 65, 67, 86, 89

race/racial identity, 8–10, 92–95, 115–116. *See
  also* ethnic identity development
racial alignment, 100–103
racial discrimination: American Indian race
  classification, 92–94; black/white paradigm, 94–95; conflated with religious oppression, 139, 141–142; danger of
  downplaying, 116–117; and ethnic identity
  development, 35, 37–38; racialization of
  religion, 97–98; and transnationalism,
  71–73. *See also* religious oppression; skin
  color; "whiteness"
racial formation, 9
racialization of religion: and Christianity, 22,
  90–91, 122; discrimination, 116, 118–119;
  harassment, 137–138; and the media,
  129–131; misrepresentation, 130–131; and
  monoethnic experience, 89–90; nature of,
  95; politics, 96–98, 103–104; and religion's
  current popularity, 2; religious oppression, 97–98, 119, 120, 126, 141–144; schools,
  23–27; sociocultural factors, 95–97,
  128–129; stereotypes, 96; violence, 140. *See
  also* religious oppression
racism: defined, 9, 98, 114; ethnic
  labels, 113–114; and foreignness, 111–112;
  institutional/societal versus individual,

99, 104; Ku Klux Klan, 94, 114–115; manifestations of, 99–100, 103; and the model minority myth, 105–107; outlook of immigrant parents on, 100–103; politics of alignment, 100–101; process and effects of, 95–96, 98–100; "real," 112–116; religious oppression, 142–143; scientific racism, 9; second-generation Indian Americans views on, 102–105; as socially unacceptable, 1–2; targeted identity, 142; victims denial of, 101, 104–105. *See also* marginalization; racial discrimination; religious discrimination; religious oppression; stereotypes

Ramayana, 56, 77
"real racism," 112–116
religion, 7–8
religious discrimination, 26–27, 121, 132–135, 141, 183–184, 197
religious oppression: Christian hegemony, 15, 123–126; delegitimization/misrepresentation/discounting, 126–131; differential treatment, 131–138; and education, 131–136, 197; and ethnic identity development, 120, 135, 136, 138, 143; gray areas, 141–144; institutional-level, 121, 124, 131–136; and lived religion, 119–120, 144; overview of, 118–123; racialization of religion, 97–98, 120, 126, 141–144; and racism, 142–143; societal, 121–122, 136–138; and socioeconomic status, 122–123; unconstitutionality of, 135; violence, 138–140
religious self, 22, 153–154
religious study: and authenticity, 77–78; and ethnic identity development, 79–81; as lived religion, 81–84
righteousness, 68–69, 73, 122
ritual practices: and the Christian norm, 127; ethnic identity development, 8; independent observance of, 84–85; and language barriers, 66, 68, 169; as lived religion, 51, 86–87; and moral compass, 65–67; role of, 85–86; and spirituality, 76, 154

scholarly theory. *See* theories of race
school conflicts, 22–27, 30–33, 38, 110
schools. *See* education system; educators
second generation, 7
sewa (service), 63, 182, 188–189, 192, 211n3
Shi'a Islam, 83
Sikhs/Sikhism: American Sikhism, 194; authenticity, 48; and Bollywood, 196; delegitimization of, 126–128; ethnic identity, 44, 89; ethnoreligious community, 30, 46, 53–54; as foreigners, 91; Hindu/Indian conflation and, 48–50, 72; immigration history of the, 17, 45–47, 93; and the Immigration Reform Act of 1965, 16, 18; independent religious study and, 28, 79, 82; and lived religion, 64, 65, 78; population statistics on, 19; post-9/11 backlash and, 97, 130–131, 139–140, 195–196; prayer languages, 60, 67; and Punjab, 17, 72, 212n12;

and racialization of religions, 96, 97, 116, 130, 142; and religious oppression, 118–119, 121–123, 126, 135; religious persecution in India of, 17; righteousness, 69; Sunday school, 77; transnational experiences, 72; Yuba City (CA) community, 17, 18
situational ethnicity, 154–155, 208n3
skin color: and assimilation, 47; and group worship, 89–90; Indian as "non-white," 93; and marginalization, 108–109, 117, 174; and religious oppression, 121, 140; and social capital, 99. *See also* "whiteness"
social capital, 52, 99
social identity development model, 171–172
society. *See* Christian hegemony
sociocultural climate: and ethnic identity development, 42–43, 50; and the model minority myth, 105–107; present-day religious, 70–71; and racial identity, 92–94; and racialization, 95–97, 128–129
socioeconomic status: and ethnoreligious community, 36–37, 42, 54–55, 57; and religious oppression, 122–123; and transnational ties, 42, 70; and "whiteness," 90–91
sociopolitical climate: and the Gulf War, 43, 128; and Hindus, 21, 87, 196; and Muslims, 174, 177, 183, 196; post-9/11 backlash and, 97, 103–104, 130–131, 139–140, 195–196; and racialization of religion, 96–98, 103–104; and religious discrimination, 183–184; and Sikhs, 97, 130–131, 139–140, 195–196
South Asian American, 7
spirituality, 65–66, 76–77, 143–144, 182
statistics on immigration, 2
stereotypes: and delegitimization, 131; effects of, 96, 117, 176, 184; and the model minority myth, 105–107
Sunday school, 30–31, 55–56, 77–79, 82
Supreme Court rulings, 16, 93–94
Swami Vivekananda, 4, 17

targeted identity, 142
terms and usage, 7–11
theories of race: gathering data for, 195; model minority myth, 105, 107, 116; need for rethinking, 1, 4, 91–92, 194
third space, 30–33, 50, 52, 56–57
transmission, 43, 48–50, 55, 58, 81
transnationalism/transnational experiences: authenticity, 50, 69–70, 157–158, 191–192; discrimination, 72–73; emotional transnationalism, 73–74; ethnic identity development, 35–37, 40, 88, 180–181, 190–191; ethnoreligious community, 54; language, 168; lived religion, 44, 70–73; role of, 51, 70–73, 75–76; social exclusion, 110–111; socioeconomics/technological development, 42, 70; through the life stages, 74–75
Transplanting Religious Traditions (Fenton), 3

United States v. Bhagat Singh Thind, 16, 93
"unmeltable ethnics," 3, 90, 117
U.S. Census Bureau, 19
U.S. Constitution: First Amendment, 135
U.S. Supreme Court, 16, 93–94

Vaisaki (festival), 43, 53
violence, 126, 138–142

white/black paradigm, 94–95, 111
"whiteness": Christian supremacy, 90–91, 117; internalized racism, 109–110; the Ku Klux Klan, 94, 114–115; marginalization, 114–115; racial alignment, 100–101, 103; religious oppression, 121; socioeconomic status, 90–91; U.S. government race classification, 93–95. *See also* racial discrimination; skin color
Winant, Howard, 8, 9

ABOUT THE AUTHOR

KHYATI Y. JOSHI is an assistant professor of education at Fairleigh Dickinson University in Teaneck, New Jersey. Before joining the faculty of FDU, she taught Asian American studies and comparative ethnic studies at Princeton University and at Columbia University's Center for the Study of Ethnicity and Race. Dr. Joshi works with teachers and school administrators on multicultural curriculum development and meeting the needs of immigrant and second-generation students. She created one of the first one-on-one mentoring programs in the United States to pair South Asian American high school students with South Asian American graduate students and young professionals, and has worked with a variety of other programs serving students of diverse backgrounds.

Dr. Joshi earned her doctoral degree in social justice education from the University of Massachusetts-Amherst, a Masters in theological studies from the Candler School of Theology at Emory University, and a B.A. in religion from Emory University. She also pursued post-graduate studies at the Hebrew University of Jerusalem and was a selected participant in the 2003–2005 Young Scholars in American Religion program at the Center for the Study of Religion and American Culture at Indiana University-Purdue University Indianapolis.